SHAKESPEARE
A Study and Research Guide

SHAKESPEARE

A Study and Research Guide
Third Edition, Revised

DAVID M. BERGERON
& GERALDO U. DE SOUSA

 UNIVERSITY PRESS OF KANSAS

Published by the University Press of Kansas (Lawrence, Kansas 66049), which was organized by the Kansas Board of Regents and is operated and funded by Emporia State University, Fort Hays State University, Kansas State University, Pittsburg State University, the University of Kansas, and Wichita State University.

Library of Congress Cataloging-in-Publication Data

Bergeron, David Moore.
  Shakespeare : a study and research guide / David M. Bergeron & Geraldo U. de Sousa.—3rd ed., rev.
    p. cm.
  Includes index.
  ISBN 0-7006-0692-0 (cloth) ISBN 0-7006-0693-9 (pbk.)
  1. Shakespeare, William, 1564–1616—Bibliography. I. Sousa, Geraldo U. de, 1952– . II. Title.
Z8811.B44 1995
[PR2894]
016.8223′3—dc20   94-37236

British Library Cataloguing in Publication Data is available.

Printed in the United States of America

10 9 8 7 6 5 4 3 2

Contents

Preface

This third edition marks the twentieth anniversary of the first edition of 1975. A comparison of this one and the first reveals not only a considerable increase in the number of books surveyed but also several changes in the direction of Shakespearean criticism. Categories of books now appear that scarcely warranted attention or were even unheard of in 1975. But the basic purpose of this book remains the same: to offer guidance in the formidable, even daunting, collection of Shakespearean criticism and scholarship. The organization of the book reflects the desirable pattern of moving from a general understanding of Shakespearean criticism to an investigation of resources to the actual writing of a critical paper. Each chapter stands alone, however; and students may dip into them as their needs dictate.

We have added over 100 new books to the 1987 edition and have created separate categories for film and television and for cultural study. There has been a sizable increase in the number of books on Shakespeare's history plays. As in the 1987 edition, we have thoroughly scrutinized every sentence, keeping, revising, or discarding as appropriate. We divided the labors of revision to make the task of covering post–1987 criticism manageable.

We received assistance from many people, beginning with colleagues and students who commented on the strengths and shortcomings of earlier editions. Geraldo de Sousa would especially like to thank his student assistants Paul Vespoli and Jeff Nienaber at Xavier University; the Office of the Vice President for Academic Affairs; and Marty Perry Ferrell, Xavier University Library. He also thanks Max Keck, Dean of the College of Arts and Science, for providing released time for work on the project. Hershini Bhana kindly let us use her fine paper on *The Tempest* for the model research paper. For their superb skill and cooperation, we thank Paula Malone, Pam LeRow, and Lynn Porter of the Wescoe Word Processing Center at the University of Kansas. We are grateful for the assistance provided by the Xavier University Library, the University of Kansas Libraries, and the Folger Shakespeare Library. In the pleasant surroundings of the Folger, we essentially brought this project to its conclusion.

Two final caveats remain. First, only book-length studies were evaluated and typically only studies of groups of plays (thus, no evaluation of books on *Othello;* rather, only studies on the tragedies). Second, our subjective but informed judgment determined which books to include and what to say about them. On this score, opinions will surely vary.

As with the earlier editions, this guide truly belongs to our students, who over the years have challenged and stimulated our thinking about Shakespeare and have often shared our enthusiasm for the subject.

October 1994   *David M. Bergeron*
                                                 Geraldo U. de Sousa

CHAPTER ONE
The Subject in Context

In confronting the criticism and scholarship currently available on Shakespeare, one may be surprised to learn that such productivity is largely a twentieth-century phenomenon. Books, editions, and essays now proliferate at an astronomical rate—some 5,000 new items published in 1992 alone. Gone are the days when professional scholars could reasonably expect to attain some sort of mastery over the material being produced on the subject; they now stand in danger of being engulfed in a sea of criticism, often unable to distinguish the sharp rocks from the sheltering boulders. We seem not to have world enough and time to separate the important from the unimportant, and we look in vain for a guide. But a moratorium on publication would be both unrealistic and undesirable; thus, students of Shakespeare simply must come to terms with the material.

CRITICISM IN SHAKESPEARE'S TIME

What accounts for the lack of criticism during the dramatist's own lifetime? Of course, people did have opinions about Shakespeare and his work. Robert Greene, in fact, rather testily refers to him in 1592 as "an upstart Crow"; and in 1598, Francis Meres, in *Palladis Tamia,* praises Shakespeare's "sugred Sonnets" and judges him to be the most excellent of the English writers of comedy and tragedy. Ben Jonson, a fellow dramatist and a classicist, complains occasionally of Shakespeare's violation of the traditional unities of time, place, and action; but in verses prepared for the publication of the first collected edition of Shakespeare's plays, the Folio of 1623, Jonson praises Shakespeare effusively, claiming, "He was not of an age, but for all time!"

At least two reasons can explain the lack of extensive early critical writing about Shakespeare. First, no well-established tradition of literary criticism existed in the sixteenth century. Grammarians and rhetoricians defined different literary forms, but that is not criticism. Philip Sidney's *An Apology for Poetry* in the early 1580s remains the major statement of the century. Unfortunately, he wrote before the full flowering of English Renaissance drama and thus praises *Gorboduc* as the finest English tragedy. Not until John Dryden in the 1660s did pieces of sustained criticism appear. The period between Sidney and Dryden, although not a critical wasteland, resulted in little of importance. Thomas Heywood's *An Apology for Actors* (1612) offers a justification for drama but breaks no new critical ground. Curiously, this most brilliant period of English literary history provoked little practical or theoretical criticism—perhaps because no English professors wandered loose in the country.

Further, people generally did not recognize drama as literature; hence they saw no particular need to discuss it seriously as a literary form. They found it difficult to intellectualize about mere "plays" that they saw at "playhouses." The location of theaters next to bear-baiting and bull-baiting arenas offers a striking commentary on the relationship between sport and play. A spectator might watch *Hamlet* at the Globe one afternoon and the next day watch a bear being torn apart by dogs in a nearby arena. At least one dramatist, however, took his plays (and himself) seriously: in 1616, Ben Jonson published a folio collection of his drama, which he had the audacity to entitle *The Works of Benjamin Jonson*. The term "works" typically designated serious poetry or prose, not plays. Even the editors of the 1623 folio collection of Shakespeare's drama entitled it *Mr. William Shakespeare's Comedies, Histories, & Tragedies*. Readers esteemed poetry as worthy literature, but drama suffered a fate as a highly ephemeral art, a notion supported by evidence that merely a fraction of plays ever got printed. Only half (eighteen) of Shakespeare's plays appeared in print during his lifetime. With this general disregard for drama as literature—but not a disregard for drama itself, which became extremely popular— one understands the absence of elaborate research and criticism about Shakespeare.

THE EIGHTEENTH AND NINETEENTH CENTURIES

The eighteenth century gave rise to the first serious and extensive research on Shakespeare, most of which focused on editing. Obviously, establishing a sound text must precede criticism. Nicholas Rowe's edition of 1709 is the first "edition" of Shakespeare; it includes a brief biography of Shakespeare, generally regarded as the first formal biography. Lewis Theobald made significant contributions as an editor, but unfortunately, he is most remembered for being the target of Alexander Pope's *The Dunciad* (1728). He had made the mistake of pointing out the shortcomings of Pope's own edition of Shakespeare (1725). In the latter part of the century, Edward Capell, George Steevens, and Edmond Malone contributed important editions. Malone also worked on the problem of the chronology of Shakespeare's plays, still an unresolved and vexing problem, though we have a generally accepted order. These serious editors ultimately established the groundwork for continuing investigation. Pope and Samuel Johnson—whose often whimsical, highly subjective editorial practices included free alteration of the text—have fallen into disrepute as editors, although Johnson's notes retain some value.

Not surprisingly, the nineteenth century spawned even more editions, many of which offered nothing new. But the Cambridge edition—issued in 1864 as the one-volume Globe text, edited by Clark, Glover, and Wright—has achieved high status. In fact, it became the standard text on which many twentieth-century editions have been based; its line numbering system is only now being altered in favor of continuous through-line numbering (it may take another generation or two before we surrender the Globe's system altogether). That century also

saw the founding in Germany and England of societies devoted
to research and criticism of Shakespeare: in Weimar, the
Deutsche Shakespeare-Gesellschaft, founded in 1865 and publisher of the *Shakespeare Jahrbuch;* in England, the Shakespeare
Society, founded in 1840, and the "New Shakspere Society,"
founded in 1873 by F. J. Furnivall. Despite the bickering and
contentiousness of the English members, these societies
opened up new territory by recognizing the importance of
Elizabethan documents and by seeking information on Shakespeare's fellow dramatists. Furnivall's group, caught up in the
late-nineteenth-century belief in science, sought scientific tests
to measure and account for Shakespeare's verse in the hope of
establishing chronology and settling questions of authorship.
Led by the industrious Frederick Fleay, the society placed its
faith in metrical tests that may seem to us either naive and
touching or simply misplaced. Other scholars in England and
elsewhere pursued various kinds of linguistic studies that led to
the publication of important glossaries and lexicons.

THE TWENTIETH CENTURY

The twentieth century gets fuller attention below in the discussion of the various schools of criticism. (By "school," we
mean simply a group whose participants share common critical
ground, not an organized effort as such.) The present century
has been exceptionally productive in many areas of scholarship.
The publications concerned exclusively with Shakespeare—
Shakespeare Survey, Shakespeare Quarterly, Shakespeare Bulletin, and
Shakespeare Studies—have all appeared in the past fifty years. The
Shakespeare Association of America became a national organization in the early 1970s; it sponsors annual meetings and encourages research.

Scholars unearthed important documents pertaining to
Shakespeare's life in the early decades of the century, largely because of the indefatigable research of Charles Wallace, E. K.
Chambers, and Leslie Hotson. Perhaps partly because of this
kind of research, the twentieth century has been the period of
Shakespearean biography, giving us the first full-fledged treatments of his life. In 1985, one scholar argued for Shakespeare's

residence in Lancashire among Catholics during the presumed "lost years," and another discovered a poem allegedly written by Shakespeare. The late 1980s also witnessed the discovery and excavation of the foundations of the Globe and Rose theaters on the South Bank in London.

The twentieth century has given rise to important studies in psychology, language, rhetoric, imagery, and feminism and gender. This has also been a time of textual and bibliographical studies, opening avenues of research and speculation undreamed of in previous centuries. Indeed, when we write the history of twentieth-century Shakespearean scholarship, textual research and theory may be deemed the most significant contribution for its overall impact—both for the questions it has raised and for some of the answers it has provided.

SHAKESPEARE IN THE CLASSROOM

For those students who have been forced to march through *Julius Caesar* and *Macbeth* in high school, it may be cause for chagrin, reassurance, exasperation, or whatever to learn that such has not always been the lot of high school students. The teaching of Shakespeare is a relatively new activity, but it now seems natural for secondary schools and colleges to offer instruction in Shakespeare. (Of course, the study of American literature in American colleges is even more recent.) Seventeenth- and eighteenth-century schools did not teach Shakespeare, primarily because education had a classical orientation; yet clearly people read Shakespeare—witness the spate of editions. His works did not become a regular subject of instruction in England until after 1858, which marked the beginning of the Oxford and Cambridge Local Examinations. Similarly, in the United States, Shakespeare became part of the curriculum in the mid-nineteenth century, but even then in a very limited fashion. In both England and the United States, the early teaching focused on such things as plot, historical background, characters, grammar, and rhetoric and on the plays as vehicles for instruction in elocution. In a word, one seldom studied the plays as dramatic art, but rather as a means of illustrating something else. As early as 1825, the study of Shakespeare appeared in courses in moral philosophy at the University of Virginia, but not until 1857 did a separate course on Shakespeare appear in the school of history and general literature. Cornell University had a course in Shakespeare by 1868; Princeton, 1869; Johns Hopkins, 1877; and Columbia, 1882. The first PhD degree for a dissertation on Shakespeare went to Robert Grant of Harvard University in 1876 for his work on the Sonnets; the second PhD for work on Shakespeare went to S. B. Weeks, who graduated in 1888 from the University of North Carolina. Interestingly, a number of American and English students received PhD degrees from German universities for their studies of Shakespeare during this same period.

By the end of the nineteenth century, the teaching of Shakespeare became widespread in the United States, with most schools offering at least one play as part of the curriculum. One teacher in particular helped move the teaching of Shakespeare away from its early, somewhat narrow concerns: George Lyman Kittredge, a popular teacher at Harvard for nearly fifty years (1888–1936). Although no one excelled Kittredge in knowledge about Shakespeare's language, his approach in the classroom was not strictly philological; he emphasized an understanding and appreciation of Shakespeare's dramatic artistry. Not surprisingly, the growth of research about Shakespeare has gone hand in hand with the expansion of the teaching of Shakespeare. The productive critics and scholars of the past few decades have been, for the most part, teachers of Shakespeare. This contrasts with the general situation in the eighteenth and nineteenth centuries, when many of the critics were poets, men of letters, or simply amateur lovers of literature.

SOME CRITICAL APPROACHES

In defining some of the critical approaches to Shakespeare, one must be aware that most critics fit into more than one school of criticism. One senses a growing awareness of the need for eclectic criticism; that is, criticism that uses several different methods in interpreting Shakespeare. A sobering account and analysis of recent criticism can be found in Richard Levin's *New Readings vs. Old Plays: Recent Trends in the Reinterpretation of En-*

glish Renaissance Drama (U of Chicago P, 1979), much of which focuses on Shakespeare. Even if one does not entirely agree with Levin's sometimes bleak assessment, one has to admit that he makes some telling points about excesses in criticism. Brian Vickers in *Appropriating Shakespeare: Contemporary Critical Quarrels* (Yale UP, 1993) also assesses contemporary criticism and finds much of it wanting. Often the problem boils down to the mistaken and regrettable view that some *one* method exists that will yield the best results or even reveal the truth.

The diversity of Shakespearean scholarship and criticism becomes apparent in chapter 2, but it might be helpful to outline and group some of the types of modern criticism.

HISTORICAL CRITICISM

We can call one large category of criticism *historical,* with its several subcategories. The emphasis on history comes partly as a reaction to the excesses of a highly romanticized, somewhat sentimental Shakespeare who emerged from some nineteenth-century criticism, which often took no note of the context in which Shakespeare wrote. Historical criticism ideally steers a course between a Shakespeare exclusively Elizabethan, whom we can apprehend only if we become Elizabethans, and Shakespeare our contemporary. This approach has validity only insofar as it leads us into the plays and poems. Context cannot substitute for text.

Biography constitutes one major area of historical research. What facts do we have of Shakespeare's life? Who constituted his family and friends? What was life like in Stratford, in London? Documents discovered in this century have filled in some of the gaps, and a large number of biographies have been written. The pursuit of the life of the world's best-known writer seems valid in and of itself, though some biographies have contributed little to our store of knowledge. With hard facts about Shakespeare frustratingly few, many critics have searched the works themselves to try to gather information about the man. But such an approach abandons historical criticism in favor of a more speculative and conjectural procedure.

Much effort has gone into getting an accurate picture of the social, economic, political, intellectual, and cultural life of the

Shakespearean era. Today we have a better-informed view than did those in earlier centuries. As a man who came under royal patronage in 1603, Shakespeare had to be keenly aware of the political world; but whether he set out in his histories to offer political propaganda or teachings remains open to debate. The strong nationalism of the Elizabethan reign, which can be easily documented, must have had some impact on Shakespeare. Whether he understood economic theory, he surely understood practical finance, for we can now document his economic success and his property holdings. The social and economic rise of actors and dramatists adds another variable to the historical equation, providing new status to a group that had been deemed vagabonds. Knowledge of the sports and customs of the people helps in understanding parts of particular plays and the whole impulse toward dramatic entertainment. Shakespeare's philosophical assumptions and predilections also make a difference in his drama, but how do we know them? By reading his literary and philosophical contemporaries, a number of scholars have drawn a composite, a paradigm, of what the "worldview" might have been. But to claim that Shakespeare himself adhered to any system seems problematical, and the "evidence" from the plays kicks up about as much dust as it settles. Certainly Elizabethan ideas about the scientific, moral, political, and psychological world differ from twentieth-century assumptions. Historical knowledge of such areas at least provides a hedge against egregious error, though it does not provide any sure-fire interpretation. Again, we must somehow understand the dramatist's context without believing that it provides the only means by which he can be understood and enjoyed.

Influenced by anthropology, Marxism, or political ideology, a number of critics have been moved to consider what defines history. Is it a construct of facts, of paradigms, or is it much more problematical? These critics, sometimes labeled neohistoricists, insist that no opposition exists between literature and history; indeed, literature helps create society. This idea differs radically from older historical assumptions that Shakespeare's work reflected society, such as that found in E. M. W. Tillyard's perspective. Critics engaged in the new historicism hope to escape the trap of reductionism that afflicts some earlier historical studies. Instead of searching for a paradigm, the newer critics focus on the complex and sometimes indeterminate nature of Renaissance culture. They explore the interaction between state and culture, often finding the theater to be a prime location for the representation and legitimation of power. The new historicism witnesses a convergence of concern for politics, cultural anthropology, historical fact, and literary theory, and an expanding awareness of the function of literature in society.

THEATRICAL CRITICISM

Knowing the historical details of the era also involves learning about the *theater.* The major research on the theaters, acting companies, and actors has occurred in the twentieth century; previous criticism had largely ignored the Elizabethan theater. Yet Shakespeare, as a complete man of the theater, had to face practical, day-to-day problems that in many ways shaped his art. The presence of actor Richard Burbage in Shakespeare's group helped make possible such great tragic roles as Hamlet, Lear, Othello, and Macbeth. One obviously does not create dramatic roles that no one in the company can play.

What were the theater buildings like? What advantages, what limitations, did they offer? Clearly the jutting platform stage made the soliloquy and the aside plausible dramatic devices because it placed the actor in close proximity to members of the audience, allowing him to communicate confidentially with them. What, if anything, happened to Shakespeare's drama when the King's Men also began to perform regularly at the private, indoor Blackfriars Theater in addition to the Globe Theater? Critics occasionally observe that Shakespeare wrote for the box office, and he certainly appealed to the audiences. But who made up the audiences—what social and economic groups with what tastes and expectations? Further, what about Shakespeare's fellow dramatists? How well did he know them and their work? What influence did they have on him? With whom did he collaborate? Learning more about the drama of the time means understanding that many of Shakespeare's dramatic conventions and techniques derived from widely accepted practices.

Another approach of theatrical criticism explores the stage history of plays since the seventeenth century and documents changing stage traditions and interpretations. How the great actors of the past have come to terms with Shakespearean characters reveals dimensions and subtleties that may not have been appreciated before. The staging of plays can involve historical study as one tries to reconstruct the likely performance in the Elizabethan theater, or it can be immediately practical, as in the mounting of a contemporary production. Much of performance criticism has focused on the practical problems of mounting a performance. Either way, one has to grapple with and resolve certain issues that a reader may simply pass over. For example, how does one stage the supposed plunging of Gloucester from the cliff at Dover in *King Lear?* And what about the Ghost in *Hamlet*—should he be a character on stage or an offstage voice? Theater criticism in particular attempts to answer an almost endless list of such questions.

A subcategory includes film and television. The twentieth century has created these new ways of producing Shakespeare, and the critical interpretations of certain films and film directors have multiplied. The BBC Shakespeare series for television has made the plays available to millions of people worldwide. Critics try to assess the contribution and limitations of this new form, including how film and television versions compare with stage productions.

GENRE CRITICISM

As the evidence in chapter 2 suggests, a vast amount of critical energy has been expended in the study of the *genres:* comedy, history, tragedy, and sonnet. Critics often create subcategories within the genres, such as problem comedies, satirical tragedies, Roman plays, Romances, pastoral comedies, tragicomedies. We have yet to reach the full extent of Polonius's famous list of such forms in *Hamlet.* What definitions and practical understanding of these forms prevailed in the Elizabethan period? Did Aristotle's critical theory of tragedy or that of the Italian critics of the sixteenth century influence practitioners of the art? How does Shakespearean tragedy differ from Aristotle's description or our knowledge of Greek tragedy? We may observe that *Romeo and Juliet* differs from the later tragedy *Hamlet*. Does this reveal some sort of development in Shakespeare's practice of writing tragedies? Similar questions can be raised about the other genres. Comedy may be defined by its themes, structure, and form; or one might emphasize the comic characters as the most distinguishing feature of these plays. How do Shakespeare's comedies differ from, say, Jonson's in spirit and in form? What defines a history play, and what about its precursors? Who else wrote plays about English history? Conceivably, Shakespeare had little systematic theory of form, being more concerned with getting another play finished than with whether it fit some conception of genre. Some critics have suggested that we should not refer to Shakespearean tragedy or comedy but, instead, to Shakespearean tragedies or comedies—that each has an independent existence not tied to those that went before or came after. Whatever conclusions we reach about Shakespeare's critical knowledge of literary theory, we can safely assume that he did not first immerse himself in critical treatises and then proceed to write.

An increasing number of studies challenge the notion that genre differentiation depends on fixed, stable boundaries. We have been aware for quite a while that violations of genre boundary occur often in Shakespeare—comic elements in tragedy, tragic elements in comedy, for example—but only in the last few years have critics turned their attention to mixed forms to understand the double problem of boundary definition and genre differentiation. This problem can be tackled from a variety of critical approaches and methods. Historical criticism helps us understand genre theory in the Renaissance. Other critics have focused on the archaic or archeological strata embedded in the works themselves, thus helping us understand the ways in which Shakespeare both represents and departs from inherited patterns. Many interesting questions have been posed: to what extent does one form or genre develop in opposition to another? How do comedy and tragedy overlap in terms of structure? Where does romance fit with the other genres? The influence of poststructuralist and deconstructionist critics has been felt, particularly in the notion that the text simultaneously erects and erases boundaries in a process often referred to as "closure." The full implications of genre boundary and differentiation studies remain to be determined.

ANALYSES OF LANGUAGE AND IMAGERY

Partly in reaction to excesses of pedantic biographical and historical criticism, a wave designated "new criticism" hit the critical shores in the early decades of the twentieth century. It places priority on the intensive exploration of poetic *language* (and, of course, encompasses much more than just Shakespearean criticism). Proponents of new criticism believe that the reader ought not be so concerned with biography or the historical milieu in which the writer wrote; instead, the sensitive reader should respond to the drama (or whatever) as poetry. To oversimplify, the reader ideally sits down with no other paraphernalia than the text itself (probably shorn of footnotes) and comes to terms with the work of art. The potential rewards and risks seem quite great. Such an approach reminds us that Shakespeare excelled as a master poet, but it risks forgetting that he functioned also as a master dramatist. At its most extreme, this critical method makes each play an expanded metaphysical poem. Probably no other school of criticism, however, has had so profound an impact on the practical matter of teaching Shakespeare. It has led to specialized studies of Shakespeare's verse—meter and rhythm—and how these elements contribute to our apprehending the poetic meaning. A number of books and essays have explored the intricacies of Shakespeare's language—his use of word play, ambiguity, paradox, verbal irony. The design of the Elizabethan theater itself encouraged an emphasis on language, as it provided a platform stage that allowed the audience to focus fully on what the actors said. The drama could thus in the best sense be deemed "wordy." With limited printing and limited literacy, this era emphasized oral communication, with the theater functioning as an obvious manifestation. Sensitivity to the word governed those who sat or stood in the Globe.

The work on language includes the study and analysis of *imagery*. This critical approach got its greatest impetus in the 1930s, when several seminal studies appeared. Today, commenting on the plays' images has become a widespread practice, and many books pursue this particular critical method. Some studies have examined or isolated individual images or groups of images, documenting, for example, the extensive sun imagery in *Richard II,* disease imagery in *Hamlet,* and garden imagery in the history plays. Patterns of repeated imagery, often referred to as iterative images, reveal a meaningful order. Or particular images may be grouped together several times in a play. Some critics seize on a single image as shaping the whole structure. For example, the image of evil in *Richard III* may be so pervasive as to imply an ordering of the play around it.

The dramatist obviously uses images to comment on theme and character. One cannot recall the image of Richard II as "glistering Phaeton" without understanding something about his dramatic character, or the constant images of storm that accompany Lear without perceiving that they reflect the tempest in his mind. In other words, seldom does Shakespeare use images merely as decoration; they have some dramatic function. Recent studies have underscored the significance of visual images produced in the staging of the plays—gestures, poses, costume. As Richard and Bolingbroke together momentarily hold the crown in Act IV of *Richard II,* they offer a striking emblem of the struggle for kingship and testify to the compelling power invested in the symbol of the crown. The larger view of Shakespeare's imagery has attempted to trace his development as a dramatist through his use of imagery: from early, fitful moments when the images seem mainly decorative to the full integration of images with dramatic action, character, and theme.

Reacting to these traditional views of language, one critical movement, referred to as poststructuralism or deconstruction, focuses on differences, oppositions, and antitheses as it asks ever more challenging questions about the ways in which the text differs from itself. Questioning, probing, and reading against the grain of the text's language, poststructuralists examine the means by which the text achieves stability. Deconstruction focuses on such oppositions as writing/speech, signifier/signified, literature/criticism, reader/writer and challenges the desire for unity, a center, and metaphysical truths. Although unable to escape this desire for unity and center, we must recognize that the centering equilibrium exists only for a moment. Poststructuralism challenges many traditional assumptions about language, imagery, text, and literature itself. A number of studies using poststructuralist strategies with regard to Shakespeare have appeared.

THE STUDY OF CHARACTER

In addition to matters of generic form and language, many critics concentrate on the study of *character.* Indeed, this may be one of the oldest critical approaches. Analysis of character inextricably links with the nature of drama itself. Although Aristotle insists that plot constitutes the soul of drama, the experiences of readers and theatergoers suggest that a striking character may be the most memorable element of a drama. The characters seem so real that some critics choose to discuss them as if they are real rather than fictional persons, or as if they have an existence beyond the play. An extreme case occurred in a mid-nineteenth-century study of the childhoods of Shakespeare's female characters. Obviously, one potential problem with this critical approach emerges as a variation of "woods-for-treeism," that is, gaining a dominant character but losing the whole play. What motivates Iago? What causes the sudden onslaught of irrational jealousy in Leontes? The questions could continue, since we obviously have a keen interest in character motivation. How much ink has been spilled trying to explain what Hamlet does (or doesn't) and why he does it (or doesn't)? Judging by what has been written, Hamlet remains perhaps the most fascinating character in all of Western literature—an extraordinary testimony to the creation of character.

PSYCHOLOGICAL CRITICISM

Concern for character leads to *psychological* criticism. The complex psychology of character in Renaissance drama, and in Shakespeare in particular, remains one of the striking features that sets it apart from medieval drama. Thanks to Freud, we can rather casually hold the opinion, whether valid or not, that Hamlet suffers from the Oedipus complex (Freud drew generously from Shakespeare in his writings). Psychoanalytical criticism has thrown off sparks of illumination, but whether they catch fire or merely fizzle often depends on how well the critic remembers that these are fictional characters. Complications occur because of the characters' inability to respond to psychoanalytical questioning except in the voices and words that the dramatist has given them. Some studies have sought to define Renaissance psychology and then view the plays in that light. In order to understand many of the references in the plays, one needs a rudimentary knowledge of Elizabethan psychology—the theory of the humors, for example. But reading all the Renaissance treatises on melancholy cannot finally explain our reaction to Hamlet or the construction of his character.

Recent psychological studies have focused on such questions as identity, doubling, sexuality, and personality development. Inevitably, some critics have examined family structure and its psychological implications: problems of parent-child relationships, paternal narcissism, fratricidal rivalry, and especially father-daughter bonds. Some less well-founded studies have attempted to move from the plays to say something about the psychological development of Shakespeare himself. Obviously, psychological understanding of the characters has informed theatrical productions of the plays.

THEMATIC AND MYTHIC CRITICISM

In a pursuit of *thematic* criticism, a small but controversial group of critics has taken what can be termed the "Christian" approach to Shakespeare. For generations, Shakespeare has been examined for the instruction he has to offer about righteous living. Indeed, in the early days of teaching his plays, this became one of the purposes. For some time, preachers with varying degrees of actual knowledge have borrowed freely from Shakespeare, usually a quotation to drive home a point. Much of the early response includes the notion that to be a good writer one must first be a good man. Shakespeare grew up in the midst of a solidly Christian culture; but we know nothing about his personal religious practices or beliefs except that he was baptized, married, and buried in the Church of England. Studies have indicated Shakespeare's extensive knowledge of the Bible as reflected in his plays and poems; that provokes no controversy. When critics interpret a work in specific Christian theological terms difficulty ensues. Do the endings of certain plays or the overall themes seem specifically Christian? Does the Duke in *Measure for Measure* represent God's providence? Does Othello find salvation? One could go on raising such debatable questions. The whole nature of "Christian tragedy" is critically vexing, and the idea seems contradictory to some. The Romances have been read as religious allegories; Christ symbols have been found here and there. The pitfalls of this particular critical approach should be obvious without denying that, in its more sensible moments, it has provided new perspectives on the plays. Other critics have examined dramatic themes not necessarily colored by religion, including jealousy, justice, love, education, patience, duty, moral obligation, suffering, revenge, transformation, reconciliation, politics, substitution, inheritance, and greed. Thematic criticism argues for the importance of ideas in the plays.

Mythic criticism asserts that Shakespeare participates in and reflects myths common to different civilizations. Drama itself seems a form of ritual, or at least it contains ritualistic qualities as it establishes a participatory relationship between actors and audience. Shakespeare's use of classical myths and ancient mythology appears obvious in the plays. On occasion, he seems to have had a specific myth in mind that ordered and structured the play, such as his dependence on the Pyramus and Thisbe and the Venus and Adonis stories. The legends of King Lear and Cymbeline come from a shadowy pseudohistory that Shakespeare fashions into drama. Critics have found, especially in the comedies or in a figure such as Falstaff, reflections and embodiments of a Saturnalian myth. The whole process of social and holiday indulgence may reflect customs and practices current in Shakespeare's own time. The necessary aesthetic distinctions between a holiday occasion and formal drama have led to fascinating criticism. The myth of the seasons has been seen to underlie the nature of comedy and tragedy, with the winter's tale of tragedy in opposition to the summer, life-renewing spirit of comedy. Such criticism explores issues of anthropology and collective psychology. This mode of analysis runs the risk, as do other methods, of forgetting the theater. But if these critical approaches even approximate the truth, they should give the lie, once and for all, to the idea that Shakespeare wrote as an untutored genius.

FEMINIST AND GENDER CRITICISM

The 1980s witnessed an explosion in book-length studies that analyze Shakespeare from a *feminist* perspective or that at least have a *gender-based* approach to his works. Feminist criticism confronts two primary questions: what does it mean to be a female character in Shakespeare's fictional world, and what does it mean to be a female reader of Shakespeare at the end of the twentieth century? The first question had been broached earlier, but not in a satisfactory or sophisticated manner. As a result of these fundamental questions, feminist criticism has relied heavily on historical and psychological approaches. Thus, a number of critics have tried to ascertain the position and plight of women in Shakespeare's time: what social conditions prevailed? What influence did women exercise in marriage, in commerce, in politics? What effect did the system of patriarchy have on women?

If one can answer these questions—and they are not as simple or straightforward as they seem—then how does one square this understanding with the way Shakespeare portrays women in his works? Do the plays reflect the actual world, contradict it, criticize it, or what? Does Shakespeare show sympathy toward women in ways that his society and his contemporaries did not? Could he be a feminist? What does it mean if some of Shakespeare's female characters appear strong and powerful when the historical record indicates that society expected women to be meek and docile?

Feminist critics have also explored on a psychological basis what it meant or means to be a woman. Can some feminine principle be recognized and defined that operates in the plays? Do the males feel threatened, endangered psychologically, by the presence of this opposing force? What does it mean to the male characters that women have the power of birth, given to them by nature? Do women envy men, desiring their aggressiveness and prowess? What role do female characters play in sexual relationships? What defines the father-daughter bond?

Additionally, feminist critics have tried to assess the relationship between gender and genre. Some have argued that the plays depict comic women and tragic men because one generic form seems particularly compatible with the feminine principle and the other suits the masculine perspective. But how do gender and genre connect in mixed forms, such as the history plays and the Romances? Does understanding gender help us interpret the structure of the plays? Do some particularly strong women cross generic boundaries?

The studies listed and discussed in chapter 2 reveal the diversity of the questions raised and approaches tried by feminist critics. Also, part of the contribution of such critics has been simply to counteract decades of male bias and insensitivity in the practice of criticism.

CULTURAL STUDY

Emerging in part from feminist and historicist studies and influenced by anthropology, *cultural study,* a relatively new critical approach, focuses on cultural practices, those social practices that impinge on the theater. These may include seasonal festivities, courtship rituals, hospitality, human sexuality, and everything in between. What formed the basic understanding of the body from the viewpoints of medicine and of physical desire? What did Shakespeare's society understand about sexuality? How did it regulate sexual practices, and how did the drama express these concerns? What cultural mythmaking appeared in the plays of the period? Why did King James I regularly order noblemen back to their country estates so that they might practice hospitality? How did hospitality and dramatic entertainment intersect? How did conflicts about property rights and social degree affect drama?

Some of these questions scholars and critics have raised with special force in the 1990s. In a way, cultural study amalgamates and appropriates various critical approaches but has a recurring focus on actual social practices. Displaying and reflecting such practices, the Shakespearean theater stands in the vortex of social challenge and change.

TEXTUAL CRITICISM

Another school of criticism deserves attention for its exceptional impact on Shakespearean studies—*textual* criticism. The practitioners of this form of scholarship have made a major contribution in the twentieth century. Students and other readers are often unconcerned about the nature of the editions they use, and certainly the standard editions mentioned in chapter 2 will not seriously mislead anyone. But such has not always been the case, as in many earlier texts, impressionistically edited and emended according to the editor's whim, whether on poetic or moral grounds. Textual criticism remains an art, though it has developed some objective, scientific methods. Fundamentally, this approach seeks to determine what Shakespeare wrote—not questions of disputed authorship, but literally what he wrote—based on the valid belief that correct understanding and analysis depend on a sound, reliable text. In the history of Shakespearean criticism, a number of examples exist in which the critic relied on a poor and incorrect text, thus damaging interpretation.

Textual criticism, according to Fredson Bowers, confronts at least three major problems. (1) To determine the nature of the printer's copy; that is, whether the printing depended on the author's manuscript, a scribal copy, a promptbook from the theater, and so on. (2) To establish the relationship between all known copies of the text. For example, how do the three different versions of *Hamlet* relate to one another, and which provides the authoritative text on which to construct a sound edition? Or what about a single edition that survives in several copies with variant readings? (3) To understand the nature of the printing process itself in order to know what effect this might have had on the transmission of the text. What typical methods did compositors use to set a page of type? What common work habits can be discerned in a given print shop? Did that shop have one or two presses? Such questions involve descriptive or analytical bibliography, the ''science'' of the physical makeup of a book. Investigations into the printing process have led to the discovery and identification of the compositors who set the type; frequently their spelling habits and preferences appear in the text, not Shakespeare's. Study of the First Folio has isolated some six or seven different compositors and the portions of the Folio that they set.

All these matters have a profound effect on how the textual editor proceeds. Computers now assist in sorting evidence, thus providing a reliable base from which to work. In the early days of this critical movement, sometimes referred to as the "new bibliography," some believed that all problems could be resolved if we followed the methodological "rules." Less sanguine today, we watch almost every solution give rise to additional problems, but textual criticism remains an area of challenge and intellectual rigor, stimulating lively debate among its theorists and practitioners.

MAJOR SCHOLARS AND CRITICS

This section attempts to single out some of the leading scholars and critics. The vast quantity of material on Shakespeare makes any such selection perilous and difficult. The choices here, of necessity subjective but not whimsical, should not in any way be construed as indicating the "top ten" among Shakespearean critics; at best, this section underscores those who have been especially influential. In a simpler day, it may have been possible to name the outstanding Shakespearean scholar; to try to do so now risks madness. A number of the persons mentioned here receive more extensive treatment in chapter 2.

Samuel Johnson (1709–1784) epitomized and at the same time reacted against eighteenth-century neoclassical criticism. His *Preface to Shakespeare* (1765), an important critical statement, views Shakespeare as a poet of nature, holding up the mirror to manners and to life. The characters become genuine progeny of common humanity; we easily recognize them. Curiously, Johnson believed that Shakespeare's true genius lay in comedy, not tragedy. Rebutting critical tradition, Johnson exonerates Shakespeare on the issue of observing the unities and accepts the mingling of tragic and comic scenes. Although his praise outweighs his faultfinding, Johnson outlines a series of problems that he further documents in the notes of his edition. He complains of loose plots and of Shakespeare's failure to fulfill the function of moral instruction. The dramatist too readily indulges in a quibble—"the fatal Cleopatra," in Johnson's famous phrase. Johnson's concern for style and dramatic construction, his recognition of the significance of the characters, and his laying to rest the argument over the unities all indicate a keen critical mind at work.

Although he never wrote a book on Shakespeare, Samuel Taylor Coleridge (1772–1834), one of the ablest critics of any era, made a major contribution through ideas scattered in notes, parts of essays, and lectures. The final view may be somewhat fragmentary, but several basic ideas emerge. Coleridge reacts as the supreme romantic critic against earlier criticism that had honored some concept of neoclassical rules. For Coleridge, Shakespeare's organic form, not mechanical in any way, shapes and develops itself from within. Coleridge also emphasizes Shakespeare as a great poet as well as dramatist. Strangely, few before Coleridge had paid much attention to this obvious fact. The logical critical extension of such an assumption may be seen in the close reading of the poetry by the "new critics" and others. In one of his excessive moments, Coleridge likened himself to Hamlet; but in a more serious vein, he pointed the way toward an emphasis on the characters, as he observed the psychological and moral sensitivity of Shakespeare's creations. The willing suspension of disbelief constitutes poetic faith, and this doctrine has clear ramifications for our perception of drama. Scattered comments on some of the plays offer insight, but the ideas sketched above form the more permanent part of Coleridge's legacy to Shakespearean criticism.

A. C. Bradley (1851–1935) stands as a giant among critics in the early twentieth century. His work on the tragedies has become one of the major contributions of this century, though in truth, Bradley may be seen as the culmination of Victorian criticism. In any event, his detailed analyses of characters and the primacy assigned to them provide a critical approach still quite appealing. E. E. Stoll (1874–1959), in his best-known book *Art and Artifice in Shakespeare* (Cambridge UP, 1933), worked in a critical direction opposed to that of Bradley. His ideas have also had a long-range impact. He modified biographical or character criticism, insisting instead that a play must be judged in light of its milieu. He places emphasis on the dramatic conventions that Shakespeare reflects and by so doing opened the door to the development of historical criticism. On the artistic level, Stoll comments: "The greatest of dramatists is careful, not so much for the single character, as for the drama; indeed, he observes not so much the probabilities of the action, or the psychology of the character, as the psychology of the audience, for whom both action and character are framed" (168). In other words, Shakespeare's art focuses on being true to art rather than being true to life. Stoll, much more than Bradley, emphasizes Shakespeare as a man of the theater. (Stoll's book was the first major critical work by an American published by an English press.)

Several others who began in the early part of the twentieth century have made special contributions in historical research and criticism. E. K. Chambers's (1866–1954) monumental four-volume study and collection of materials on the Elizabethan stage has had a major influence on the development of scholarship. Similarly, his collection of materials relevant to Shakespeare's life remains unsurpassed. Hardin Craig (1875–1968), noted as an editor and great teacher, did much to define the philosophical and historical context in which Shakespeare wrote. That critical concern E. M. W. Tillyard (1889–1962) shared. His brief book on the Elizabethan world has become a classic statement of the orthodox, hierarchical worldview that the Elizabethans inherited. Although Tillyard wrote about the early comedies and the Romances, his influential book on the history plays is his best-known work. His vision and interpretation of the histories constituted the accepted view for some time, though it has since been challenged. It remains, nevertheless, a landmark in Shakespearean criticism.

The new directions in bibliographical and textual studies gained impetus from a number of scholars, among them R. B. McKerrow (1872–1940), A. W. Pollard (1859–1944), W. W. Greg (1875–1959), and John Dover Wilson (1881–1969). Singling out individual works remains difficult, because these scholars produced many and various books. McKerrow's introductory guide to bibliography and Pollard's (in collaboration with Redgrave) *Short Title Catalogue* of all the books printed in England, Scotland, and Ireland between 1475 and 1640 have both been of enormous help and have made additional research possible. Greg's influential essay on the rationale of the copy text, his bibliography of English printed drama to the Restoration, and his book on the First Folio have been major contributions to textual studies. Wilson, who produced books on *Hamlet* and on the comedies, explored many new avenues of textual theory as editor of the New Cambridge edition of Shakespeare.

The early analyses of Shakespeare's imagery by Caroline Spurgeon (1869–1942) and Wolfgang Clemen (1909–1990) (both discussed in chapter 2) influenced many later critical studies. Spurgeon's arguments have been much modified, but most studies of imagery start with her book. Unfortunately, she uses imagery to reach conclusions about Shakespeare the man, not content to analyze what the images reveal about the drama. Clemen's book, published in German in 1936 and translated into English in 1951, explores the development of the dramatist's use of imagery. G. Wilson Knight (1897–1985), whose productive critical career also began in the 1930s, studied imagery imaginatively. But to categorize Knight as a critic who investigated the dramatist's imagery unduly restricts one's view of him. His highly metaphysical, religious, symbolic, spatial vision of the drama does not fit neatly into any single category, though he emphasizes imagery in a number of his essays. He never fails to offer insight into the drama or poetry, even if one finally disagrees with him.

More recent years have witnessed enormous productivity, but only a few persons can be singled out for their contributions. G. E. Bentley and Alfred Harbage deserve special recognition. Bentley, in his seven-volume compilation of material on the Jacobean and Caroline stage, provides an impressive base from which additional research has sprung. His other books on the Shakespearean stage and on the profession of the dramatist during this period use some of his research materials and present an analysis of significant theatrical problems. Harbage not only edited certain plays and served as general editor of the Pelican Shakespeare but also contributed important historical studies, principally, *Shakespeare's Audience* (1941), *As They Liked It* (1947), and *Shakespeare and the Rival Traditions* (1952). Harbage's view of the makeup of the theater and the audience and his thesis of a profound cleavage between public and private theaters have provoked challenge, but his contributions remain considerable.

Geoffrey Bullough and S. Schoenbaum also work in a historical tradition. Bullough's multivolume collection on Shakespeare's narrative and dramatic sources constitutes a major piece of scholarship, providing a sound text of and extensive guide to the sources—a work not likely to be supplanted. Schoenbaum revised Harbage's *Annals of English Drama*, but his major work exclusively on Shakespeare has been his work on Shakespeare biography. In one book he sifts through the mass of materials concerned with constructing a life of Shakespeare. Given the increasing number of biographies, certainly the time had come for such a survey and assessment of them. Schoenbaum handles the subject with skill and wit. He has become *the* biographer of Shakespeare.

The present era has yielded many important textual studies. Among the principal contributors have been Fredson Bowers and Charlton Hinman. This period of bibliographical research, often called the "age of Bowers," testifies to the impact of his work. His principles of bibliography and techniques of editing have been much imitated. His editorship of *Studies in Bibliography* provided an outlet for research and set high standards for it. The culmination of Hinman's work came in his two-volume study of the printing and proofreading of the Shakespeare First Folio. The monumental examination of several dozen copies of the Folio yielded conclusions about how the printer put the book together and many other details associated with its publication. Additional studies now supplement Hinman's study of the compositors who set the type for the book.

The post–World War II explosion of Shakespearean criticism makes it impossible to single out the most outstanding critics of this era. Critical fortunes have a way of waxing and waning, but the contribution of research and scholarship may be easier to assess. The materials evaluated in chapter 2 provide a partial basis for grasping contributions in Shakespearean criticism in the latter half of the twentieth century. Depending on one's perspective, the productivity of Shakespearean critics may be either a curse or a blessing, a burden or an embarrassment of riches. Time may be the final arbiter of which critical studies survive and have influence.

Only a willingness to suffer the fate of fools who rush in where angels fear to tread would lead one to speculate about where Shakespearean criticism (or anything else) will be in the twenty-first century. We will doubtless have more editions of Shakespeare, and we will have critical studies that pour old wine into new bottles. Probably we will witness more interdisciplinary studies that link Shakespeare's works with other art forms—music, pictorial art and iconography, even other dramatic forms—that explore the full range of cultural implications (past and present) of Shakespeare's art, that examine the psychological and practical consequences of gender awareness. If we are lucky, we will have criticism that asks questions as yet undreamed of. A hundred years ago, who could have foreseen the diversity and richness of current criticism?

Part of the beauty and mystery of Shakespeare's art derives from its never-ceasing appeal and its ability to stimulate the intellect and emotions of people far removed from one another in time and place. Each passing decade and each passing century verify Jonson's seemingly extravagant claim that Shakespeare was "not of an age, but for all time."

CHAPTER TWO
A Guide to the Resources

This is the heart of the matter. This chapter presents a selection of some of the most valuable and useful books, arranged under the following categories: bibliographies and reference guides, editions, studies in the genres (comedies, romances, histories, tragedies, sonnets), studies of groups and movements, interdisciplinary studies, periodicals, and biographical studies. With a few exceptions, no essays are included, only books. Students should consult the appropriate bibliographies to gain access to potentially helpful essays in periodicals. Students trying to track down a particular critic should consult the index of authors.

Obviously, summarizing and analyzing these scores of books involve paraphrasing the authors' ideas and sometimes direct or indirect quotations. Names of publishers and dates of publication immediately follow each reference. Below is a list of abbreviations for the titles of Shakespeare's works:

Ado	*Much Ado about Nothing*
Ant.	*Antony and Cleopatra*
AWW	*All's Well That Ends Well*
AYL	*As You Like It*
Cor.	*Coriolanus*
Cym.	*Cymbeline*
Err.	*Comedy of Errors*
Ham.	*Hamlet*
1H4	*Henry IV, Part 1*

2H4	*Henry IV, Part 2*
H5	*Henry V*
1H6	*Henry VI, Part 1*
2H6	*Henry VI, Part 2*
3H6	*Henry VI, Part 3*
H8	*Henry VIII*
JC	*Julius Caesar*
Jn.	*King John*
LLL	*Love's Labor's Lost*
Lr.	*King Lear*
Luc.	*The Rape of Lucrece*
Mac.	*Macbeth*
MM	*Measure for Measure*
MND	*A Midsummer Night's Dream*
MV	*The Merchant of Venice*
Oth.	*Othello*
Per.	*Pericles*
R2	*Richard II*
R3	*Richard III*
Rom.	*Romeo and Juliet*
Shr.	*The Taming of the Shrew*
TGV	*Two Gentlemen of Verona*
Tim.	*Timon of Athens*
Tit.	*Titus Andronicus*
Tmp.	*The Tempest*
TN	*Twelfth Night*
TNK	*Two Noble Kinsmen*
Tro.	*Troilus and Cressida*
Ven.	*Venus and Adonis*
Wiv.	*The Merry Wives of Windsor*
WT	*The Winter's Tale*

BIBLIOGRAPHY AND REFERENCE GUIDES

Joseph Rosenblum, *Shakespeare: An Annotated Bibliography* (Salem P, 1992), provides the most recent bibliography. This book arranges items by topics, such as reference works, editions, biographies, and general studies, and then lists the individual plays. Rosenblum includes books and articles.

Shakespeare bibliography takes a giant step into the electronic age with the appearance of the first installment of *World Shakespeare Bibliography on CD-ROM, 1900–Present* (Cambridge UP, 1995), ed. James L. Harner. The first disk covers the period 1990–1993 in hypercard format for CD-ROM. This bibliography grows out of the annual ones prepared for *Shakespeare Quarterly.*

Part of the Goldentree Bibliography series, David Bevington's *Shakespeare* (AHM Publishing, 1978) offers nearly 4,700 entries arranged by topics (such as bibliographies; social, political, and intellectual background; biography; editions and textual criticism; and studies in genre) and then entries on the plays and poems. Bevington uses asterisks to mark those items that he considers indispensable; otherwise, there is little annotation. For a number of the plays, Bevington creates subtopics of criticism, thereby assisting in sorting out the criticism. Clear and easy to use, this bibliography makes a good starting point for a survey of Shakespearean material published between 1930 and 1977. One may find additional items in Andrew M. McLean's *Shakespeare: Annotated Bibliographies and Media Guide for Teachers* (National Council of Teachers of English, 1980), which is a three-part bibliography: (1) an extensive bibliography on teaching Shakespeare in high school and college, (2) a listing of Shakespeare in films and on television, and (3) a guide to media for teaching Shakespeare (audiovisual materials).

A Selective Bibliography of Shakespeare, prepared by James G. McManaway and Jeanne Addison Roberts (UP of Virginia, 1975), contains some 4,500 items covering the period 1930 to 1970, with a few exceptions. The table of contents reveals the organization of the book, which surveys material on individual plays and poems and specific topics. Some of the entries have annotations.

Larry S. Champion's *The Essential Shakespeare: An Annotated Bibliography of Major Modern Studies,* 2d ed. (G. K. Hall, 1993) includes 1,800 entries in its 540-plus pages. Champion covers the period 1900 to 1991 and annotates what he considers to be the significant works in scholarship and criticism. He begins with a general studies section and then moves to the individual works arranged by genre. His annotations, primarily descriptive rather than evaluative, are thorough and helpful.

Much more extensive, but now outdated, is Gordon Ross Smith's *A Classified Shakespeare Bibliography, 1936–1958* (Pennsylvania State UP, 1963). Over 20,000 items appear in this book. On pp. xlix–li, Smith discusses the use of the bibliography and its methods of compilation; on pp. vii–xli, the two broad categories "General" and "Works" are broken down, which should make it easier to find references on specific topics. For example, under the heading "General," entries appear on bibliography, surveys of scholarship, life, sources, stage, literary taste, influence, criticism, and the Bacon controversy. This bibliography examines works individually and also includes a category on the chronology of the drama.

Smith's bibliography continues the earlier one by Walter Ebisch and Levin Schücking, *A Shakespeare Bibliography* (Clarendon, 1931), which had a cutoff date of 1929. Clarendon Press published a supplement to this bibliography in 1937, covering the years 1930 to 1935. Eight pages outline the contents of the volume. The classification categories resemble those adopted by Smith, so students should be able to thread their way through both bibliographies if they know the format of one of them (even so, they can be a bit perplexing).

William Jaggard compiled the first full-fledged bibliography on Shakespeare: *Shakespeare Bibliography* (Shakespeare P, 1911; later reprints). Jaggard boasts of over 36,000 entries and references and claims that the book is "so simply arranged that a child can use it"–a dubious claim. The entries appear alphabetically, according to author, title, and subject. Under the heading "Shakespeare," separate works are listed first, arranged alphabetically and with each item in chronological order. Jaggard is especially strong on early editions of the plays but not very useful on matters of criticism or interpretation.

Ronald Berman produced what he calls a "discursive bibliography," *A Reader's Guide to Shakespeare's Plays,* revised edition (Scott Foresman, 1973; originally published, 1965). Berman treats each play in terms of text, editions, sources, criticism, and staging, with criticism getting the main attention. He covers articles as well as books and does not hide his critical opinion of the material he reviews. Not an enumerative bibliography as such, this one offers a narrative guide to the scholarship and criticism of the plays.

Bruce Sajdak, *Shakespeare Index: An Annotated Bibliography of Critical Articles on the Plays, 1959–1983* (Kraus, 1992), includes a citation and author index in volume 1, arranged by play and by year of publication of the critical article. Volume 2 provides character, scene, and subject indexes. These volumes offer excellent information about articles published in periodicals in the years included.

Stanley Wells's *Shakespeare: Bibliographical Guide* (Oxford UP, 1990) provides nineteen discursive essays by various people on text, performance, early comedies, middle comedies, and certain individual plays (for example, *Ham., Lr., Oth.,* and *Mac.*). Each essay concludes with a list of references, citing articles as well as books. The book closes with a piece on critical developments.

The Garland Shakespeare Bibliographies, general editor William L. Godshalk (Garland, 1980–), offer extensive annotated bibliographies of Shakespeare criticism since 1940 for their respective plays. A general introduction assesses critical trends and offers an overview. Thorough indexes enable the user to retrieve information easily.

An ongoing project, *The Biblioteca Shakespeariana* (Microforms International), is a series of 3,000 works on Shakespeare reproduced on microfiche. Some thirty units, including one on Shakespeare bibliography, make up the series. Other topics include Shakespeare's life and society, Shakespeare's texts, Shakespeare's reading, Shakespeare in performance, and Shakespearean scholarship and criticism. Various editors have chosen the material to be reproduced. In the section on bibliographies, for example, six major bibliographies are reproduced in their entirety on microfiche.

Although not specifically prepared for that purpose, the *Folger Shakespeare Library: Catalog of the Shakespeare Collections,* 2 vols. (G. K. Hall, 1972), serves not only as a guide to one of the world's greatest Shakespeare collections but also as a bibliography. Volume 1 covers the hundreds of editions of Shakespeare, both collections and individual plays, all arranged chronologically. Volume 2 treats Shakespeare as a subject, with some fifteen categories, and Shakespeare as the first word of a title.

The Cambridge Bibliography of English Literature, vol. 1, edited by F. W. Bateson (Cambridge UP, 1940, with a supplement in 1957), offers a generous section on Shakespeare (pp. 540–608; Supplement, pp. 257–93). Bateson surveys such topics as bibliography, life, works, and criticism; and the entries are arranged both alphabetically and chronologically with cross-references to the appropriate parts of the Ebisch and Schücking bibliography. The most recent version of this bibliography is *The New Cambridge Bibliography of English Literature,* edited by George Watson (Cambridge UP, 1974). In volume 1, the extensive Shakespeare bibliography may be found in columns 1473–1636.

A specialized bibliography, John W. Velz's *Shakespeare and the Classical Tradition: A Critical Guide to Commentary, 1660–1960* (U of Minnesota P, 1968) attempts to gather, classify, summarize, and appraise the commentary that has been written since 1660. The entries are arranged alphabetically by author under nine different categories, all geared toward the topic of Shakespeare's participation in the classical tradition. Velz includes a valuable index. His book greatly expands the earlier one by Selma Guttman, *The Foreign Sources of Shakespeare's Works: An Annotated Bibliography of the Commentary Written on This Subject between 1904 and 1940* (Columbia UP, 1947; reprint, 1968). Guttman lists the foreign authors and the pertinent editions and translations that could have been known by Shakespeare. This bibliography includes foreign sources other than classical ones.

In addition to these sources that cover long periods, other publications list or comment on Shakespearean items annually. Students should consult these publications to bring their research up-to-date. The *Shakespeare Quarterly,* published since 1950 and now under the auspices of the Folger Library, contains an extensive "Annotated World Bibliography" on Shakespeare. The subject index aids the researcher in tracking down potentially useful essays or books. There is a *Cumulative Index* to volumes 1–15 (1950–1964) of the *Quarterly* itself, prepared by Martin Seymour-Smith (AMS P, 1969), which offers easy access to the articles, reviews, and notes of the journal. Each year, the Modern Language Association produces the *MLA International Bibliography,* sometimes filed separately from the journal *PMLA.* The annual bibliography began in volume 37

(1922). The section on Shakespeare has entries on general topics and on the individual works. The *Shakespeare Association Bulletin,* published between 1924 and 1949 by the Shakespeare Association of America, also contains annual bibliographies. The *Annual Bibliography of English Language and Literature,* which began in 1920, is published by the Modern Humanities Research Association. This bibliography surveys nearly 800 journals and contains a section on Shakespeare. The English Association publishes *Year's Work in English Studies,* begun in 1919–1920, which presents in narrative form a summary and evaluation of materials published on Shakespeare, arranged under such categories as editions, textual matters, sources, bibliography, criticism, theater, and reprints. This book includes helpful indexes as well. Beginning in volume 19 (1922) and continuing through volume 66 (1969), *Studies in Philology* published annual Renaissance bibliographies that, of course, had sections on Shakespeare.

Students may want to consult more general bibliographies (often kept in special reference sections in college libraries). *The Reader's Guide to Periodical Literature* surveys popular magazines. Another H. Wilson publication, the *Essay and General Literature Index,* analyzes the content of books that are listed at the back of the publication. Since it is often difficult to determine the exact contents of a book by its title, this guide aids in efficient research. Published since 1960, *An Index to Book Reviews in the Humanities* arranges entries by author and includes the editions of Shakespeare under his name. *The British Humanities Index,* published quarterly by the Library Association of London, contains a section on Shakespeare. The front of the issue lists all surveyed British publications, a number of which are not covered in the *MLA Bibliography.* The *Social Sciences and Humanities Index,* issued four times a year, has a section on Shakespeare and a convenient list of all the periodicals indexed in it. Begun in 1938, *Dissertation Abstracts International* offers a guide to PhD theses. The simplest way to use it is to look in the index under "Shakespeare" for a list of all the pertinent dissertations. *Dissertations in English and American Literature, 1865–1964,* prepared by Lawrence F. McNamee (Bowker, 1968), also provides access to graduate theses. A 1969 supplement covering the years 1964 to 1968 includes a section on Shakespeare.

Much research involves some specialized knowledge of Shakespeare's language, and several books provide the means of understanding the patterns of usage and the peculiarities of Elizabethan English. With the advent of computers, new studies and analyses of Shakespeare's language have become possible; one of the results is the publication of new concordances to his works. These concordances record each word that Shakespeare uses, where he uses it, and the frequency of its use. The first new one to be completed is Marvin Spevack's *A Complete and Systematic Concordance to the Works of Shakespeare*, 9 vols. (Olms, 1968–1980). Volume 1 provides drama and character concordances to the comedies; volume 2, to the histories and nondramatic works; and volume 3, to the tragedies plus *Per., TNK,* and *Sir Thomas More.* Volumes 4–6 provide an alphabetical listing of all the words used by Shakespeare; volume 7, stage directions and speech prefixes; volume 8, the bad quartos; and volume 9, substantive variants. Spevack's work uses the Riverside Shakespeare edition for its references. *The Harvard Concordance to Shakespeare* (Harvard UP, 1973) is a one-volume abridgment of Spevack's concordance. The *Oxford Shakespeare Concordances* (Clarendon, 1969–1973), prepared by T. H. Howard-Hill, are published in individual volumes for each play, with the copy-text being the one chosen for the Oxford Old Spelling Shakespeare edition.

Other books also deal with Shakespeare's language and offer reference sources. E. A. Abbott, *A Shakespearian Grammar* (1870; reprint Dover, 1966), remains the standard grammar. It surveys the various grammatical constructions and includes a section on prosody. It contains illustrations from the plays and poems and often compares Shakespeare's usage with Early English and Middle English. In his book *Shakespeare's Vocabulary: Its Etymological Elements* (1903; reprint AMS P, 1966), Eilert Ekwall explores the derivation of Shakespeare's language.

G. L. Brook's *The Language of Shakespeare* (Andre Deutsch, 1976), a somewhat technical book, examines matters of syntax, accidence, word formation, rhetoric, dialects, pronunciation, spelling, and punctuation. On matters of syntax, Brook notes that Elizabethans preferred vigor to logic. He also discusses concord, word order, ellipsis, functional shift, nouns, pronouns, and other parts of speech. With regard to punctuation, Brook reminds us that the Elizabethan system was rhetorical. The influence of regional dialects can be found in Shakespeare's plays in vocabulary and pronunciation and, to a much lesser extent, in syntax and semantics.

A valuable reference book is Helge Kökeritz, *Shakespeare's Pronunciation* (Yale UP, 1953), which provides a comprehensive account of Shakespeare's pronunciation and presents the relevant phonological evidence for the reconstructions. Kökeritz believes that an adequate knowledge of pronunciation is essential for an understanding of the text and prosody.

Disputing some of Kökeritz's conclusions, Fausto Cercignani, in *Shakespeare's Works and Elizabethan Pronunciation* (Clarendon, 1981), sets out to examine the question of pronunciation in light of contemporary external evidence and in the wider framework of historical English phonology. In contrast to Kökeritz, who argues that Shakespeare's pronunciation closely resembled modern English, Cercignani argues that the types of speech reflected in Shakespeare's works and in those of contemporary writers on orthography and pronunciation reveal considerable discrepancies between Elizabethan and present-day standard usage. Most of the book examines and describes Shakespeare's phonology, the use of vowels and consonants.

A handy guide is C. T. Onions, *A Shakespeare Glossary* (Clarendon, 1911), enlarged and revised by Robert D. Eagleson (Clarendon, 1986). It is based on usages from the *Oxford English Dictionary*. Onions gives definitions of words with their location in Shakespeare's text; these references are sometimes supplemented with evidence from other contemporary writers. Comparable but much more extensive is Alexander Schmidt, *Shakespeare Lexicon*, 3d ed., revised by Gregor Sarrazin (1901; reprint Blom, 1968). All words are listed with definitions and citations to Shakespeare's text (Schmidt cites the Globe edition).

Another book that deals with definitions, but of a very special kind, is Eric Partridge's *Shakespeare's Bawdy,* 2d ed. (Routledge & Kegan Paul, 1968; 1st ed., 1947). Partridge includes an essay on the sexual and bawdy in Shakespeare, but the major portion of the book is a 180-page glossary, listing every word suspected of bawdy possibilities. Partridge provides definitions with references to location in the plays and poems. He certainly sheds quite a different light on Shakespeare.

E. A. M. Colman, in *The Dramatic Use of Bawdy in Shakespeare* (Longman, 1974), explores Shakespeare's development in the use of bawdy language in his plays and poems. Eventually, Colman argues, the dramatist made such language one of the most potent weapons in his dramatic armory. In order to trace development, Colman treats the plays more or less chronologically and includes a separate discussion of the Sonnets and poems.

Building on Morris Tilley's *A Dictionary of the Proverbs in England in the Sixteenth and Seventeenth Centuries* and subsequent studies, R. W. Dent, in his *Shakespeare's Proverbial Language: An Index* (U of California P, 1981), lists all the known proverbs, play by play, in Shakespeare's canon. Appendixes give the actual proverbs, cite possible origins, and cross-reference them to the plays. Dent's introduction indicates the principles by which he compiled this valuable index.

Of enormous value is *The Reader's Encyclopedia of Shakespeare,* edited by O. J. Campbell and Edward H. Quinn (Crowell, 1966; published in London by Methuen with the title *A Shakespeare Encyclopaedia*). This compendium of information covers a vast range of subjects and people, arranged alphabetically from "Aaron" to "Zuccarelli." It also includes excellent sections that review criticism and scholarship, arranged by century, as well as topics that comment on the various schools of criticism. The appendixes provide a chronology of events, transcripts of relevant documents, and a thirty-page selected bibliography. Charles Boyce, in *Shakespeare A to Z* (Dell, 1990), offers a similar guide of some 3,000 entries, including play summaries and commentary on characters, theaters, actors, and Shakespeare's contemporaries.

Three collections of essays offer students a good view of the critical and scholarly terrain. The earliest one is *A Companion to Shakespeare Studies,* edited by Harley Granville-Barker and G. B. Harrison (Cambridge UP, 1934). This book gives a fair sampling of where scholarship was in the early 1930s and offers valuable introductions to several topics—biography, theater,

Shakespeare's dramatic art, Elizabethan English, music, historical background, sources, text, the drama of his time, and Shakespearean criticism and scholarship. Among the outstanding contributors of essays are Pollard, Harrison, Granville-Barker, T. S. Eliot, and Sisson. A follow-up volume, *A New Companion to Shakespeare Studies,* edited by Kenneth Muir and S. Schoenbaum (Cambridge UP, 1971), contains a series of eighteen essays on comparable topics. Essayists include Schoenbaum, Hosley, G. K. Hunter, Bevington, Bradbrook, Ure, Sprague, and Sternfeld. Like its predecessors, the most recent version, *The Cambridge Companion to Shakespeare Studies* (Cambridge UP, 1986), edited by Stanley Wells, pursues some of the same topics. This new collection, however, contains a fuller treatment of Shakespearean criticism, including an essay on new critical approaches. These volumes include reading lists and help researchers who are trying to assess fact and critical opinion on various subjects.

In the three-volume set *William Shakespeare: His World, His Work, His Influence,* edited by John F. Andrews (Scribner's, 1985), sixty writers explore various topics in a series of essays. Topics range from Shakespeare's culture, education, music, theater companies, language, contemporaries, psychology, criticism, texts, and theater productions to contemporary issues in Shakespearean interpretation. Each article concludes with a select bibliography. Volume 3 includes a comprehensive index.

Mark Van Doren's *Shakespeare* (Holt, 1939) is a stimulating book of criticism. Van Doren writes on the poems and on each play; he is especially sensitive to the poetry of the drama.

In *How to Read Shakespeare* (McGraw-Hill, 1971), Maurice Charney covers such matters as the presented play: text and subtext, dramatic conventions, poetry of the theater, and Shakespeare's characters. This is a lively, sensible guide to the art of reading Shakespeare, generously illustrated with examples from the plays as practical demonstrations of the points being discussed. Charney has also written *All of Shakespeare* (Columbia UP, 1993), based on his thirty-five years of teaching. It offers pithy and stimulating commentaries on all the plays and poems. This book makes an excellent starting point for students who are trying to get ideas about the plays. In a sense,

Charney's book serves as a sequel to Van Doren's earlier survey of the plays.

In *William Shakespeare: A Reader's Guide,* Alfred Harbage (Farrar, Straus, 1963) explores the components of a Shakespearean play—its words, lines, and script—and suggests how the reader can learn to confront these vital elements. Harbage comments extensively on fourteen plays, frequently scene by scene, demonstrating how one reads and understands each play.

Russ McDonald, in *The Bedford Companion to Shakespeare Studies* (St. Martin's, 1996), provides essential background and covers a wide range of topics. He confronts the question of authorship, the nature of the playhouses, textual problems, Shakespeare's reading, the different kinds of drama, dramatic language, and various social issues. This book gives students an excellent, informed perspective from which to approach the plays.

David M. Zesmer's *Guide to Shakespeare* (Barnes & Noble, 1976) serves as a fine introduction. Zesmer surveys the major subjects, including Shakespeare's life, theater, philosophical ideas, problems of the text, chronology, and the likely sources. In subsequent chapters, he moves through the entire canon, beginning with the narrative and lyric poems and closing with the Romances. Generous footnotes provide the key to many other sources that can be consulted. Zesmer offers a commentary and interpretation of each work, varying from fewer than two pages on *Err.* to fourteen pages on *Ham.*

EDITIONS

The importance of reliable editions of Shakespeare to the researcher cannot be overestimated. For one thing, students may be assured of having a satisfactory text; furthermore, they may find valuable introductory materials and notes in many of the editions.

Both the Oxford and Cambridge University presses are in the process of publishing individual texts of each play, edited by various scholars. Oxford University Press has also issued the single-volume *William Shakespeare: The Complete Works* (Oxford

UP, 1986), edited by Stanley Wells and Gary Taylor. Two additional 1987 volumes accompany it: an original-spelling edition of the plays, and a volume of textual apparatus entitled *William Shakespeare: A Textual Companion*. The volume of modern spelling represents several years' work and a complete rethinking and reediting of the works. Because it offers very brief introductions and no commentary notes, undergraduate students may not find this edition as helpful as others. It will in all likelihood prove controversial, because the editors have made some radical departures from the standard procedure in Shakespeare editions. For example, they include both the quarto (1608) and Folio (1623) texts of *Lr.*; and they use the Folio text of *Ham.*, believing it to be the more theatrical version of the play. The text of *Per.* has been "reconstructed" by including lines from George Wilkins's prose version of the story. *H8* has been renamed *All Is True*. The editors were not timid in their decisions; the scholarly community will decide whether they were right.

In *The Riverside Shakespeare* (Houghton Mifflin, 1974), general editor G. Blakemore Evans reexamines the original editions and collates all major editions since the Nicholas Rowe edition of 1709. In addition, Harry Levin contributes a general introduction that includes consideration of Shakespeare's heritage, biography, linguistic medium, style, theatrical setting, and artistic development. Evans writes an essay on Shakespeare's text and includes a useful glossary of bibliographical terms. Herschel Baker prepared the introduction and notes for the histories; Frank Kermode, for the tragedies; Hallett Smith, for the Romances and poems; and Anne Barton, the introductions for the comedies. The volume includes extensive appendixes, such as the comprehensive essay by Charles Shattuck on stage history from 1660 to the present, and a selected bibliography.

David Bevington has completely revised Hardin Craig's edition of *The Complete Works of Shakespeare*, 4th ed. (HarperCollins, 1992; original ed., 1951). This new edition involves a complete reediting and resetting of the earlier edition and includes a new set of interpretive notes. Bevington writes on life in Shakespeare's England, drama before Shakespeare, London theaters and dramatic companies, the order of the plays, Shakespearean criticism, editors and editions, and Shakespeare's English. The appendixes contain materials on the canon, dates, sources, and stage history. Students will find the thirty-page bibliography, arranged topically, helpful. Bevington includes an interpretive essay before each play and more general ones for the various stages in Shakespeare's development. Both this and the Riverside edition are handsomely produced books.

In *The Complete Signet Classic Shakespeare* (Harcourt Brace Jovanovich, 1972), general editor Sylvan Barnet brings together Signet's previously issued single volumes in a one-volume hardback edition. The edition has multiple editors for the plays, which are arranged chronologically (including *TNK*, a play increasingly assigned to Shakespeare). Barnet contributes a long introductory essay covering such topics as Shakespeare's life, canon, theaters and actors, dramatic background, style and structure, Shakespeare's English, intellectual background, comedies, history plays, tragedies, nondramatic works, and texts. Interpretive essays by the various editors precede the texts and include information on the sources and a note on the text, with some textual variants recorded. The edition includes fourteen pages of suggested references on topics and on individual plays and poems.

The Complete Pelican text, issued as a single-volume edition in 1969, is entitled *William Shakespeare: The Complete Works*, general editor Alfred Harbage (Penguin, 1969). It has been widely adopted for classroom use. This represents a revision of the original paperback texts. The introductory matter has essays by Ernest Strathmann on the intellectual and political background, Frank Wadsworth on Shakespeare's life, Bernard Beckerman on Shakespeare's theater, Harbage on Shakespeare's technique, and Cyrus Hoy on the original texts. The plays appear according to genre categories, and each play has a brief critical introduction by the individual editor.

Peter Alexander's *The Complete Works* (Collins, 1951) has been much praised by textual scholars, but students will not find the kinds of apparatus available in the editions mentioned above. Alexander follows the order of the First Folio but also includes *Per.* and the poems. He writes a brief introduction and includes a glossary at the end of the book. Some scholars view this edition as one of the most authoritative produced in this century.

Another highly influential edition is George Lyman Kittredge's *The Complete Works of Shakespeare* (Ginn, 1936). Kittredge reveals his great knowledge of Elizabethan English in the glossary of the book. He arranges the plays in their Folio order and includes *TNK,* which makes this one of the earliest editions to do so. Several generations have grown used to the Kittredge text. Recognizing its earned popularity, the publishers had it revised in 1971 by Irving Ribner (Xerox, 1971), who radically altered and simplified Kittredge's text and notes, thus producing a quite different edition, which has been rather harshly reviewed by a number of scholars.

Noted both for its bold imagination and for its occasional eccentricity, the New Cambridge edition of Shakespeare appeared in separate volumes, spanning over forty years (Cambridge UP, 1921–1966). It was edited by Arthur Quiller-Couch and John Dover Wilson, with Wilson doing most of the volumes. These texts have extensive introductions involving interpretation, sources, and stage history; the volumes also contain discussion of textual problems, commentary notes, and a glossary.

Two other series demand special attention. The New Variorum edition, begun in 1871 ("new" here as opposed to some of the earlier variorum editions), is still incomplete. Some of the early volumes are being reedited as a project under the auspices of the Modern Language Association. These single volumes contain the most extensive discussion of the plays available. Their textual and commentary notes not only offer explanations but also trace historically the reaction to the particular problem—either text or meaning. The volumes conclude with an inclusive textual history, stage history, and history of criticism.

Somewhat less imposing but equally valuable are the editions that constitute the *Arden Shakespeare.* The original Arden editions were published between 1899 and 1924, with W. J. Craig as the first general editor. The New Arden editions began in 1951, with H. F. Brooks and Harold Jenkins as the general editors. Richard Proudfoot now serves as general editor, as reediting begins. Because so many people have been involved in this project, the quality of individual volumes varies; but taken together, they form a most impressive edition. Students will find a treasure-house of information about textual matters, source studies, brief stage histories, and interpretations, as well as valuable commentary notes.

Although not an edition in the sense of the others cited in this section, the latest facsimile edition of Shakespeare's First Folio, prepared by Charlton Hinman, deserves attention. *The First Folio of Shakespeare: The Norton Facsimile* (Norton, 1968) is the most reliable of the facsimile editions that have been published. Hinman drew from the vast collection of Folios housed at the Folger Shakespeare Library in Washington, D.C. By carefully picking the pages to be photographed, he produced an "ideal" Folio—that is, examples of the best pages. Hinman's facsimile is thus unlike any one single copy of the Folio. In his introduction, he writes about the Folio and its contents, the printing and proofreading of the book, and the facsimile itself. The original Folio made not only literary history but printing history as well, and this facsimile earns its place in the history of facsimile printing. Hinman establishes in it a through-line numbering system for the texts, which may eventually replace the more traditional act and scene designations. The skill and care evident throughout this book bring credit to the editor and the publisher.

STUDIES IN THE GENRES

In the discussion that follows, we analyze and summarize books that cover more than one play. For essays or books exclusively on individual works, students should consult the standard bibliographies, which offer commentary on critical studies. Not to be overlooked are the editions of the plays, both the complete texts and particularly single editions of individual plays, such as the valuable Arden, Oxford, and Cambridge editions mentioned earlier in this chapter.

The commentary here begins with the earliest, most significant study on the comedies, Romances, histories, and tragedies, in order to demonstrate the initial foundation of the critical approaches. Other books appear as they complement or react against the first one, treat certain categories of the plays (such as early and late), and deal with topics or techniques common to that particular genre. A wide diversity of critical approaches occurs, illustrating not only the dramatist's but also the critics' infinite variety.

COMEDIES

Neither this section nor any of the others attempts a history of criticism of the comedies or the other genres; nevertheless, as students review the books below, some ideas will emerge about how critics have treated Shakespeare's comedies. Some critics dwell on the theory of comedy and Shakespearean comedy in particular. Others are more concerned with the dramatic techniques involved in making comedy work. Shakespeare's development as a comic dramatist interests a number of critics, as do the basic comic themes and comic structure. After examining the first major book on the comedies, the discussion proceeds to those studies that pursue other techniques in the comedies. Books that touch on all the periods of the comedies come next; then the focus narrows to a chronological pattern, moving from critical studies of early romantic comedies to the "problem," or middle, comedies. Finally, the section closes with books that focus on specific approaches, such as psychoanalytic, Marxist, and phenomenological.

A convenient review of criticism, though now in need of updating, is John Russell Brown, "The Interpretation of Shakespeare's Comedies," *Shakespeare Survey* 8 (1955): 1–13. Anthologies of criticism include the one edited by Laurence Lerner, *Shakespeare's Comedies: An Anthology of Modern Criticism* (Penguin, 1967), which contains essays on ten comedies through *TN* and five essays on the nature of comedy. An anthology prepared by Kenneth Muir, *Shakespeare: The Comedies* (Prentice-Hall, 1965), covers the whole range of Shakespearean comedy; it includes a selected bibliography. Herbert Weil, in *Discussions of Shakespeare's Romantic Comedy* (Heath, 1966), focuses on the early comedies through *TN,* including excerpts from eighteenth- and nineteenth-century critics. The collection by David Palmer and Malcolm Bradbury, *Shakespearian Comedy,* Stratford-upon-Avon Studies 14 (Arnold, 1972), has nine original essays on the comedies and bibliographical notes. Gary

Waller has edited *Shakespeare's Comedies* (Longman, 1991); it includes reprints of essays on plays ranging from *Err.* to *MM*.

The first full-scale modern critical effort devoted to the comedies, H. B. Charlton, *Shakespearean Comedy* (Methuen, 1938), traces Shakespeare's growth as a comic dramatist. The essays that make up this book were originally eight lectures presented at the John Rylands Library over the course of eight years. Charlton sometimes seems victimized by his effort to trace a kind of evolutionary process, especially when he juggles chronology to place *TN, Ado,* and *AYL* after the "problem" comedies in order to find in this group the final "consummation" of Shakespeare's art.

Charlton sees the following qualities in the comedies: realistic temper, love, concern for the present; the objective is to attain mastery of circumstances. Chapter 1 emphasizes romanticism, specifically *TGV*. Elizabethan romantic comedy was an attempt to adapt the world of romance to the service of comedy. Charlton sees in *Err., Shr.,* and *LLL* a "recoil" from romanticism; and he later designates *Shr.* as a signpost along the road to the most mature achievements. *MND* is Shakespeare's first masterpiece, revealing his promise as the world's finest comic dramatist. Charlton finds *MV* somewhat troublesome, especially the ambiguity of Shylock, which makes the dramatist's intentions unclear. He devotes one lecture to Falstaff but takes an unusually serious attitude toward him, finding Falstaff's denial of the value of honor, faith, love, and truth a kind of comic failure. In contrast, he argues against the supposed cynicism, bitterness, and darkness of *Tro., AWW,* and *MM;* he views them as Shakespeare's effort to recover the spirit of comedy after the misleading comedy of Falstaff. All this ultimately leads to Shakespeare's artistic consummation in *AYL, TN,* and *Ado*—his greatest triumphs in comedy.

Northrop Frye's "The Argument of Comedy" in *English Institute Essays 1948* (Columbia UP, 1949), pp. 58–73, has had a profound effect on the criticism of the comedies. This essay has been much anthologized and is enlarged and revised in Frye's *Anatomy of Criticism* (Princeton UP, 1957), pp. 163–86. A theoretical essay about the nature of comedy, it serves as a prime example of the mythic approach to criticism. According to Frye, the action of comedy begins in a world represented as a normal world, moves into the "green world," goes into a metamorphosis there in which the comic resolution occurs, and returns to the normal world. In ritualistic terms, this process represents the victory of summer over winter. The essential comic resolution is an individual release that is also a social reconciliation. The ritual pattern behind the catharsis of comedy is the resurrection that follows death, the epiphany or manifestation of the risen hero. The fundamental pattern of our existence, according to Frye, is comic; tragedy exists as implicit or uncompleted comedy.

Frye greatly expands this whole thesis in his book on the comedies, *A Natural Perspective: The Development of Shakespearean Comedy and Romance* (Columbia UP, 1965). Believing that Shakespeare was primarily interested in dramatic structure, Frye also emphasizes this approach as opposed to moral ideas, images, vision, and theme. Anything that has the comic structure is a comedy, whether especially "happy" or not. This point leads Frye to several curious conclusions: for example, declaring *Tim.* a comedy instead of a tragedy. As he had suggested in the essay, Frye argues that the mythical or primitive basis of comedy is a movement toward the rebirth and renewal of the powers of nature in which a festive mood predominates. The movement of comedy, not only cyclical but also dialectical, lifts us to a higher world of the spirit. The emphasis falls on reconciliation, the birth of a new society, frequently displayed in a marriage. In such a process the "anticomic" elements, such as Shylock and Malvolio, have to be removed so that the resolution may occur.

C. L. Barber's *Shakespeare's Festive Comedy* (Princeton UP, 1959) in some ways complements Frye's position. In this study of dramatic form and its relationship to social custom, Barber explores how Elizabethan social and holiday customs contributed to the form of festive comedy. The study focuses on *LLL, MND, MV, H4, AYL,* and *TN.* These plays are distinguished by the use of forms of experience that can be termed Saturnalian, hence "festive." The basic pattern of the comedies appears in the formula, through release to clarification. The "clarification" achieved by the festive comedies corresponds to the release they dramatize: a heightened awareness of the relation between humankind and "nature"—the nature celebrated on holidays.

In the first three chapters, Barber examines Elizabethan holiday traditions, and two chapters give examples of holiday shows. Barber chooses plays that demonstrate the translation from social into artistic form. Shakespeare's comedies are not holiday shows but carefully structured drama. For example, *LLL* is not a show because Berowne can stand outside the sport and ruefully lament its sporting nature. In *MND*, the magical May game expresses the will in nature that consummates in marriage; the play brings out the underlying magical meanings of ritual but keeps the comedy human. Barber notes how Shylock remains outside the festive force, complicating *MV*. But Shylock is comic insofar as he exhibits what should be human degraded into mechanism. Though in disguise, Rosalind in *AYL* has a function similar to that of Berowne. Barber emphasizes the liberty of Arden as the play itself articulates a feeling for the rhythms of life. *TN* explores both misrule and liberty. For Barber, Shakespeare's comedy makes distinctions between false and true freedom and realizes anew the powers in human nature and society that make good the risks of courtesy and liberty.

In *Shakespeare and the Traditions of Comedy* (Cambridge UP, 1976), Leo Salingar explores the development of Shakespearean comedy, which brings into unison a diversity of traditions. From the medieval romance tradition, Shakespeare got the romantic elements; from the Roman playwrights, his sense of comic irony; and from the Renaissance, his feeling for comedy as festivity. Medieval romance provided Shakespeare with a point of departure, offering him two elements that would occupy center stage in his comedies—namely, prolonged trials by Fortune and the division and reintegration of a family. Classical comedy gave him a preoccupation with errors and mistaken identity. Finally, from the Renaissance writers, he got the double plot, which the Italians had elaborated on; from Italian *novelle*, he borrowed stories about broken nuptials and crises involving the law.

Salingar divides Shakespearean comedy into three groups, according to the types of source material that interested Shakespeare as he wrote: (1) the woodland plays (*TGV, AYL, MND,* and *LLL*), whose actions take place in a park or woodland, the leading idea for which came from Thomas Lodge's *Rosalynde* or from other works such as Montemayor's *Diana*, Sidney's *Arcadia*, or earlier romances; (2) plays of classical origin (*Err.*, *Shr.*, and *Wiv.*), derived from classical or Italian learned comedies, which use the Renaissance double plot and the classical notion of comedy as a matter of "errors" due to trickery, disguise, or Fortune; and (3) problem plays or novella plays (*MV*, *Ado*, *AWW*, and *MM*), written between 1596 and 1604, which derive directly from Italian *novelle*. Although they rely on trickery and disguise, more serious elements appear: recourse to the law and prominent trial scenes, broken nuptials, interrupted completion of marriage, and plots revolving around the authority of a prince. Salingar traces Shakespeare's interest in what he calls the "complex of the judge and the nun" from *Err.* to *MM*. This conflict in his mind over the claims of love and the claims of law in Elizabethan society becomes one of Shakespeare's central preoccupations.

Alexander Leggatt's *Shakespeare's Comedy of Love* (Methuen, 1973) considers each play as an experiment in the treatment of love and the dynamics of art, convention, and human nature. Each play has a dominant comic strategy—for example, dislocation in *Err.* and *TGV*. *Err.* interweaves the fantastic and the commonplace. *TGV* places love against a background that ranges from hostile to indifferent; though mocked and displaced, love still remains the center of the play. Such dislocation creates comic tension. *Shr.* relies on traditional comic conventions; but some characters are able to manipulate convention and therefore transcend it, such as Katherina, who acquires a new identity as she crosses the border between one type of experience and another. *LLL*, though a formal play, constantly questions conventions. Its ultimate effect subsumes a delight in the changes and surprises of life. *MND*, a play that shows characters trapped in different kinds of perception and understanding, relies on dislocation, which becomes a double instrument of celebration and mockery. *MV* also explores the interplay of convention and human reality, combining complex characters and formalized action. Unlike *AYL*, which relies heavily on conventional comic intrigue, *TN* depends on plot complications and shows characters locked in their limited understanding. This play presents a fragmented world of confined spaces, self-enclosed perceptions, and barriers, which at least some of the characters must transcend. In his last chapter, Leggatt turns briefly to the dark comedies and the Romances, showing, for example, that the final plays return to an emphasis on convention and patterns of artifice.

Antic Fables: Patterns of Evasion in Shakespeare's Comedies (St. Martin's, 1980), by A. P. Riemer, discusses the uniqueness and individuality of Shakespeare's comedies from *Err.* to *Tmp.* Throughout his career, Shakespeare incorporates, changes, or challenges the usual conventions of the comic form; therefore, each play represents an attempt to write a particular type of play in an unexpected manner and in such a way that its novelty engenders delight. Fascinated with "playfulness" and "playing," Shakespeare in *Err.*, for example, uses the conventions of farce, transforming the usual ingredients of the genre. In fact, all comedies employ a similar witty transformation of the conventions of comic drama. *LLL* is a comedy without a normal ending; *Shr.* plays with levels of theatrical illusion through its use of the play-within-a-play device; *MND* mingles an amazing variety of comic motifs and characters.

The comedies of the middle period seem radically to violate conventional comic modes: *MM*, which is a comedy because it has a happy ending, displaces comic conventions and can be considered an experiment in comic form. *AWW* may be regarded as Shakespeare's most abstract comedy. In it, Shakespeare turns the usual conventions of love-comedy upside down, and the play contains a broad pattern of reversals. Such violations and reversals of conventions inevitably lead to excess. In *AYL*, we have the gratuitous arrival of the youngest of the de Boys brothers and the indecorous appearance of Hymen. According to Riemer, however, *WT* best exemplifies Shakespeare's skills. Finally, Riemer looks at the plays as emblems of art—how the plays turn to themselves as Shakespeare shows a preoccupation with the illusory power of art.

In *Shakespeare's Comedies of Play* (Columbia UP, 1981), J. Dennis Huston argues that the defining quality of *Err.*, *LLL*, *Shr.*, *MND*, and *Ado* derives from their playfulness. Shakespeare examines not only the idea of the play but also the idea of play itself. These works show Shakespeare playing with the contingencies of plot, staging an almost endless series of plays within plays, manipulating conventions and expectations in order to play with the audiences' responses. He engages his characters in games of elaborate wordplay, offering events and characters out of the play worlds of fairy tale and make-believe, playing with the difficulties and challenges of playwriting by drawing attention to them.

Err. plays almost exclusively with the dramatic possibilities of plot; *LLL* concentrates on language and the uses to which humans put it as they construct schemes and pageants to suit reality to their desires; *Shr.* and *MND* show a celebration of the possibilities of the theatrical medium itself. *Ado* resembles the early plays, especially *Shr.*, hence its inclusion in this study, suggesting that Shakespeare may have had the outlines of *Shr.* in mind while writing *Ado.* Huston traces a change in Shakespeare's career. The early plays celebrate an absolute self-assurance and joy in play making, but *Ado* qualifies this exuberant optimism. In this work, the powers of the artist figure noticeably diminish. These powers, Shakespeare suggests, may be turned as much to deception as to vision, as much to destruction as to creation. In *Ado,* all reality does not submit to the playwright's almost magical energies and powers. This view of the possibilities of art and the intractability of reality shows a mature dramatist.

In *Comic Transformations in Shakespeare* (Methuen, 1980), Ruth Nevo examines ten early comedies in order to explore a theory of the dynamic of comic form and to demonstrate Shakespeare's development. She sees the plays as experiments that show a gradual conquest of the medium. She argues that Shakespeare developed his own comic form out of the Donatan formula of comic plots and the battle of the sexes. But he modifies the Donatan formula in that the protagonists do not know what they want; they discover as they go along. As a result, formal development becomes a continual, unfolding process of disclosure for the protagonist and the audience. The eventual recognition is retrospective as well as immediate for the protagonist and integrative for the audience.

The protagonists of Shakespeare's comedies become increasingly more self-perceptive, more aware of having gained in wisdom and insight. The early comedies culminate with *MND.*

Nevo considers *Ado, AYL,* and *TN* masterpieces, as Shakespeare's praise of Folly. These plays exhibit an Erastian transvaluation in a battle of the sexes in which neither contender suffers defeat. The three plays epitomize Shakespeare's achievement in the invention of a New Comedy. She says that Shakespeare's plays represent an increasing experiment with a restorative, cathartic effect. Thus Shakespeare saves us from the trap of bipolarity, of mutually exclusive alternatives.

The Metamorphoses of Shakespearean Comedy (Princeton UP, 1985), by William C. Carroll, argues that virtually every comedy and two Romances investigate a mode of metamorphosis or transformation. To Carroll, metamorphosis is more than mundane forms of change, such as natural mutability and normal human maturation; instead, metamorphosis entails fearful liberation and implausible possibilities, expressing itself in terms of a duality—both destroyer and creator. It figures as a kind of death or dissolution of identity yet at the same time leads to the enchantments of love. In Shakespearean comedy, love cannot remain unfulfilled—an endless and unsatisfied longing—because it would be a one-way metamorphosis, a suspension in otherness or self-alienation. Instead, love is harnessed into marriage, a paradoxical state in which two must become one but also remain two, in which the self is given and therefore lost but miraculously received back. *Shr.* contains the central issue of a psychological transformation—the "taming" of a shrew into a wife. In fact, all the comedies suggest how marriage becomes a type of metamorphosis. In *Err.* and *TN,* Shakespeare focuses on doubling, disguise, and mistaken identity not only as plot devices of intrigue but also as new and subtle versions of transformation. In chapter 4, "Forget To Be a Woman," Carroll explores the metamorphoses of Shakespeare's heroines. *MND* contains almost every type of metamorphosis. This play shows the monstrous as a temporal and dramatic stage that the characters must pass through. Finally, Carroll looks at the changes of romance in *WT* and *Tmp.*

Also exploring metamorphosis, Roger L. Cox finds a connecting thread among the comedies: the transformation plots in which one or more characters change significantly through education or magic. Cox examines such plots as time-lapse metaphors in his *Shakespeare's Comic Changes: The Time-Lapse*

Metaphor as Plot Device (U of Georgia P, 1991). The transformation plot derives as a by-product of Shakespeare's fascination with metaphor and language. The comic plots reflect an interest in three principal types of change: Ovidian metamorphosis (farce—*Shr.*, *MND*), moral and intellectual growth (romantic comedy—*AYL*, *Ado*, *AWW*), and religious awakening (romance—*MM*, *WT*, *Tmp.*). A time-lapse metaphor sums up the main plot of *Shr.*: "Kate the shrew becomes Kate the ideal wife." No play has a greater emphasis on costume, disguise, role switching, and role reversal than *Shr. MND*, *MV*, and *AYL* include three important variables: strongly contrasted settings, benevolent and effective manipulator figures, and self-consciousness (or lack of it) on the part of characters who change. The transformation of Bertram becomes the main event in *AWW*. The statue scene at the end of *WT* can be understood as the dramatization of a time-lapse metaphor. Cox also devotes one chapter to the Henriad history plays.

Thomas McFarland groups the comedies around a common motif in *Shakespeare's Pastoral Comedy* (U of North Carolina P, 1972). He devotes considerable space to a theoretical and historical discussion of both the pastoral and comedy. Shakespeare uses the pastoral to strengthen and deepen comedy itself. The compatibility of comedy and pastoral resides in a common tendency toward artificiality; also, they both function as social microcosms and emphasize the affections of the sexes. By bringing the two forms together in pastoral comedy, Shakespeare achieves what neither form alone could accomplish. McFarland discusses five plays: *LLL*, *MND*, *AYL*, *WT*, and *Tmp*. In these plays, the reciprocity of social and religious concern becomes the common denominator of the plays' significance. The ideal setting in *LLL* counteracts the formlessness of the play and helps mold it. Theseus in *MND* declares from the beginning the existence of a state of comic and pastoral grace, and the play as a whole is less formed and more evanescent than *LLL*. *AYL* represents a darkening of action and tone; the play labors to keep its comic balance. Jaques's presence threatens as well as criticizes the pastoral environment. Acts IV and V bring about pastoral redemption in *WT*. In *Tmp.*, the two great realities of Shakespeare's comic vision—movement toward social concord and the recognition of disharmony and disruption—

come together in a final confrontation. The play reaffirms the happiness of *MND* as it reasserts the enchantment of brotherhood and social harmony.

In *The Heart's Forest: A Study of Shakespeare's Pastoral Plays* (Yale UP, 1972), David P. Young studies four plays (*AYL, Lr., WT,* and *Tmp.*) in relation to the pastoral tradition, arguing for close thematic, structural, and stylistic similarities between these plays and the pastoral. Like pastoral works, these plays concern the exile of some of the central characters into a natural setting, their sojourn in that setting, and their eventual return. The plays also show a dual concern with innocence and happiness and a preoccupation with dualities, alternatives, and contrasts: urban versus rural, court versus country, and so forth. Differences in the treatment of the pastoral in the four plays can be accounted for by the influence of other genres and different stages of Shakespeare's career, as well as variations in the pastoral design introduced by Shakespeare's experimentation. According to Young, these plays are indeed versions of the pastoral in a more literal sense than that used by William Empson.

In a topical approach, Robert G. Hunter, in *Shakespeare and the Comedy of Forgiveness* (Columbia UP, 1965), concentrates on six plays: *Ado, AWW, MM, WT, Cym.,* and *Tmp.* Hunter sees these comedies as constituting a special genre. They resemble their medieval prototypes, which help define the nature of Shakespeare's version. Hunter devotes one chapter to the medieval heritage and another to the pre-Shakespearean dramatic examples. He purports to show how the doctrine of forgiveness inspired the development of a literary form and to demonstrate the importance of a sympathetic understanding of that doctrine for the success of these works. *Ado* was the first comedy of forgiveness, and from *AWW* onward, Shakespeare's work in comedy remained entirely within the tradition. *Ado* threatens by strife the fabric of society, but love and order finally return after a revelation of truth and a consequent repentance and forgiveness. In *AWW,* Shakespeare deliberately changes his source into a comedy of forgiveness. The total effect of *Cym.* depends absolutely on a sympathetic understanding of Posthumus's contrition and an emotional involvement in his forgiveness (Hunter sees this play as the most overtly

Christian of the romantic comedies of forgiveness). The resurrection of Hermione in *WT* is Shakespeare's most inspired moment of reconciliation and forgiveness. The charity that makes possible the happy ending of *MM* has as its source the knowledge and acceptance of our common humanity. *Tmp.* explores the themes of forgiveness and romantic love in two separate actions, and Hunter argues that Alonso is the principal one forgiven. Hunter rather successfully avoids some of the pitfalls that often beset critics who take an overtly "Christian" approach to Shakespeare.

In *Shakespeare's Comedies* (Clarendon, 1960), Bertrand Evans focuses principally on dramatic technique. He examines all the comedies, which he approaches through one of Shakespeare's dramaturgical characteristics: the use of awareness and control. Evans calls Shakespeare's technique "discrepant awareness," which may involve disguise and, of course, irony. Disguise is only one of several means at the dramatist's disposal for creating a structure of discrepant awareness. Irony emerges as one of the results and effects of this exploitation of different levels of awareness among the characters. After *Err.*, Shakespeare regularly exposes at the outset the existence of the potential solvent. *MND* is the first time that Shakespeare uses an outside force that interferes with and controls the affairs of humans. The climactic peak in the mature comedies regularly rises in the final scene of Act III, the opening scene of Act IV, or both. At this moment the exploitation of discrepant awareness achieves its peak. *TN* represents the summit of Shakespeare's dramatic technique, for he sustains Viola's masquerade through the whole play. Evans notes that Helena in *AWW* is pivotal in Shakespeare's development because after her, heroines do not control the world of their plays; instead, this role passes to benevolent, omniscient, omnipotent men like Prospero.

Several other books cover all the comedies, though taking a different approach from Evans's. Larry S. Champion's *The Evolution of Shakespeare's Comedy: A Study in Dramatic Perspective* (Harvard UP, 1970) includes forty-five pages of notes that evaluate critics and point the way to other books and essays. Champion groups the plays in four categories: comedies of action, comedies of identity, problem comedies, and comedies of transformation. In tracing the dramatist's evolution, he focuses on *Err., TGV, MND, Ado, TN, AWW, MM, WT,* and *Tmp.* The earliest comedies are essentially situation comedies in which the humor arises from action rather than character. In the second group, the plots emphasize problems of identity rather than physical action. The problem comedies present comically controlled character delineation on the level of transformation; a central character sins but gains eventual pardon after experiencing a comic catharsis on a moral level. The character development in the final comedies, which include sin and sacrificial forgiveness, involves a transformation of values. Champion emphasizes the idea of a character who serves as a "comic pointer," who provides the perspective for the audience.

S. C. Sen Gupta, in *Shakespearian Comedy* (Oxford UP, 1972; original, 1950), also surveys all the periods of Shakespeare's comic development. He devotes the first two chapters to discussing theories of comedy and the development of English comedy from its beginnings in medieval drama. Sen Gupta argues that for control of plot, English comedy had to await the classical influence of Plautus and Terence. The principal characteristics of Elizabethan comedy are its richness and variety; and Shakespearean comedy excels in its multiplicity: its characterization, its unity and diversity, its logic and inconsistency. For Sen Gupta, Shakespearean comedy means the art of exploration, usually of a personal sort, with Falstaff as the dramatist's greatest comic character.

John Russell Brown, in *Shakespeare and His Comedies,* 2d ed. (Methuen, 1962; 1st ed., 1957), argues against the importance of characterization. In his survey of the whole range of comedy, Brown emphasizes the implicit judgments made in the plays; such judgments, Brown believes, reflect the dramatist's attitudes toward life. Brown draws on many of Shakespeare's other works in order to provide a basis for the judgments about the comedies. He suggests in a chapter on structure that the comedies often resemble the history plays. The ideal of love's wealth becomes the principal judgment of *MV. MND* and *Ado* both explore the truth of love: the lovers establish their own truth, which seems to them most reasonable. *AYL* culminates in the fullest celebration of the ideal of love's order. These three judgments recur in *TN* as it repeats characters, situations, and devices from the earlier comedies. *AWW, MM,* and *Tro.* involve the ordeal of love and imperfect responses to love. The final Romances share, albeit differently, most of the implicit judgments of the earlier comedies. But *Tmp.* seems to be an exception to the pattern, because the main action here turns on the conflict between Prospero's virtue and his desire for vengeance.

Examining the early comedies, critics try to determine the salient features of the plays from *Err.* through *TN* that represent experimentation. In *Shakespeare's Early Comedies* (Chatto & Windus, 1965), E. M. W. Tillyard discusses *Err., Shr., TGV, LLL,* and *MV.* The first two chapters examine the background and range of Shakespeare's comedy. Tillyard does not pursue a consistent theme or structure; instead, he examines the plays as separate entities. The admixture of the status of mind proper to romance makes Shakespearean comedy different from other great comedy. In *Err.,* Shakespeare follows what was to be his permanent instinct: never forsake the norm of social life. *Shr.* is not quite consistent, not completely realized or worked out. In the approach to the theme of friendship in *TGV,* Shakespeare does not allow this theme to remain pure or uncorrected. The two main themes of adolescence and verbal excess in *LLL* interconnect, and this comedy belongs to the central area of social comedy. Tillyard finds Shylock appropriate to the romantic comedy in which he appears.

Peter G. Phialas, in *Shakespeare's Romantic Comedies: The Development of Their Form and Meaning* (U of North Carolina P, 1966), sets out to define the distinctive qualities of the romantic comedies by analyzing the action. Phialas believes that we can trace a steady progress in Shakespeare's ability to develop comic character and adjust it to the expression of the central comic theme and in his ability to develop dramatic structure. The principal theme presents the lovers' ideal against the fact of human's physical being; hence the importance and centrality of love. Phialas includes *Err.* and *Shr.* because they prefigure some of the significant features of romantic comedy. *TGV* is the first "romantic comedy" because it explores the theme of forgiveness and reconciliation. *LLL* involves the committing of a comic error that leads to reversal and recognition. Part of the superiority of *MND* is the device of the play-within-the-play.

In its achievement of a cohesive plot, *MV* surpasses the earlier plays. *Ado* carries further the attempt to elicit from its audience highly complex responses to its stage action. *AYL* has an important pastoral theme, which emphasizes and qualifies the theme of romance and romantic love; the play illustrates the successful form of romantic comedy. *TN* has a distinguished reflectiveness, which at moments tends toward gravity; its chief theme is education in the ways of the disdainful lover as well as the romantic lover.

R. Chris Hassel, Jr., in *Faith and Folly in Shakespeare's Romantic Comedies* (U of Georgia P, 1980), examines the Christian dimensions of Shakespearean romantic comedy and Shakespeare's indebtedness to Pauline and Erasmian teachings on faith and folly. Accordingly, the inevitably flawed characters progress through exposure and humiliation to a humble awareness and acknowledgment of their common folly. Hassel examines six comedies. *LLL* is the richest in doctrinal allusions, presenting the doctrinal controversy of love versus charity, with the characters' eventual discovery of the wisdom of folly. *MND* explores the opposition between imagination and religious faith. *Ado, AYL,* and *TN* focus on the paradox of faith and folly. Finally, *MV* examines the doctrinal controversy about the nature and efficacy of communion, to which it alludes. In this play, Shakespeare embraces ambiguity: namely, the characters' failure to achieve comic wisdom and humbly to acknowledge their imperfections. In the concluding chapter, Hassel explores the larger implications of Shakespeare's allusions to Christian doctrine.

Published in his eightieth year, John Dover Wilson's *Shakespeare's Happy Comedies* (Faber & Faber; Northwestern UP, 1962) attempts to define the nature of Shakespeare's comic genius and discusses the neglect of Shakespearean comedy. The "happy" ones include *Err., TGV, LLL, MV, AYL, TN, MND, Wiv.,* and *Ado*. Wilson defines Shakespeare's comedy as emotional, tender, fanciful, and human. The earliest comedies share the quality of serene happiness, which is liable to develop into merriment in the conclusion yet threatens to become serious at times. The main ingredients of the happy comedies are a Continental or Mediterranean background (except *Wiv.*), clownishness and foolery, quibbling by the gentry, merchants and mercantile life, and love and friendship among persons of high rank. Wilson views *LLL* as Shakespeare's most elaborate and sustained essay in satire and burlesque, with an emphasis on the "feast of languages." He believes that *Wiv.* is the nearest Shakespeare came to writing a comedy after the fashion of Jonson. Shylock ought to be regarded as a tragic, not a comical, figure (but one wonders what happens to the "happiness" of the comedy then). Wilson finds Malvolio the most interesting character in *TN* and Feste the subtlest of all fools. *Ado* is a grand game, and *AYL* has a vein of mockery in the midst of its pastoral romance. Based on his analysis of these particular comedies, Wilson concludes that Shakespeare delighted in experiment and would not be tied to a system.

John A. Hart's *Dramatic Structure in Shakespeare's Romantic Comedies* (Carnegie-Mellon UP, 1980) focuses on the dramatic structure of *MND, MV, AYL,* and *TN. TGV* and *LLL* receive brief attention. Structure, to Hart, means a combination of locations (setting, limitations of characters, and exercise of authority or power). Shakespeare presents each world as self-contained and whole within its own terms; but he makes sure that we never mistake it for all of experience, since he sets it against an alternative world, equally whole and equally limited. His technique enables him to present but not to judge, satirize, or moralize. Instead, he creates a variety of exactly described worlds, each partial and limited, and each sharing some of the attitudes that the entire world of experience may exhibit.

In *Shakespeare's Comic Rites* (Cambridge UP, 1984), Edward Berry argues that Shakespeare's romantic comedies (*Err., Shr., TGV, LLL, MND, Ado, AYL,* and *TN*) incorporate rites of passage. These comedies focus on courtship and marriage, the separation of central characters from their familiar setting, psychic turmoil as the main obstacle to their fulfillment in love, turmoil depicted through role-playing and disguise, paradoxes of clowning, symbolic dislocations in place and time, and rites and customs of marriage. These elements, borrowed from rites of passage, provide endless variations and help explain the distinctive and peculiarly deep appeal of the romantic comedies. Chapter 1 focuses on the three phases of rites of passage: separation, transition, and incorporation. Chapter 2 is on separations, and chapters 3 and 4 address courtship as a transitional experience. Chapters 5 and 6 also examine transitional matters, discussing the role of clowns and fools and the temporal and spatial dimensions of the comic experience. Chapter 7 examines rites of incorporation that end the plays, and the conclusion explores "social criticism" and the ways history can help us understand art.

Emphasizing form rather than character, Ralph Berry, in *Shakespeare's Comedies: Explorations in Form* (Princeton UP, 1972), covers ten plays from *Err.* to *TN*. He treats them as separate entities rather than evolving a common form or structure. Berry emphasizes the organic form of each play, and each analysis attempts to detect the governing idea of the comedy and relate it to the action that expresses it. The central technique of the comedies concerns the relation of the overtly comic parts to the rest of the play, usually an extension of the social function of a jester: to criticize the behavior of social superiors. The grand theme of the comedies is illusion and its opposite, reality. Berry specifically argues against the "festive comedy" approach of C. L. Barber, believing it inadequate and incomplete. Berry pays special attention to the language of the plays—*LLL* and *MV*, for example. Although Berry does not trace a particular development, he does see in *TN* a recapitulation and restatement of the themes that have been apparent since *Err.* He sees the comedies as a means of preparing for the tragedies—that is, the effect, if not the purpose, of them.

Several studies deal specifically with that group of comedies known, for better or worse, as "problem comedies"—usually *AWW, MM*, and *Tro*. A survey of the criticism can be found in Michael Jamieson, "The Problem Plays, 1920–1970," *Shakespeare Survey* 25 (1972): 1–10. The first full-scale treatment of this group is William W. Lawrence, *Shakespeare's Problem Comedies* (Macmillan, 1931; revised, Penguin, 1969). Lawrence bases his designation on the suggestion first made by F. S. Boas in *Shakespeare and His Predecessors* (London, 1896).

The term "problem play" is useful for those plays that clearly do not fall into the category of tragedy yet are too serious and analytic to fit the commonly accepted conception of comedy. The controlling spirit must be realism. The essential characteristic is a perplexing and distressing complication in human life presented in a spirit of high seriousness. The play probes the complicated interrelations of character and action in a situation admitting of different ethical interpretations. These plays represent a radical departure in Shakespeare's art.

Lawrence's treatment of the plays relies heavily on an analysis of the probable sources and traditions for these plays. In *AWW,* Helena appears noble and heroic, and Bertram changes in a wholly conventional manner. This tells the story of a noble woman passing through great afflictions into happiness. Two movements make up the play: the Healing of the King and the Fulfillment of the Tasks, which Lawrence finds traditional. *MM*'s tone, less depressing than tragic, can best be understood in light of earlier traditions and social usages. Sympathy for the frailties of mankind penetrates the play. Both plots of *Tro.* point to failure. The last act is weak dramatically but strong psychologically. Lawrence also examines part of *Cym.* and the other Romances briefly. He speculates on why Shakespeare wrote these plays at this particular time. Lawrence is strongest on his historical approach and weakest in actually analyzing the plays.

E. M. W. Tillyard includes *Ham.* in *Shakespeare's Problem Plays* (U of Toronto P, 1950). He suggests that *Ham.* and *Tro.* are problem plays because they display interesting problems; *AWW* and *MM,* because they are problems. Tillyard admits that he uses the term "problem play" vaguely and equivocally. Some of the qualities that these plays share include concern with religious dogma, abstract speculation, or both; serious tone, revealing a strong awareness of evil; and an acute interest in observing and recording the details of human nature. Tillyard finds *Ham.* not tragic in the fullest sense. Explication preoccupies the play, which forces it out of the realm of tragedy. Tillyard's discussion of *Tro.* has to do mainly with sources, though he does deny the classification of the play as a tragical satire. *AWW* has a defective poetical style, and *MM* has an inconsistent style. He observes in the book's epilogue that the theme of mercy and forgiveness observable in *AWW* and *MM* points the way toward the Romances.

Ernest Schanzer's *The Problem Plays of Shakespeare* (Routledge & Kegan Paul, 1963) takes Tillyard and others to task. His problem plays include *JC, MM,* and *Ant.,* which should make the reader wary of any set group deemed to be problem plays.

Schanzer finds Tillyard too vague; and although he agrees with Lawrence that the "problem" should be confined to the sphere of ethics, he believes that the plays Lawrence groups together do not fit this assumption. Schanzer contends that one should look for a satisfactory definition of the term and then see which, if any, plays fit. Ambiguity of audience response is one of the characteristics that the author finds—an ambiguity produced by the presentation of a moral problem that leaves the audience uncertain of its moral bearings. Thus audience responses to the protagonists and main actions remain not so much mixed as uncertain and divided.

William B. Toole, in *Shakespeare's Problem Plays: Studies in Form and Meaning* (Mouton, 1966), argues that these problem plays, as religious plays, betray a considerable indebtedness to medieval morality drama. Toole goes back to the Tillyard group of plays and, in his first two chapters, sketches the background for his argument—an investigation of *The Divine Comedy* and medieval drama, which form the basis for his "Christian" approach to these plays. He sees *Ham.* as a Christian tragedy that explores the problem and consequences of original sin. In *AWW* and *MM,* Shakespeare makes explicit what is implicit in the morality play; they represent the medieval comic pattern in dramatic form. Because the world of *Tro.* lacks the implication of redemption, it remains a tragedy, quite different from the other problem plays.

As the subtitle of Richard P. Wheeler's *Shakespeare's Development and the Problem Comedies: Turn and Counter-Turn* (U of California P, 1981) indicates, Wheeler focuses on mutually balancing movements in Shakespeare's plays: attraction and repulsion, union and separation, trust and autonomy, love and authority. He examines *AWW* and *MM* to demonstrate that their problematic resolutions illustrate larger patterns of Shakespeare's development as a dramatist. He argues that our reading of one play depends on an interpretive context constructed from the others. In *AWW,* Bertram embodies in embryonic form the essential components of a romantic rebel who can thrive only by rejecting the society that shaped him. Bertram must be reinstated, however; for he threatens precisely those social and domestic values celebrated in the festive comedies. The psychological underpinnings of Bertram's rejection of Helena create for Shakespeare an unprecedented conflict between Bertram's experience and the demands of comic form. Wheeler places *AWW* in the context of earlier comedies, the Sonnets, and the Romances to help us understand the implications of Shakespeare's dramatization of psychological conflict. In *MM*, conflict converges most sharply on a sexually naive young man thrust into a new relation to authority. It dramatizes an un-purged tension between sexuality and the moral order. In the rest of the book, Wheeler explores trends in Shakespeare's de-velopment as a writer.

Although Joseph Westlund's *Shakespeare's Reparative Come-dies: A Psychoanalytic View of the Middle Plays* (U of Chicago P, 1984) purports to be a psychoanalytic reading of the plays, it can be better described as reader response because of its focus on the comedy's effect on an audience. The role of reparation and the therapeutic effect of Shakespeare's plays interest West-lund. He defines reparation as the ability to recognize a de-structive impulse, to feel guilt for real or imagined destructive-ness, and to attempt to repair the damage. By seeing the characters through this reparative strategy, the audience can work out its own problems and bring about reparation. The success of these plays depends on the various strategies whereby potentially destructive feelings in the viewers are an-ticipated, contained, and transcended.

MV explores the problems of excessive trust and mistrust. *Ado* suggests that control can be both good and bad—bad when it deprives characters of their autonomy, forcing them to isolate themselves to avoid being manipulated beyond endur-ance. *AYL* presents a world of wish fulfillment in which the re-parative impulses integrate into a way of life, thus making us feel sane and wonderful. In *TN*, the characters idealize; they lose touch with reality and imagine perfection where it does not exist. But the play suggests that we must want to believe in the existence of a world where idealizations, however unrealis-tic, prove true. *TN* has a reparative effect because this play makes us see a distinction between an idealized object and a good object. *AWW* and *MM* present a more skeptical view. The former fully reveals the dangers of inventing what one wants, of idealizing others beyond a reasonable extension of ac-tual traits. The latter deeply frustrates our desires for certainties and for clearly ideal, or nonideal, figures. Shakespeare thus explores the eternal struggle between fusion, on the one hand, and isolation, on the other.

In *Shakespeare's Universe of Discourse: Language-Games in the Comedies* (Cambridge UP, 1984), Keir Elam explores the centrality of discourse—that is, "language in use" in both Elizabethan culture and Shakespeare. His study rests on Ludwig Wittgenstein's conception of language not only as action but also in action. He adopts Wittgenstein's notion of language "game" to indicate any form of language use that is subject to its own rules and defined within a behavioral context. Elam explores several classes of linguistic activities in the plays, including theatrical, semantic, pragmatic, and figural games. These games occur within well-defined frames. Elam describes a game-frame dialectic, exploiting language as activity and as object. Apparent in Shakespeare's use of language are various forms of reflexivity or metalanguage—language commenting on itself. Elam studies *Err., AYL, Shr., LLL, MM, MV, Wiv., MND, Ado, TN,* and *TGV.*

Karen Newman, in *Shakespeare's Rhetoric of Comic Character: Dramatic Convention in Classical and Renaissance Comedy* (Methuen, 1985), examines rhetorical devices that Shakespeare uses in soliloquies and monologic fragments to create what she refers to as the "lifelikeness of Shakespearean character." Such soliloquies and monologic fragments contain a rhetoric of consciousness. This rhetoric shows the characters' divided minds through particular features that the audience perceives as signs of psychological complexity and realism. She examines the rhetorical features that represent an inner life to both reader and audience in *MM, AYL, TN,* and *Ado.*

Traditional readings of the comedies identify a primary world and a secondary or "green" world in which the conflicts of the primary world are resolved. In *A Marxist Study of Shakespeare's Comedies* (Macmillan, 1979), Elliot Krieger sees these two worlds as part of the same reality. The changes that take place in the secondary world seem to resolve the conflicts of the primary world, but in fact they do not. The protagonists develop "a second world strategy," which protects them from change and perpetuates their interests. The protagonists in *MV, MND, AYL, TN,* and *1H4* transform their environments into manifestations of their subjective needs. This secondary world thus advances the interests of the ruling classes and is antagonistic to the interests of other classes. The comedies examine the process through which a class creates and perpetuates its ideology.

W. Thomas MacCary, in *Friends and Lovers: The Phenomenology of Desire in Shakespearean Comedy* (Columbia UP, 1985), studies nine comedies and *WT* from a phenomenological standpoint. MacCary explores the complex relations between erotic orientation and identity, showing the dynamics of love relationships in the comedies as a series of assimilations and differentiations between self and other. In the plays examined, we see the action from the point of view of one character, a young man, who must learn to love. The characters start out by not knowing themselves or their appropriate objects of desire, and so they learn to love. Shakespeare takes his young heroes through four stages of object desire: they love themselves (or seek themselves); they love images of themselves in twins or friends; they love those same images in transvestized young women; and finally they learn to love young women in all their specific, unique, and complex virtues. In the early comedies (*Err., TGV, LLL, Shr.*), Shakespeare focuses on the danger of a young man committing himself—his happiness, his whole identity—to a young woman in courtship and marriage. In the mature comedies (*MND, Ado, MV, AYL*), he shows how the lovers must fight against preconceived notions of female sexuality and yield, in some cases, the lead in love to the lady. Finally, *WT* brings all the concerns of the previous plays together.

In *Unconformities in Shakespeare's Early Comedies* (St. Martin's, 1986), Kristian Smidt offers a fascinating sequel to his rich book on the history plays. He examines Shakespeare's methods of composition and revision of his manuscripts and the inconsistencies present in the texts of *TGV, Shr., LLL, MND, Wiv.,* and *MV.* The term "unconformities," borrowed from geology, refers to breaks, disruptions, and irregularities in narrative continuity; contradictions in causality or effect; impossible sequences of events; and unexplained or unexpected changes in characterization. Formal irregularities such as meaningless repetitions and shifts in speech styles and language pattern often mark the sites of unconformities. These "faults"—both in the geological and in the aesthetic sense—are not necessarily defects because they give rise to a sense of depth, urgency, or pressure and add to the complexity of the drama.

Marilyn L. Williamson, in *The Patriarchy of Shakespeare's Comedies* (Wayne State UP, 1986), focuses on the male mechanisms of control over female sexuality. Changes in audience demand and interest and sociohistorical conditions govern Shakespeare's development from the romantic comedies to the problem plays to the Romances. In the romantic comedies, men appear as rivals and women as property in marriage. In the problem plays, written after King James had come to the throne, powerful male figures try to control the sexuality of their subjects and children, with marriage becoming a means of regulating society. The Romances mythologize the power of fathers and rulers as "the patriarchy seeks to appropriate to itself the *reproductive* powers of women" (113).

Two books focus on comedy and revenge. Linda Anderson, in *A Kind of Wild Justice: Revenge in Shakespeare's Comedies* (U of Delaware P, 1987), contends that revenge is a central element of comic intrigue. Revenge can be retaliatory or reformatory; it ranges from trivial acts of revenge on family, friends, and lovers in the early comedies to more serious threats in the romantic comedies and problem plays. In *Err., Shr., TGV, LLL,* and *MND,* revenge functions both as a simple plot device and as a corrective social instrument. In *MV, Wiv., Ado, AYL,* and *TN,* avengers protect defenseless characters or society from outsiders who want to inflict serious harm on the comic spirit. In *Tro., AWW,* and *MM,* where at least one character threatens others, revenge seems curtailed and justice is not served. Anderson argues that erring or evil characters experience little revenge; hence the audience's dissatisfaction with the resolutions of such plays. Anderson provides a useful overview of the revenge motif in Elizabethan culture and art and its connection to the legal systems represented in the plays.

From a different perspective, G. Beiner, in *Shakespeare's Agonistic Comedy: Poetics, Analysis, Criticism* (Fairleigh Dickinson UP, 1993), examines the dichotomy between reparative and punitive comedy and develops a poetics of "agonistic comedy," a subgenre of the comedy of love. In comedies from *Err.* to *TN,* Shakespeare uses an agonistic or punitive strategy, which emerges as a distinctive pattern within the comedy of love. Characters such as Shylock, Falstaff, and Malvolio signal the existence and function of an agonistic strategy or agon, which involves the punishment and eventual exclusion of a negative antagonist. The agon complements the comedy of love without displacing it. Although present in all the romantic comedies, agonistic comedy finds its nucleus in *Wiv.*, *MV*, and *TN*.

Barbara Freedman brings together psychoanalysis, film theory, and postmodernism in *Staging the Gaze: Postmodernism, Psychoanalysis, and Shakespearean Comedy* (Cornell UP, 1991). She discusses what Jacques Lacan terms "the gaze" and our desire for mastery. The comedies tempt spectators with the desire for mastery as privileged voyeurs, only to expose such a desire as an illusion by presenting onstage audiences, characters, plots, and themes as "sites of misrecognition" and error. Onstage audiences in *Shr.* and *MND* subvert the position of the viewer. Misleading visual appearance, such as the use of identical twins in *Err.* and *TN* and of visual disguise and illusion in *Shr.* and *MND*, dislocates and confounds the audience's perspective. Freedman also discusses emerging models of Renaissance subjectivity and developments in optics and perspective painting.

Ejner J. Jensen, in *Shakespeare and the Ends of Comedy* (Indiana UP, 1991), argues that the critical emphasis on closure seems to undermine and reject the spirit of comedy. He sees the end as a necessary and inevitable part of the total work, but not the most important part. In the comedies, the dramatic process is much more important than the finality of closure. In *MV*, the dramatic power lies in the particularity of the action, and meaning arises not in the closing scenes but from the progression of the action toward a conclusion. The true pleasure and power of *Ado* emerge from progression and comic preparation. Similarly, if we emphasize closure, we sacrifice the comic and theatrical vitality of *AYL*, *TN*, and *MM*. The ending of a play does not carry the burden of its meaning; rather, as in *MM*, the closing scenes recapitulate a pattern established throughout the drama.

Taking a sociological approach, Anthony J. Lewis, in *The Love Story in Shakespearean Comedy* (UP of Kentucky, 1992), discusses sexuality and gender relations in all the comedies and in the Romances, especially emphasizing *Cym*. These plays present five phases in love relationships. In the initial phase, involving familial ties, the hero undergoes a separation from his father, whereas the heroine, whose social status is often higher than the hero's, endures attempted patriarchal control and restraint. The next phase involves the hero's rejection of the heroine and the resulting separation of the lovers. The psychological effects of the separation and a gender inversion follow. The hero, in a descent with clear social and psychological consequences, assumes the ideology or position of the illegitimate, whereas the heroine, acting decisively, saves him from self-destruction. The fourth phase involves the lovers' attempts to communicate physically or spiritually with each other. Finally, the lovers reunite after the hero assumes his social and familial position: women cease to be the enemy, and celibacy is forsaken for heterosexuality.

Camille Wells Slights's *Shakespeare's Comic Commonwealths* (U of Toronto P, 1993) examines the social dimensions of the comedies, especially the problems and satisfactions of living in an ordered commonwealth. The comedies, she argues, are neither subversions nor endorsements of English Renaissance ideology; yet they present characters who find happiness within undemocratic, racist, and sexist societies. She explores a number of topics related to the social bases and concerns of the comedies, such as a pattern of conflict and conciliation in the struggle between savagery and civilization, autonomy and dependence, and isolation and community. *Err.* and *Shr.* contrast the civilized and the uncivilized. *Err.* stresses the importance of belonging to society but not the need to reform it, and *Shr.* centers on the conflict between savage and civilized impulses. *TGV* and *LLL* emphasize the activities, manners, and values of those in the upper echelons of a society. *MND* and *MV* blend the foreign and the familiar. *MND* makes the mysterious and fantastic familiar while making incidents and situations from common life seem strange. Its characters achieve happiness through stability despite subjective inconstancy and differences. In *MV*, social heterogeneity becomes an intractable problem, and desired change becomes unavoidably painful. In *AWW* and *Ado*, outsiders attempt to exert control over local communities, whereas in *AYL* and *TN,* characters try to re-build a society that has disintegrated.

ROMANCES

Critics have grouped another series of comedies, the final Romances, *Per., Cym., WT,* and *Tmp.* Philip Edwards surveys the criticism of these plays in "Shakespeare's Romances: 1900–1957," *Shakespeare Survey* 11 (1958): 1–18. A similar survey by F. David Hoeniger in *Shakespeare Survey* 29 (1976): 1–10 covers the years since 1958. *Shakespeare's Romances Reconsidered* (U of Nebraska P, 1978), a collection of essays edited by Carol McGinnis Kay and Henry E. Jacobs, contains eleven essays on the plays, including one that surveys critical approaches that have been taken in the Romances, and a helpful bibliography of over 600 items.

Robert M. Adams, *Shakespeare: The Four Romances* (Norton, 1989), provides an engaging introduction to Shakespeare's last plays. Although Adams offers no overall thesis, he often gives connections between the plays. Mainly he provides sensible and intelligent readings of each play, with special emphasis on their presumed sources. This book makes a good starting point.

Derek Traversi presents detailed analyses of the plays in *Shakespeare: The Last Phase* (Stanford UP, 1955). He suggests that at the heart of the plays lies the conception of an organic relationship between breakdown and reconciliation and that the plays, completely removed from realism, are properly definable in symbolic terms. *Per.* experiments in poetic symbolism, asserting nothing less than a concept of spiritual resurrection. *Cym.* presents the theme of loss and reconciliation in Cymbeline's sons and daughter. *WT,* a finished achievement, explores the divisions that time and passion create in love and friendship and the final healing of these divisions. For Traversi, *Tmp.* represents a further and logical development in the symbolic technique. In the final part, the sublimation of the human state, foreshadowed in Miranda's romantic vision, merges into the full symbolic structure of the play.

In one of his first books, *Shakespeare's Last Plays* (Chatto & Windus, 1938), E. M. W. Tillyard also discusses these final plays, though he omits *Per.* because of uncertainty about the reliability of the text. He comments on the plays first under the heading "The Tragic Pattern." The old order collapses in the last plays as thoroughly as in the main group of tragedies, and this element of destruction sets them apart from the earlier comedies. But the total scheme is prosperity, destruction, and recreation; Tillyard illustrates how this works in each play. He admits in the "Planes of Reality" chapter that to speak of different planes implies a state of mind akin to the religious and renders probable a certain amount of symbolism, but he does not suggest religious dogmatism. He finds the planes somewhat blurred in *Cym.* but set in striking and successful contrast in *WT.* In *Tmp.*, they form a brilliant pattern of bold contrasts, subtle contrasts, and delicate transition.

G. Wilson Knight, in *The Crown of Life: Essays in Interpretation of Shakespeare's Final Plays* (Methuen, 1948; original, 1947), adds *H8* to the group, arguing that it is the culmination of the vision implicit in the Romances. This book includes Knight's much earlier essay "Myth and Miracle" (1929), which lays the groundwork for much of his criticism as it defines the belief that Shakespeare, moved by vision, not fancy, creates not merely entertainment but myth in the Platonic sense. Thus, in the final plays, the dramatist expresses a direct vision about the significance of life. Present in *Per.* are the depth and realism of tragedy within the structure of romance; it might be called a Shakespearean morality play. Great nature—unpossessive, ever-new, creative—is the overruling deity in *WT,* against which Leontes has offended. Resurrection does not occur until Leontes completes his repentance and Perdita returns. Knight emphasizes in *Cym.* the Vision of Jupiter, which underscores the play's theological impressionism. But he lavishes the greatest praise on *Tmp.*, which he calls the most perfect work of art and the most crystal act of mystic vision in our literature. He insists on the identification of Prospero with Shakespeare; through this play, Shakespeare looks inward and traces the past progress of his own soul. On this point, however, many critics would demur. The play itself, Knight suggests, is poor in metaphor because it *is* metaphor.

Less mystical but not less spiritual, Joan Hartwig's *Shakespeare's Tragicomic Vision* (Louisiana State UP, 1972) attempts to see the final plays within the confines of the genre of tragicomedy, one of the most elusive forms to define. Part of her approach revolves around audience perception of the stage reality; somehow the audience is able to hold apparently opposite responses in equilibrium. The plays use illusion to illuminate the world of the actual, but the audience is aware of the difference. The final vision of the plays reunites the realm of human action and the realm of the divine. Hartwig emphasizes in *Per.* the dramatist's control of the audience and his techniques for doing this as he creates a conscious distance between staged illusion and the audience. Like the others, this play creates the achievement of "joy," shared with the audience. The discrepancy between humans' true nature and outward appearances dominates *Cym.* At the end of *WT,* Paulina fuses illusion and reality into joyful truth; she builds the imaginative excitement required of tragicomic recognition. The audience suspends its rational judgment so that for a special moment it may glimpse the wonder in the world of human actions. Prospero as magician and man incorporates the power and presence of divinity. All the major emphases of Shakespeare's tragicomic vision occur in *Tmp.* with great self-consciousness. The play, in effect, begins at the denouement of the other Romances. Looking over the final plays, one may observe that the dramatist moves from direct supernatural manifestation to human embodiment (Prospero). Also, he changes the almost totally passive hero in Pericles to the thoroughly active Prospero, who participates in providential knowledge. Hartwig's approach is refreshing as she abandons the impulse to mythic vision in favor of how we the audience perceive and participate in these tragicomedies.

In his *Shakespeare: The Dark Comedies to the Last Plays: From Satire to Celebration* (UP of Virginia, 1971), R. A. Foakes argues that Shakespeare in his later plays learns how to liberate himself from a commitment to characters presented with psychological and linguistic consistency in order to achieve different kinds of effects, especially distancing the audience from the characters. Foakes focuses on the last plays as structures designed for performance. Thus the author moves from *AWW, MM,* and *Tro.* through satiric plays by other dramatists to arrive eventually at a discussion of Shakespeare's Romances. Documenting the satiric detachment in the problem comedies enables Foakes to sketch the achievement of the last plays. He also finds that the late tragedies, such as *Cor.*, form a natural link between dark comedies and the last plays. The masque in *Tmp.* may be taken to exemplify in the final plays Shakespeare's move away from character emphasis and a search for motives toward a visionary sense of wonder, also evident in the restoration of Hermione in *WT.*

In the opening chapter of *Shakespearean Romance* (Princeton UP, 1972), Howard Felperin seeks to answer this question: what are we to make of romance as a literary genre? He traces the three strands of romance that intersect Shakespeare: classical romance, medieval chivalric romance, and medieval religious drama. In subsequent chapters, Felperin establishes the pervasive presence of romance within Shakespeare's entire work, even within the major tragedies, arguing in part that the Romances would not have been possible without the preceding tragedies. *Cor.*, *Tim.*, and *Ant.* make a clear transition from tragedy to romance. With this well-established background, Felperin then turns to the final plays. He traces *Per.*'s indebtedness to early religious drama and shows how the focus of the play changes to Pericles as man, husband, and father. *Per.* also reveals Shakespeare reassessing the premises on which his art had always been based. *Cym.* and *H8* illustrate some of the problems that arise from the conflation of history and romance. Felperin nevertheless finds the action of *Cym.* highly unified on three levels: sexual or romance plot proper, the familial and dynastic level, and the level of international politics. In *Cym.*, the values of romance ultimately determine the value of history; a similar observation can be made about *H8*. This latter play ends in the golden world of romance: the mythic realm of a Tudor golden age. In its combination of romantic design and mimetic fidelity to life as we know it, *WT* not only transcends *Per.* and *Cym.* but also represents a breakthrough in Shakespeare's romantic art. This play fulfills the conventions of romance while testing them rigorously against the touchstone of reality. *Tmp.* asks to be seen as glittering illusion or as essential reality, and its cast divides the possibilities of response among its members. In some ways, the play is also an ironic commentary on Renaissance travel literature. The art of power and the power of art become in Prospero's hands one and the same thing. Felperin agues that *Tmp.* finally resists all attempts to allegorize or idealize experience, thereby illustrating the limitations of the idealizing imagination. The world that emerges in the final scene is neither so brave nor so new as Prospero himself could have wished.

In a book strong on background material, *Shakespeare's Romances* (Huntington Library, 1972) by Hallett Smith explores the romance tradition, the pastoral world, and the connections between comedy and romance and between tragedy and romance. Smith establishes that Shakespeare's Romances evolve in a natural way from the tragedies and also from the comedies. He develops fully the relationship between *WT* and Greene's *Pandosto*. Problems of reality and illusion inhere in both *MND* and *Tmp.* The final two chapters concern scenery and landscape and language and style of the Romances. Smith uses landscape to signify the world that is described in visual terms but not shown on the stage, and he finds *Tmp.* to be the greatest achievement in landscape. In the Romances, Shakespeare's style achieves a new complexity and beauty, bringing about in the audience a heightened awareness of the improbable, the incredible, and the marvelous.

Douglas L. Peterson, in *Time, Tide, and Tempest: A Study of Shakespeare's Romances* (Huntington Library, 1973), explores the modes of dramatic illusion in the Romances, the problem of time, and the emblematic nature of these plays, which often involve the participation of the audience. Peterson suggests that generative and destructive love becomes the means by which the principal characters in the last plays influence the processes of growth and decay. Shakespeare depicts humans' position within the natural order metaphorically in terms of time. Peterson sees *Per.* as a complex emblem, with Gower as a guide who controls audience perspective. Each of these plays discloses structures deriving from the dual aspects of time: duration and occasion. Shakespeare celebrates the power of a love grounded in trust. *Cym.* also shifts from representational to emblematic narrative. Peterson finds the turning point to be when Pisanio renews Imogen's faith and she decides to seek out Lucius; the action then moves steadily toward the restoration of trust and the reconstruction of the social order. *WT* emphasizes the dependence of seeing on belief, the confirmation of nobility through action, and natural love and concord as the only basis of community. Generative powers of love begin the process of renewal in the play after Leontes has nearly destroyed himself and the kingdom. Peterson views *Tmp.* as the culmination of the issues that he has singled out in analyzing the other Romances. He argues that consideration of the past as memory and its influence on the future leads to the deepest concerns of the play. Prospero's use of time reveals his belief in a purpose and meaning in the flow of events, and his decision to forgive illustrates the dependency of the restoration pattern on faith. Peterson also explores ways in which Prospero resembles Shakespeare.

Believing that the meanings of the Romances intricately connect with their form, Barbara A. Mowat, in *The Dramaturgy of Shakespeare's Romances* (U of Georgia P, 1976), examines *Cym.*, *WT*, and *Tmp.* for their dramatic tactics and strategy. Each chapter concentrates on a separate dramaturgical issue. Mowat first explores how these plays exhibit a careful blending of tragic and comic effects, thereby offering a double perspective on life. Shakespeare's tactics include soliloquies and other presentational devices. In *Tmp.*, for example, the most important presentational devices are the spectacles. Through these various techniques, Shakespeare makes an audience's experience parallel that of the characters on stage. One primary strategy avoids the midplay climax, common in most of Shakespeare's plays, which upsets dramatic expectations. The persistent use of narrative devices in these plays in part accounts for their characteristic quality: witness Prospero's function as narrator in *Tmp.* Adding these tactics and strategies together, Mowat argues that the Romances are a kind of "open form" drama, a drama that goes against standard dramaturgical practices. Prospero, for instance, opens the closed form of his play. Like the characters, we also experience bewilderment and uncertainty in the face of the unstable, true-false world of romance. Mowat convincingly argues that the meanings are contingent on the play's dramaturgy.

In an introductory chapter of *Beyond Tragedy: Structure and Experience in Shakespeare's Romances* (UP of Kentucky, 1981), Robert W. Uphaus examines the qualities that define romance and the ways in which Shakespeare's Romances move beyond tragedy, projecting a sense of destiny in the guise of Providence. Analyzing *Mac., Lr.,* and *Ant.,* Uphaus shows how these tragedies introduce elements that intimate the idea of romance. *Per.* remains a skeletal romance, one in which all the conventions of romance are displayed though rarely individualized. But *Cym.,* with its prominent emphases on dysfunction and mortality, becomes at once romance taken to its dramatic limits and a skeptical response to the optimism of *Per.* Indeed, *Cym.* parodies romance. *WT* takes romance conventions and invests them with extraordinary human significance in Shakespeare's most defiant romance. Paradoxically, Prospero's art in *Tmp.* performs the dissolution of art in such a way that the imaginative representation or fiction of romance becomes the actual experience or fact of romance. The characters and the audience participate in ways uncommon to the other Romances: *Tmp.* becomes its own hierophancy. *H8* constitutes a historical version of the literary experience of romance; thus, for example, Act V presents a hierophantic spectacle of the triumph of a new Protestant order. All the plays, as Uphaus persuasively argues, take us beyond tragedy.

Frances A. Yates's approach to the last plays in her *Majesty and Magic in Shakespeare's Last Plays* (Shambhala, 1978; published in 1975 by Routledge & Kegan Paul under the title *Shakespeare's Last Plays: A New Approach*) can be characterized as historical-topical. She argues for an Elizabethan revival in the early years of King James's reign and that this harkening back pervades Shakespeare's final plays. Thus, the preoccupation with royal children in the Romances parallels what was occurring in the Jacobean court as James sought to arrange suitable marriages first for Prince Henry and then for Princess Elizabeth. Yates even identifies the royal children in *Cym.,* the two sons and a daughter, with the children of James. Thus these plays reflect actual events in the life of the Jacobean court, according to Yates. She also suggests that Shakespeare was a wholehearted supporter of Henry and Elizabeth. In the book she focuses on *Cym., H8,* and *Tmp.;* in the last she finds a link between its practice of magic and German Rosicrucianism. This book should be read with caution and with a skeptical mind.

Gary Schmidgall's *Shakespeare and the Courtly Aesthetic* (U of

California P, 1981) pulls together information and insights from several disciplines in order to sketch the Jacobean courtly aesthetic and to determine how Shakespeare's Romances fit. Schmidgall argues that the new Jacobean court established an artistic fashion to which Shakespeare responded, especially in *Tmp.* In one chapter, Schmidgall explores themes common to courtly art: praise and encouragement of a healthy *civitas* or polis, the golden age, the dynastic or imperial theme, and the ideal of the perfect ruler. He also examines the influence that the new Jacobean royalism in the arts had on Shakespeare's late plays, noting, for example, the effect of the court masques on these plays. *Tmp.* exhibits the prominent themes and structures of courtly fiction and manifests a strong political interest. Caliban has central political significance because he symbolizes the opposite of order. Two separate chapters treat Caliban and Prospero extensively. If Caliban is the rebel capable of all ill, then Prospero is Shakespeare's vision of the ruler capable of all good. *Tmp.*, at once about the power and the vanity of art, itself contributes to the Jacobean courtly aesthetic. Schmidgall touches on all the late plays, but he emphasizes *Tmp.*

In an investigation of the topicality and intertextuality of Shakespeare's last plays, David M. Bergeron, in *Shakespeare's Romances and the Royal Family* (UP of Kansas, 1985), argues that the family of King James I constituted a "text" that Shakespeare "read" and incorporated into his drama. The issue is not one of identifying members of the Stuart royal family with characters in the plays, as Yates argued, but rather one of "representation"—how Shakespeare took the facts of the public and private lives of the royal family and represented them in the Romances. The royal family becomes part of the intertextual nature of these plays. Bergeron provides the historical and dramatic context for the last plays by examining in detail the Stuart royal family and the comic drama that immediately preceded Shakespeare's Romances. He notes the satiric nature of most of the comedy, a drama that demystifies the family and pays little attention to politics. In contrast, the romance mode of Shakespeare's final plays, including *H8*, emphasizes and celebrates royal families, which are themselves inevitably linked with politics. Indeed, these final plays intertwine politics and family as Shakespeare pursues questions of dynasty and succession. Bergeron analyzes the plays in terms of the twin issues of family and politics. From Pericles' quest in Antioch for a wife, so that he might propagate "an issue," to Henry VIII's presence at the baptism of his daughter Elizabeth, Shakespeare examines the politics of royal families, especially how the future will be secured by the royal children such as Marina, Imogen, Florizel and Perdita, Miranda and Ferdinand, and Elizabeth. The royal children redeem their kingdoms by providing much-desired stability. Bergeron points out how the usually presumed sources for the final plays do not emphasize familial politics in the way that Shakespeare does, and he suggests that the text of the Stuart royal family may account for the difference. The plays contain not merely exotic romances of remote places and times; rather, they are dramas that reflect the political world of their creation. *H8*, Bergeron argues, culminates the concern for politics and family in these plays, focusing on an actual English royal family, one linked explicitly with the Stuart royal family.

Emphasizing reverie as the mode of romance, Ruth Nevo, in *Shakespeare's Other Language* (Methuen, 1987), examines fantasy in the final plays. In *Per.*, fantasy is always death-driven; the play captures the rhythm of the vicissitudes of human life: separation, dispossession, return under the cross of guilt. Thaisa's recovery is a rebirth fantasy, and Pericles needs a rebirth for himself. *Cym.* contains fantasies of dispersed and reassembled families, of split and recuperated identities. Posthumus's dream is a transparent wish fulfillment. The play transforms the forces of death and dissolution into a reaffirmation of procreative life. The second part of *WT* redeems yet repeats the first part. In Bohemia, the second chance comes through the second generation and a second genre. The fictive resurrection of Hermione effects a real resurrection in Leontes—fantasy realized. Prospero engineers the wish-fulfillment fantasy in *Tmp.*, a play in which fantasy serves heuristic purposes. Prospero's design for human regeneration achieves its end in this Shakespeare's most indissolubly tragicomic drama.

In a revised version of a book first published in 1987, Marco Mincoff in *Things Supernatural and Causeless: Shakespearean Romance* (U of Delaware P, 1992) explores the late plays' relationship to their sources. For example, Mincoff examines the link of *Cym.* to Beaumont's *Philaster.* He finds human blindness to be at the root of suffering in *Cym.* and notes the importance of the appearance of Jupiter. *WT* emphasizes the guiding hand of Providence in a play that focuses on time's effect on human existence. Mincoff sees Prospero in an unpleasant light, a rather hollow facade.

Shakespeare's linguistic dramaturgy forms the focus of Maurice Hunt's *Shakespeare's Romance of the Word* (Bucknell UP, 1990). Potent words at the end of each Romance make possible characters' secular salvation. Antiochus's riddle in *Per.* has a destructive effect on Pericles, a parody of the nurturing word. Marina introduces her father to the restorative virtues of a story retold. *Cym.*'s troublesome style reveals the problematic interaction of thought and speech, but Jupiter's words offer a liberating perspective. The word, first lacking and misleading, becomes the means to grace in *WT.* Hunt sees linguistic deficiency as the actual subject of the play's first episode. Polixenes and Camillo respect language, but Leontes exhibits linguistic totalitarianism. Hermione's words in the last scene possess the signature of peace. *Tmp.* shows mankind's vulnerability to corrupting words, but Ariel's words eventually accomplish Prospero's change of attitude and bring about his redemptive design.

Cynthia Marshall, in *Last Things and Last Plays: Shakespearean Eschatology* (Southern Illinois UP, 1991), argues that the last plays represent the eschatological concerns of a culture heavily imbued with apocalypticism and focused on judgment, the afterlife, and attitudes about time. Each of the final plays features the apparent death of a central character and a period of mourning and loss. *Cym.* explores the apocalyptic concerns of Advent. Posthumus moves from a legalistic view of sin to an acceptance of grace, which demands an act of self-forgiveness. The play closes with a vision of the social aspects of Judgment Day. *WT* provides the most emphatic instance of physical reunion; only here do we find the simultaneous restoration of the body and restoration of the family in the statue scene. Marshall suggests that the concept of the seven ages of the world informs *Per.* It incorporates the symbolic history of the human race into the history of one man, Pericles. A dialectic of loss and recovery governs *Tmp.* This play presents an anatomy of Renaissance conceptions of the ideal society. In the duality of time and timelessness, Prospero ultimately abandons his attempt to control the future.

Roger Warren's *Staging Shakespeare's Late Plays* (Clarendon, 1990) documents an immediate stage history of these plays, based on his attendance at rehearsals and performances of National Theatre productions in 1988 and the Stratford, Ontario, productions of 1986. Warren offers a gold mine of information about how directors make production decisions and how these emerge in actual performance. This book underscores the theatricality of the final plays. On the basis of his experience, Warren concludes that the plays emphasize the sense of the central characters going on spiritual journeys, voyages of discovery and self-discovery.

In his fourth volume on this subject, Kristian Smidt assumes in *Unconformities in Shakespeare's Later Comedies* (St. Martin's, 1993) that Shakespeare arrived at unity of theme, conservation of character, and continuity of plot, despite some broken continuity in story line. Smidt analyzes several comedies, beginning with *Ado,* and then moves to the Romances. He focuses on the supernatural in *Per.* and finds the theme of quest crucial. The unconformities in *Cym.* arise from complications in plot, and the characters oscillate between romance and realism. Smidt argues that *WT* shows evidence of revision to include the restoration of Hermione. Prospero's behavior provides a divided picture: benevolent but temperamental and irascible. Shakespeare evidently engaged in a fair amount of revision of his plays.

HISTORIES

To this day, defining the history play as a genre remains imprecise. The dramatist's use of possible sources has been explored extensively. Which chronicle histories did he conceivably consult? How did he use them? How does the dramatic art correspond to the chronicle account or whatever other source might have been used? These plays, grounded in English history, have provoked much research into contemporary political theory and how the apparent assumptions of the plays do or do not reflect current political thought. Did Shakespeare teach his fellow Elizabethans some lessons about their own political world? How did the dramatist regard the function of Providence in the working out of history? Critics have certainly been divided on this issue. The plays seem to serve the cause of Tudor nationalism, but by intention or coincidence? Does a coherent political system emerge from the plays, or do they serve propaganda? Of interest to critics has also been Shakespeare's developing artistry as illustrated in the histories.

A review of criticism can be found in Harold Jenkins, "Shakespeare's History Plays, 1900–1951," *Shakespeare Survey* 6 (1953): 1–15. *Shakespeare: The Histories: A Collection of Critical Essays* (Prentice-Hall, 1965), edited by Eugene M. Waith, reprints eleven essays, Waith's introduction, and a brief selected bibliography. Irving Ribner's *The English History Play in the Age of Shakespeare,* 2d ed. (Barnes & Noble, 1965; 1st ed., 1957), outlines a dramatic context in which Shakespeare participated. In the opening chapter, Ribner discusses history and drama in Shakespeare's age; then he turns to the emergence of the genre, which Ribner sees as greatly indebted to medieval drama, specifically morality plays. He provides a long consideration of the various history plays of the sixteenth century, including Shakespeare's. Appendix B provides a useful chronological list of extant English history plays, 1519–1653; appendix D has a select bibliography.

Peter Saccio's reference book *Shakespeare's English Kings: History, Chronicle, and Drama* (Oxford UP, 1977) contains excellent summaries of the history that forms the background of Shakespeare's ten plays on English history. Saccio begins with a sketch of fifteenth-century history and then moves through each play, recounting the history on which it rests. Such a summary helps us understand what Shakespeare did with the historical chronicle that he inherited.

All criticism of the histories emanates from E. M. W. Tillyard's pioneering work *Shakespeare's History Plays* (Chatto & Windus, 1944), whether one agrees or disagrees with it. Tillyard's became the traditional interpretation of the history plays. He devotes a large part of the book to the background: cosmic, historical, literary nondramatic, and literary dramatic. Tillyard argues that Shakespeare derived his historical vision from that he found in Hall's chronicle and that he successfully expressed a universally held scheme of history—a fundamentally religious one, whereby events evolve under a law of justice and under the ruling of God's Providence. England serves as the protagonist in the histories, especially the first tetralogy (*1H6, 2H6, 3H6,* and *R3*), producing a structure that reflects the dramatist's indebtedness to medieval morality drama.

Tillyard emphasizes the idea of a "Tudor myth" of history: namely, that the Tudors under Henry VII successfully ended the War of the Roses and brought a new unity and peace to the land. The theme of order is powerful, as is the continual insistence on cause and effect in the unfolding of history. The play *1H6* involves the testing of England, including the assumption of divine interference, whereas the problem of dissension at home develops in *2H6,* with the Duke of York as the emergent figure. In *3H6,* Shakespeare shows us chaos itself, as full-scale civil war breaks out. *R3* completes the national tetralogy and displays the working out of God's plan to restore England to prosperity, a view that does not take enough note of Richard's dramatic character. A political theme binds these four plays: order and chaos, proper political degree and civil war, and the belief that such had been God's way with England. *Jn.* offers the political problems of succession, the ethics of rebellion, and the kingly character. Tillyard finds *R2* the most formal and ceremonial of the histories, and he argues that Richard's crimes never amounted to tyranny; hence the rebellion against him was treasonous. In *H4,* Hal, first tested in the military or chivalric virtues, becomes the mean between the extremes of Hotspur and Falstaff; in the second part, he encounters the civil virtues and must choose between disorder or misrule and Order or Justice (the supreme kingly virtue). By *H5,* Shakespeare had finished the theme of England and thus could allow a concrete hero to dominate, though Tillyard finds many shortcomings in the play itself. Tillyard's criticism provides historical study in the political orthodoxy of the plays, demonstrating the dramatist's awareness and use of a providential view of history.

Lily B. Campbell's *Shakespeare's "Histories": Mirrors of Elizabethan Policy* (Huntington Library, 1947) complements Tillyard's study. It, too, sketches an orthodox political approach to the history plays but discusses only *Jn., R2, H4, H5,* and

R3. Part 1 deals with historiography and politics—the different views on the meaning of history and the English historians. For Campbell, the history play functions as a literary medium for history, concerned with politics as it mirrors patterns of behavior. In *Jn.*, Faulconbridge, not the hero, serves as a kind of vice from the moralities to prick others to action. *R2* reflects contemporary problems or concerns, namely, the deposition of a king; thus Shakespeare uses Richard to set forth the political ethics of the Tudors with regard to the rights and duties of a king. Henry IV, who was a rebel and usurper, suffers for his sins by rebellion. Meanwhile, Henry V appears as an ideal hero, and the play mirrors the English as triumphant in a righteous cause, achieving victory through the blessing of God. *R3* combines the elements of both tragedy and history.

M. M. Reese, in *The Cease of Majesty: A Study of Shakespeare's History Plays* (Arnold, 1961), largely hews to the Tillyard line. History demonstrates the logic and reason of God's control of human affairs; it also teaches through the examples of the past how to bear misfortune in the present. Reese discusses the Tudor historians—Polydore Vergil, More, Fabyan, Hall, and Holinshed—and literary works by Daniel and Drayton and *The Mirror for Magistrates*. According to Reese, the history play developed naturally from the folk dramas of the Middle Ages, the miracle and morality plays. Shakespeare's unique contribution comes from the depth and range of his penetration and the undogmatic balance of his conclusions. Through the histories, Shakespeare searches for the ideal public figure and finds in Henry V the man who most nearly fits. The parts of *H6* offer only an occasional glimpse of real people and human predicaments. Although Richard gives *R3* boisterous energy, the play is not concerned only with him. The dramatist argues in *R2* that rebellion is always wicked, but character and destiny cooperate in Bolingbroke's ruthless drive toward the crown. The real victim of Richard's tragedy is England (shades of Tillyard). *Jn.* remains unsatisfactory because it lacks a focal point. The two parts of *H4* treat the education of the Prince, and the morality pattern inheres. In *H5*, Shakespeare celebrates England's recovered majesty in the mirror of the Christian king. Consistently the plays reflect on the plight and destiny of the country, as well as occasionally presenting interesting dramatic characters.

S. C. Sen Gupta, in *Shakespeare's Historical Plays* (Oxford UP, 1964), reacts against the Tillyard school. Sen Gupta assumes that the greatness of Shakespeare consists chiefly in his ability to create men and women who have the vividness of living characters, a view of the histories that differs greatly from those who seek some pattern of morality throughout the plays. In his discussion of Tudor political philosophy, Sen Gupta doubts that the dramatist was primarily interested in propagating a particular political or moral idea. In fact, the notion that Shakespeare tried to express the Tudor view of history seems somewhat naive. The histories function neither as moral homilies nor as political treatises. They emphasize instead the personal, human aspect of events, the conflict and clash of Nature and Fortune in the lives of men and women. Sen Gupta sees in the first tetralogy an increasing tendency to simplify the network of history and to assign changes to the unpredictable element in human character. Although *3H6* remains largely a chronicle of events rather than a historical play, *R3* is the first attempt to organize the various materials of history by placing the center of interest in a tragic character. Even so, the materials remain partly recalcitrant until the end. *R2* seems a human drama—indeed, a personal tragedy—rather than a political document or a moral homily. The theme of *H4* focuses not on the education of Prince Hal and his moral struggle between virtue and vice but on the fortunes of Falstaff. In *H5,* Shakespeare presents a fusion of epic and drama, with the Chorus providing a perspective from which to view the events and personalities. Sen Gupta offers a healthy corrective by insisting that these histories are plays, not historical documents or pieces of propaganda.

Robert Ornstein, in *A Kingdom for a Stage: The Achievement of Shakespeare's History Plays* (Harvard UP, 1972), also emphasizes the aesthetic qualities of these plays. This work, in which the author discusses all the histories, reacts somewhat to the earlier critical treatments, especially Tillyard and Campbell. Ornstein argues that, for all practical purposes, Shakespeare originated the historical dramatic genre and that the histories must be judged by artistic standards and not by any effort to recreate the "Elizabethan world picture."

Ornstein doubts that Shakespeare wrote his tetralogies to set forth the Tudor myth of history, a myth that, if it existed, should more properly be called a Yorkist myth. Whatever source materials Shakespeare used, his interpretation of the past became his own. The tetralogies are themselves too separate and too different from one another to be regarded as the complementary halves of a single oddly constructed panorama of English history. Shakespeare journeys in the history plays toward artistic exploration and self-discovery, leading almost unerringly beyond politics and history to the universal themes and concerns of his most mature art. The dramatist demonstrates in the *H6* plays the possibilities of characterization and the range of dramatic and poetic techniques. In *3H6,* as Henry approaches saintliness, he becomes less a dramatic character than a moral symbol, and Richard gains a new psychological complexity. For the first time in the histories, Shakespeare's plotting in *R3* has vertical as well as horizontal form, because each step of Richard's rise and fall offers a fresh discovery of political and moral reality. As Ornstein suggests, Richard plays the moral teacher for quite a long time before he becomes the moral lesson of the play. More than simply a dramatic protagonist, Richard II is also the poetic voice of his era and the quintessential expression of its sensibility. The play presents a subtle revelation of the protagonist's nature. Ornstein finds *1H4* remarkable for its unity of vision and of plot, which embraces and demands the interplay of comedy and history, but *2H4* increases in disillusion and the debilitation of age. That Shakespeare succeeded as well as he did in celebrating English heroism in *H5* surprises us, because he also makes damaging admissions about the methods and motives of the principal characters.

In *Shakespeare's History Plays: The Family and the State* (Ohio State UP, 1971), Robert B. Pierce examines all the histories except *H8*. The discussion proceeds chronologically in order to observe the developing skill of the histories in relating the family and the state. Pierce covers three basic areas: figures and analogies based on the family and relying on the habit of seeing correspondences; scenes of family life injected into the middle of historical events; and passages and whole plays in which the family inextricably mixes with the political situation. The ideas of the plays and the craft come together with some attempt at understanding the audience's likely response. In the *H6* plays, the family functions almost entirely as a commentary on the causes and consequences of political disorder. The family in *R3* makes nemesis more than just a Senecan doom, gives it weight and ethical meaning as a force of Providence. *R2* embodies the most prominent family theme in the histories, focusing on the issue of inheritance. The play centers on fathers and sons, not only in its emphasis on orderly succession but also in its study of moral inheritance. Shakespeare displays in the *H4* plays the quest for political order as fundamentally like the quest for personal order within the family—only the scale differs. The family theme has little consequence in *H5,* which at least carries out the function of making the family an echo of political themes. Pierce sums up the argument of the book in an excellent conclusion.

Focusing on the second tetralogy, Derek Traversi, in *Shakespeare from "Richard II" to "Henry V"* (Stanford UP, 1957), sees the plays as focused on the life and career of Prince Hal. The plays pose the question: what are the personal, as distinct from the political, qualities that go into the making of a king? As the personal implications of the royal vocation in Hal progressively unfold, they constantly relate to the state of an England that at once reflects and conditions the central presentation of royalty. *R2,* with its simple plot but elaborate style, has as its most original feature the effort to diversify artificial forms, to make the elaboration of contrasted styles respond to the tensions that constitute the true tragic theme. The drama emphasizes a conflict of personalities, with the tragic impotence of the king balanced by the purposeful advance of his rival. *1H4* represents a remarkable growth in significant complexity of structure. The development into full consciousness of the effective political Prince exists against the background of the English realm, threatened by anarchy. Falstaff's disintegrating, ultimately corrupting force cannot be overcome by his exuberance. The Lord Chief Justice balances Falstaff in *2H4.* The play includes the concepts of repentance and restitution, thus marking a changing spirit from the comic to the severely moral.

H5 has as its principal theme the establishment in England of an order based on consecrated authority and crowned successfully by action against France. Like most of Shakespeare's plays of this time, this play includes concern about the mastery of passion and its relation to action. *H5* combines an acute analysis of motive in its hero with a conception of the royal office that has been carefully built up. Traversi argues that the play ends with a decided pessimism that somehow fails to attain the note of tragedy.

Michael Manheim follows a particular theme through some of the histories in *The Weak King Dilemma in the Shakespearean History Play* (Syracuse UP, 1973). He examines a group of plays that represent the ambivalence of subject toward monarch, be that monarch wanton or meek. For Manheim, this reveals the universal contradiction about monarchy, beginning to emerge in the Elizabethans of the 1590s. This critical approach also involves consideration of the manipulation of audience sympathies toward the monarch. Manheim includes in the discussion an examination of several non-Shakespearean plays, such as *Edward II* and *Woodsock*. The central dilemma of the weak king derives from whether deposition can be justified. Richard II excites first antagonism and then sympathy, once he appears vulnerable. In the death scene, the play approaches tragedy as Richard finally shows signs of new self-awareness. Bolingbroke, of course, embodies strength. The *H6* plays stretch to its limits the issue of whether an inadequate monarch ought to be deposed. Henry's weaknesses drag him down in the face of the inhumanity and strength of the nobles. In all these plays, an embedded Machiavellianism may be seen as an alternative to the weak king; the successful and strong king learns the practical lessons of a kind of Machiavellianism. *Jn.* is a transitional play, for it demonstrates a rapprochement with the new political methods, as seen chiefly in the character of the Bastard. It thus stands between *H6* and *H5*, bridging the chasm between anti-and pro-Machiavellianism. The culmination comes in *H5*, which presents a strong king not plagued by the vacillation and weakness of other kings. Henry V makes desirable and attractive his brand of strength and Machiavellianism. Manheim's shortcomings derive from his sometimes careless attention to the texts of the plays and a failure to correlate his thesis with Shakespeare's necessary dependence on some sort of source.

James Winny, in *The Player King: A Theme of Shakespeare's Histories* (Barnes & Noble, 1968), argues against Tillyard's view that the tetralogies form a coherent thematic unit embracing a moral argument. Instead, Winny believes the historical order of the six reigns irrelevant to Shakespeare's imaginative purpose, though the chronological order of the plays is important. Throughout the series (*R2* to *H5*), the king sits uneasily on the throne, under assault from rivals whose ambition he must contain if he is not to lose his crown; his task is one of personal domination. Winny focuses on the idea of the king not as a political concept but as an imaginative one, developed from play to play. In *R2,* Richard's identity seems to exist in his name and title. The shock of political disaster forces him to acknowledge the emptiness of his grand identity and to fall back toward the basic, simple human character that he has ignored. The play centers on the confrontation of a majestic imposture (Richard) by the robust reality (Bolingbroke) it has attempted to avoid. Bolingbroke as Henry IV evades some realities himself; he adopts a facade of moral responsibility and maintains an outward majesty, but Falstaff parodies this pose in his comic stateliness and aplomb. Hal debases the royal standard by submitting it to indignity and therefore continues the process initiated by the usurper, his father. But he ultimately restores dignity to both the king's office and his person. Winny finds *H5* a seriously flawed play, and he dislikes the idea of Henry as the ideal Christian king. For some reason, Shakespeare's historical matter seems intractable, and the play is most alive at those moments of uncertainty and doubt in the king.

Although it ranges through comedies and tragedies and ends with an analysis of *Tmp.,* Eileen Jorge Allman's *Player-King and Adversary: Two Faces of Play in Shakespeare* (Louisiana State UP, 1980) devotes one-third of its space to the history plays. She argues that in Shakespearean dramaturgy, Henry V culminates the history plays' decade of search for a Player-King. Compared with the Player-King, who wills his being into the perpetual enactment of metaphor, Richard II is an Audience-King, enjoying the activity before him as if it were a spectacle he had no part in. Even Bolingbroke in *R2* recreates the paralyzing split between the word and the act. Allman sees the confrontation at Flint Castle as the turning point in the play, marking the end of hope and the first awareness of futility. But this episode also points to the search for self rather than for power. Allman explores the ways in which Henry IV and Falstaff resemble each other and how Prince Hal must ultimately be free of them both. Hotspur, meanwhile, cannot see that he stands alone. Hal, trained in play, becomes in *H5* a king who enacts metaphors and heals division, who creates his own realm in the way an artist creates an imaginary landscape. Henry V creates the garden and gives the players in it free will.

In *Shakespeare's Heroical Histories: "Henry VI" and Its Literary Tradition* (Harvard UP, 1971), David Riggs emphasizes the literary, dramatic, and rhetorical traditions available to Shakespeare. In the first chapter, the author develops a set of assumptions about history and literature relevant to the actual business of making an Elizabethan history play; he considers issues of Providence and historiography. Riggs questions the assumption that a humanistic approach to history came intuitively to the Elizabethan dramatists and suggests that the providentialism of the chroniclers was more the exception than the rule. He further explores the rhetorical basis of popular history, giving special attention to Marlowe's *Tamburlaine*. Chapter 3 presents a survey of the "heroic example" from Marlowe to Richard III, distinguishing between parentage and deeds in the evolution of the Herculean hero. The trilogy of *H6* encompasses Shakespeare's presentation of "agents" who gave the reign its distinctive contours, as opposed to a consistent moral history or view of Providence. Riggs pursues through all three plays Shakespeare's treatment of the gradual deterioration of heroic idealism; this trilogy is at once an embodiment and a criticism of the literary traditions described here. In a final chapter, the author includes consideration of *R3* and *1H4*, reappraising the heroic tradition and its significance in English history; these two plays try to resolve the dilemmas. For example, *1H4* takes the erosion of traditional standards for granted and thereby redefines the intentions that lead a prince to elect the chivalric vocation. Riggs includes a helpful bibliography.

Examining the *H6–R3* tetralogy, Edward Berry, in *Patterns of Decay: Shakespeare's Early Histories* (UP of Virginia, 1975), argues for the dramatic integrity of the sequence. The conjunction of chivalric heroism and ceremonial mystique that unifies *1H6* represents an important tendency in Elizabethan thought. Stages of social disintegration appear in *2H6* in the concepts of justice and law, which erode until they collapse in the confusion of civil war. In *3H6*, Shakespeare depicts the gradual dissolution of a society at war with itself, a society in which the single bond of kinship becomes increasingly corrupted and is finally destroyed. Berry emphasizes the isolation of Richard III as *R3* explores the nature of the self alone as Richard moves from conquest to destruction. The aggressive egocentricity that gradually reduces the state to chaos ultimately destroys the self. In a final chapter, Berry assesses the relationship between these early history plays and the later ones, which become more concerned with the development of character.

Because almost every writer on the histories sooner or later says something about the role of Providence, it was both inevitable and desirable that someone would make a full study of this important issue in the plays. Henry A. Kelly's *Divine Providence in the England of Shakespeare's Histories* (Harvard UP, 1970) pursues the topic. Part 1 deals with the various "myths" of history as revealed in the contemporary accounts of fifteenth-century England. The sixteenth-century prose chroniclers Vergil, Hall, and Holinshed synthesized these views. Kelly argues against an absolute sense of the working out of divine punishment or judgment in the chroniclers, though Daniel's 1595 version of *The Civil Wars* has a strong sense of providential design. Providential themes occur in *R2*, but no final sense exists that God actively brings about any of the actions of the play. In *1H4*, the themes occasionally appear for rhetorical effect, and in *2H4*, Shakespeare does not clearly indicate that he believes either side in the conflict to have God's full approval or full condemnation. The actions of the *H6* plays do not come as some consequence of Providence from the earlier reigns; the conflicts arise as a new situation with causes of their own. Nor does *R3* demonstrate that Henry VI and his family suffer punishment because of the "sins" of his grandfather, Henry IV. Kelly suggests that the providential aspect of the Tudor myth as described by Tillyard occurs as an ex post facto Platonic form not substantiated by the drama or literature itself. Instead,

Shakespeare dramatizes the characters and thus eliminates all the purportedly objective providential judgments made by the histories on historical characters.

In his *The Lost Garden: A View of Shakespeare's English and Roman History Plays* (Macmillan, 1978), John Wilders sketches the philosophical background of Shakespeare's history plays, examining such topics as time and change; fortune and nature; prayer, prophecy, and Providence; knowledge and judgment; and dilemma and discovery. All these concepts point to the image of the lost garden. The human condition that Wilders outlines, although solving one problem, never attains the ideal. Shakespeare portrays history as a series of attempts by individuals to satisfy their need for permanence and their necessary failure. Shakespeare sees in the histories the spectacle of human failure. At the heart of his conception of politics lies the paradox that a rule of law is necessary to protect mankind from its own inherent savagery; yet few people are willing to be governed. Wilders reinforces his thematic approach with generous evidence from the history plays.

Looking at the second tetralogy (*R2–H5*), James L. Calderwood, in *Metadrama in Shakespeare's Henriad* (U of California P, 1979), finds a self-contained metadrama in which the dramatist examines his art through his art. Calderwood sees Shakespeare as solving problems of language by means of politics, which become metaphor for art. Thus in the Henriad, the main metadramatic plot centers on the "fall of speech." The sacramental language of Richard II eventually gives way to a much more pragmatic language. The debasement of kingship also involves the secularizing of language in which the relation between words and things is arbitrary, unsure, and ephemeral. A wedge driven between words and their meanings leads not merely to the fall of a king in *R2* but also to the fall of kingly speech. Bolingbroke regards words as mere vocal conveniences. To raise such questions about the function of language forces the dramatist to look at his own artistry. Falstaff, Calderwood maintains, perfectly embodies a final profane reincarnation of Shakespeare's impulse to create verbal worlds sufficient unto themselves. Hal, however, functions as an "interior" version of Shakespeare the controlling playwright. In *2H4*, Shakespeare repeats the form but not the substance of *1H4*. At Agincourt, Henry V redeems English kingship in a self-conscious way. In *H5,* the dramatist moves to rhetorical speech in which words acquire pragmatic value as instruments of action. The Epilogue reminds us of what Henry V soon loses, as it reminds us that Shakespeare's own dramatic achievements are fugitive: he must move on to other kinds of problems and attempted solutions.

Basing his analysis on J. L. Austin's work on speech acts, Joseph A. Porter, in *The Drama of Speech Acts: Shakespeare's Lancastrian Tetralogy* (U of California P, 1979), explores several dimensions of language in the *R2–H5* tetralogy. Simply stated, Porter uses "speech act" to mean an act performed in speech. He argues that this tetralogy is in part about language and its function. Talk about name, naming, title, and the like constitutes the most prominent body of references to language in *R2;* therefore, to Richard, Gaunt, and Bolingbroke, the idea of name is of great importance. For Richard, to lose the name of "king" means also to lose the name "Richard," so thoroughly do they intertwine in his mind. Richard also conceives of language poetically, as material from which to construct literary objects. Porter suggests that the overall action of the play documents the decline and fall of Richard's conception of language. His universal, unilingual, absolutist world of nomenclature and ceremonial performatives contrasts with Bolingbroke's world of tongues and silence. In *1H4,* we confront practical questions of dealing with proliferated tongues. Porter likens Hotspur to Richard II, in that Hotspur ties his ear to his own tongue and its world of figures. Prince Hal, meanwhile, responds to the existence of a variety of languages, a fact made explicit in the appearance of Rumour in *2H4.* Reporting is one of the most frequently mentioned and frequently occurring speech acts in this play. In *H5,* the variety of languages, excluded from Richard's absolutist conception of language, becomes a prominent example of the manageable order of the world. Ultimately, Porter argues that the verbal form—drama—is itself a major unifying subject or theme of the tetralogy. Or to put the issue slightly differently, the tetralogy illustrates a shift of allegiance from nondramatic to dramatic literature. Porter takes time toward the end of the book to explain his methodology and concludes with an overview of the entire tetralogy.

In a detailed analysis of the plays *R2–H5,* Herbert R. Coursen, in *The Leasing Out of England: Shakespeare's Second Henriad* (UP of America, 1982), seeks to define the world of these plays. He explores the question of the presence of God in the Henriad plays. For Coursen, this second tetralogy represents a long denouement, beginning with Richard II's defection from duty and the evocation of a paradise lost—a lost sacramental vision of the world. Bolingbroke sets up a new feudal system in England; and the political world of Henry IV consists of broken contracts, duplicity, and political calculation and miscalculation. In *2H4,* England sinks below the baseness represented by a purely commercial ethic. Henry V, inheritor of an intrinsically meaningless crown, provides an artistic simulation of true kingship; his play explores the limits of Henry's vision. In the plays of the Henriad, morality tends to succumb to power.

In *Unconformities in Shakespeare's History Plays* (Macmillan, 1982), Kristian Smidt focuses on style, governed by a belief that Shakespeare often hesitated and sometimes ran into perplexities, leading him to revise his manuscripts and even make structural alterations as the plots grew. Such a view determines Smidt's approach to all the histories. Expectation and fulfillment are the key concepts in Smidt's structural analysis. He argues, for example, that the second and third parts of *H6* were not at first envisaged as two separate plays but that Shakespeare expanded his original Henry VI–Duke of York play by stages. The succession of plays about Henry VI assumes an epic as well as dramatic character, and the traffic of relations runs both backward and forward. *R3* contains a web of stated intentions, curses, prophecies, and dreams, with most expectations fulfilled. But *Jn.* suffers from a lack of focus; the Bastard threatens the king's centrality. Smidt argues that *R2* underwent some major changes of design in the course of its shaping, and the attitude of the play as a whole remains ambiguous. Prince Hal not only redeems his own lost opinion but also helps vindicate his father's legitimacy. Smidt finds the choruses in *H5* not in complete agreement with the main body of the play and maintains that they may not have been in the original version. King Henry seems to be at least two persons: the meek and pious

Christian hero and the bragging conqueror. *H8* focuses on character rather than on plot and intrigue, and it has a shifting center. Smidt admirably confronts seeming lapses, discrepancies, or contradictions in Shakespeare's histories.

John W. Blanpied, in *Time and the Artist in Shakespeare's English Histories* (U of Delaware P, 1983), argues that the historical tetralogies have a coherence born of the dramatist's sustained attention to the evolving relationship of subject to medium, history to drama. Thus the book examines the ways in which the playwright acts in his historical material—how he manages to transform his own inevitable presence in the histories into the means of sounding out their huge and elusive energies. In his challenging analysis, Blanpied explores all the English histories except *H8*. He suggests that even though *1H6* fails to enact the central issue between the dramatist and history, it nevertheless provides the bedrock for the future. Enlarging his sense of history, Shakespeare in *2H6* adds silence, absence, impotence, and flux, qualities that demand the active involvement of the audience. The mutual dependencies of Henry, Gloucester, and York reveal that history becomes the product of interwoven human action, which drama conveys especially well. In the king-centered plays such as *R3* and *R2,* Shakespeare begins the process of searching out the meaning of history in the very art and artistry of his own plays. *R3* culminates an old parodic mode of theatricality; *R2* initiates a new, more deeply sentient one. What happens to Richard II also happens to the play: an emergence from an unconscious to a conscious process of self-destruction. In *1H4,* rebellion—more than the subject of the play, and more even than its central metaphor—becomes its style. Falstaff brings to light the design of the play's rebellious energies. In contrast, *2H4* is a play about thwarted effort, in a sense parodying *1H4,* a point that Blanpied develops persuasively. *H5* comes to us already full of its particular, scripted audience: the "audience" addressed by the Chorus becomes a part in the play. The play isolates the primary relationship of evidence and play as it has operated throughout the history sequence.

Larry S. Champion's introduction to *Perspective in Shakespeare's English Histories* (U of Georgia P, 1980) sketches the background of Shakespeare's history plays. Champion argues that from the earliest histories to *H8,* Shakespeare continually modifies his dramatic design, balancing the sweep of history with effective psychology of character. In separate chapters, Champion analyzes all the histories, noting, for example, that Henry VI's ambivalence modulates to provoke a complex response from audiences. In both *R3* and *R2,* Shakespeare narrows the focus in order to explore fully the principal characters; in these plays, he also moves significantly toward his profound tragedies. In the *H4* plays and *H5,* Shakespeare essentially returns to the broad perspective and the skeletal characterization of the early histories, but he achieves a level of genuine human complexity by manipulating and modifying the spectators' angle of vision. Champion examines the techniques of detachment in *H8.* Throughout his discussion, he pays attention to dramatic techniques, such as soliloquies, and how these shape the play's perspective.

Larry Champion's more recent book, *"The Noise of Threatening Drum": Dramatic Strategy and Political Ideology in Shakespeare and the English Chronicle Plays* (U of Delaware P, 1990), examines several non-Shakespearean chronicle plays as well as Shakespeare's. It focuses on how the chronicle plays permit a multiplicity of ideological responses and offer a discourse on authority. Shakespeare intensifies political factionalism by revealing the class division inherent in feudal society. Jack Cade's rebellion in *2H6* reveals a society that has virtually collapsed from within; this crisis of authority reaches its greatest depths in *3H6. R2* debunks the idea of divine right, whereas *Jn.* reveals the historical process determined by fundamental self-interest. The Lancastrian forces in the Henriad plays try to invest power with a pragmatic and theoretical acceptability. In *H5,* we see monarchic power in the service of martial imperialism. Shakespeare weaves together dramatic strategy and political ideology.

The opening chapter of C. G. Thayer's *Shakespearean Politics: Government and Misgovernment in the Great Histories* (Ohio UP, 1983) concentrates on the death of divine kingship in *R2.* The book examines the second tetralogy, *R2–H5.* This tetralogy undercuts the idea of passive obedience and reinforces the emerging strength of the sovereign, epitomized in Henry V. The whole movement goes from injustice to justice, according to Thayer. Richard II differs from his successors because they deserve obedience and he does not. Passive obedience runs counter to good government and human dignity. Richard, Thayer argues, suffers from the psychopathology of divine kingship; but Bolingbroke forces Richard out of games and into the objective facts of life. In *R2,* the king's follies wound the state; in *H4,* the wounds begin to heal; in *H5,* the state again becomes a healthy organism. Thayer suggests that Henry V as the antithesis of Richard II has special relevance for the political world of 1599.

Robert Rentoul Reed, Jr., in *Crime and God's Judgment in Shakespeare* (UP of Kentucky, 1984), examines matters of guilt, conscience, and divine retribution in several of the history plays and in *Ham.* and *Mac.* Reed assumes the divine function of conscience and analyzes the histories as an eight-part epic with the fundamental theme of political homicide, prompted by self-interest, and God's ultimate judgment upon the perpetrator or his heirs. Reed emphasizes the theme in the histories of inherited guilt from generation to generation, and he suggests that Richard and Carlisle in *R2* possess a divinely granted clairvoyance in their prophecies. The theme of *nobilitas,* Reed observes, emerges as a unifying motif in Shakespeare's double tetralogy: its qualities of valor and selflessness betoken manhood. Reed basically argues that concepts of God's judgment control the principal destinies of each play's world. Thus, Bolingbroke functions as an agent of God, avenging Gloucester's murder. Reed also traces the responses to the death of Richard II through the histories. In *H5,* we find Shakespeare's most complete statement of the Lancastrian dread of God's vengeance for the death of Richard. The Wars of the Roses in the *H6* plays become an arena of vengeance and unwarranted bloodshed. The Ghosts that appear to Richard III, signs of God's judgment, paralyze his capacity to focus on the objective at hand.

In an intricately and persuasively argued book, Graham Holderness, in *Shakespeare's History* (St. Martin's, 1985), fulfills two tasks: to describe as precisely as possible the production of Shakespeare's historiography, and to demonstrate the fate of those historiographical texts in history, particularly the story of their subsequent reproduction. He focuses primarily on the *R2–H5* tetralogy and argues that specific historical conditions attending the genesis of Shakespeare's drama inscribed patterns of meaning into it. In so doing, Holderness devotes considerable time to confronting the principal critics of the histories, especially Tillyard, and exposes their own often nationalistic biases in their interpretations. Examining the Tudor historians, he concludes that these sources for Shakespeare were more complex than we often assume. Therefore, Shakespeare's history plays do not just reflect a cultural debate; they intervene in that debate, contributing to the historiographical effort to reconstruct the past. Specifically, these plays embody a conscious understanding of feudal society as a peculiar historical formulation, and they analyze that society. *R2* reflects Shakespeare's sophisticated understanding of medieval history, and it dramatizes the process of the destruction of the concept of divine monarchy. The play epitomizes the struggle between royal authority and feudal power. Holderness observes that Richard, as a historian, constructs and creates the myth of his own tragic history.

The *H4* plays show a continuation of the struggle between sovereign and nobles, complicated by the change of dynasty. Bolingbroke's earlier victory only centralizes and deepens the unstable and contradictory forces of the society he hopes to rule. Falstaff, in his function as carnival, constitutes a constant focus of opposition to the official and serious tone of authority and power. Holderness sees the eventual collision of Hal and Falstaff as the inevitable confrontation of patrician and plebeian dramatic discourses, or ruling-class and popular cultures. He views Henry V as a feudal overlord, not the ideal Renaissance prince; the play's historical vision provides an image of the declining feudal society of the fifteenth century. The remainder of the book examines how critics and theater producers have treated these history plays in the reproduction of history.

Paul N. Siegel, in *Shakespeare's English and Roman History Plays: A Marxist Approach* (Fairleigh Dickinson UP, 1986), distinguishes himself from other critics who examine the historical and political backgrounds of Shakespeare's plays. Siegel believes that class struggle is the "motor force" of history and that the ruling ideas of an age come from the ideas of the ruling class. He thus analyzes the interaction of the history plays with their culture and with the economic base of the political structure.

Siegel argues that Shakespeare not only demonstrates the changing relationship between monarchy, aristocracy, and the bourgeoisie but also shows the changes in his own time and foreshadows the bourgeoisie helping to overthrow a Stuart king. From such a perspective, Richard III is very much of the new capitalist world, obsessed with financial language and attitudes; but his energy is that of the bourgeoisie. In *Cor.*, Shakespeare shows the class struggle present in the early Roman republic. The social systems depicted in these plays mark only stages in the development of human society.

Shakespeare manages to find a pattern in the untidy events of history. So argues Alexander Leggatt in *Shakespeare's Political Drama: The History Plays and the Roman Plays* (Routledge, 1988). Leggatt examines all the histories, except *Jn.*, as well as *JC, Ant.*, and *Cor.* Through these, Leggatt explores how drama helped shape Shakespeare's political thinking, a thinking that is exploratory rather than prescriptive. Leggatt defines Shakespeare's politics as a search for power and authority by the politicians themselves. In *2H6*, Cade ironically becomes one of Shakespeare's most articulate social critics. Richard's capacity for long-range planning in *R3* and his mastery of the political situation go along with his extraordinary theatrical control. But Richard eventually loses control, unable to function as the center of social and political relationships; and Richmond takes the play from Richard. In a play of pervasive self-consciousness about language, Richard and Bolingbroke in *R2* shift kingship into a theatrical arena, as Richard gives away his identity with the crown. With misinformation as a recurring motif in the *H4* plays, Shakespeare also examines the underlying futility in the rebel cause. By the end, not only Hal turns against Falstaff; so does the play. Heroic and realistic visions conflict in *H5*, making judgment difficult. *H8* continues the pattern of the Roman plays: the interplay of greatness and frailty, of public and private interests.

Phyllis Rackin writes in *Stages of History: Shakespeare's English Chronicles* (Cornell UP, 1990) of the conflict in the history plays between older and newer conceptions of history, the basic conflict occurring between a providential and a Machiavellian view of history. In the sequence of plays from *H6* to *H5*, Shakespeare replaces the providential narrative with a self-referential cycle that questions the project of history mythmaking. The order in which Shakespeare wrote these plays follows the progress of Renaissance historiography toward an increasingly self-conscious and skeptical attitude. Indeed, in *R3*, Rackin argues, Shakespeare reconstructs the history that he has already written. Richard finds himself trapped in a world governed by Providence. The historical conflict finds its representation in *R2* in the battle between Richard and Bolingbroke. Rackin pays particular attention to the situation of women in the histories; ordinarily, they represent a threat to the legitimacy of patriarchal succession. The plays focus on heroic men, marginalizing the role of wives and mothers; but Shakespeare does give women a voice. *1H6*, for example, shows Joan as an emblem of social and spiritual transgression; the conflict between England and France becomes a conflict between masculine and feminine values. *Jn.* reveals deep anxieties about female power and authority, reflecting its crisis in patriarchal authority. Rackin also examines the place of the theater itself in the historical debate.

Donald G. Watson emphasizes theatrical dimensions in *Shakespeare's Early History Plays: Politics at Play on the Elizabethan Stage* (U of Georgia P, 1990). In Watson's view, the stage serves as a site for dramatized interpretations of history and as an arena for exploring contemporary issues. *1H6* becomes dramatic by exploring the gap between professed intention and true motive; the factionalism within the English nobility complicates the play's politics. The commoners in *2H6* threaten boundaries between social groups and undermine generic unity by challenging the coherence of history. Watson argues that Henry VI and Margaret arrive at the margins of history by different paths. The opening speeches of *3H6* establish the tone of this drama of mutilation. Henry becomes a choric figure but also a much more human character, whereas Richard perceives and acts on the opportunities provided by the fragmentation of order and the absence of ideology. Shakespeare concentrates on acting, deceit, and politics as performance in *R3*. The last two acts demonstrate Richard's failure to play the king, manage the theatrical symbols of royalty, and command the powers of sovereignty. Watson views *Jn.* as a highly theatrical melodrama of political history. Throughout these plays, Shakespeare exploits the paradoxes of politics in order to dramatize fully the irony of history.

Robert C. Jones explores the viability of heroic renewal in *These Valiant Dead: Renewing the Past in Shakespeare's Histories* (U of Iowa P, 1991). *1H6,* for example, opens with a lament for the lost leader Henry V, whose model offers a potential for sustaining and reviving his grand heritage. Talbot keeps the heroic spirit alive in the play. Jack Cade in *2H6* parodies the disregard for history's authority that pervades the nobility; no positive memory of the English past survives. Memory floods the world of *R3,* but its continuity moves by retribution rather than renewal. Margaret becomes memory's most insistent voice. In *Jn.,* the Bastard vividly renews the memory of Richard I; this character exposes the imperfections of the world around him by commenting on them and by being an exemplary contrast to them. *R2* shows the loss of meaningful contact with the positive force that the past should have. Although *1H4* is unique in its total abstinence from any recollection of the valiant dead, *2H4* is an emphatically retrospective play. Primarily, this latter play remembers the lost leader Hotspur. The shaping of history both in the making and in the telling adds to Henry's stature as heroic king in *H5,* even as he teases us with complexity and sometimes ambiguity.

Jonathan Hart concentrates on the second tetralogy, *R2–H5,* in his *Theater and World: The Problematics of Shakespeare's History* (Northeastern UP, 1991). He explores the fall into language and temporality, the issue of drama versus history, and the relationship of the history play and the problem play. Language in these plays shows contradiction, limitation, and lack of communication. Hart examines in detail the function of irony. Shakespeare creates different genres within the history play: tragedy in *R2,* comedy in *1H4,* satire in *2H4,* and problem play in *H5.* Because of its self-reflexive nature, the second tetralogy examines its own limitations and potentialities, as Shakespeare elaborates the problems of trying to represent history on the stage (especially in *H5*). How characters respond to the idea of kingship helps define them; indeed, *R2* seems to be a series of crises over the meaning of kingship. In the afterword, Hart discusses how interpretations of the history plays have changed, with special attention to new historicism.

Barbara Hodgdon includes rich examples of theatrical productions in *The End Crowns All: Closure and Contradiction in Shakespeare's History* (Princeton UP, 1991) and examines all the history plays in light of their endings. Hodgdon operates on two premises: that representation of sovereignty on the stage closes with and addresses the immense prestige and power of monarchy, and that closure in the history play constitutes a territory that generates and seeks to legitimize new kings. *Jn.* confronts the question of legitimacy by hollowing out John's mythic Tudor identity to reveal its precarious and contradictory shape. The *H6* plays privilege "chronicle closure," based largely on Hall's history. Closure in these plays criticizes power and its principles. *2H6* shifts from female misrule to another form of festival inversion: Cade's transgressive commonwealth. The last scene in *3H6* embraces and intensifies a number of signs associated with comic closure, especially the creation of a new family. But the close of *R3* masks the claims of royal successor; only the play's design endorses Richmond's kingship. *R2* evades the dynastic rift caused by Bolingbroke's accession; the final movement of closure sets king against king, scene against scene, ending against beginning. Falstaff's presence at Shrewsbury in *1H4* gives the lie to and refutes chivalric signs; he becomes the central character in *2H4*, helping the play to expose history as possible misrepresentation. The dialectic of genres in *H5* enables the play to interrogate its own dismantling and mystification of history. The Epilogue makes explicit that what completes or succeeds represented history is another history play. *H8* offers a final vision of England's future under Elizabeth, implying her redemptive potential.

W. F. Bolton's *Shakespeare's English: Language in the History Plays* (Basil Blackwell, 1992) is a linguistic analysis of ten history plays, focusing on linguistic data and linguistic concepts. Bolton begins with sound patterns in *R3* and then examines the linguistic structure of *R2*. He explores the vocabulary of *Jn.*, the rhetoric of the three parts of *H6*, the linguistic variety of *1H4* and *2H4*, "language and nation" in *H5*, and the "pragmatics" of *H8*. He responds in part to the earlier work of Kökeritz and Cercignani.

TRAGEDIES

Criticism of the tragedies has often focused on the study of characters. Indeed, the leading protagonists of the tragedies capture our memory; and their motives, psychology, and spirit produce fascination both on the stage and in the printed text. The great actors of any generation aspire to the role of some Shakespearean tragic hero. Critics have examined both the spirit and the form of tragedy and have marked Shakespeare's development as a writer of tragedies. Questions of influence from his contemporary dramatists and from tragic theories have been discussed. Several critics have grouped common themes that bind together certain of the tragedies. Matters of style and imagery have likewise been considered.

An extremely helpful review of criticism of the tragedies can be found in *The Major Shakespearean Tragedies: A Critical Bibliography* (Free Press, 1973), edited by Edward Quinn, James Ruoff, and Joseph Grennen. This book reviews and evaluates criticism and scholarship on *Ham., Lr., Oth.,* and *Mac.* The work on each play comprises five categories: criticism, editions, text, sources, and staging. The emphasis is on criticism, treated chronologically, usually starting with the eighteenth century. An index to the critics accompanies the discussion of each play. An essay by Clifford Leech, "Studies in Shakespearian and Other Jacobean Tragedy, 1918–1972: A Retrospect," *Shakespeare Survey* 26 (1973): 1–9, also reviews criticism. Specialized studies can be found in Leech's essay "Studies in *Hamlet,* 1901–1955," *Shakespeare Survey* 9 (1956): 1–15, and in Helen Gardner, "*Othello:* A Retrospect, 1900—67," *Shakespeare Survey* 21 (1968): 1–11. Anthologies of tragedy criticism include Laurence Lerner, ed., *Shakespeare's Tragedies: An Anthology of Modern Criticism* (Penguin, 1963), which contains essays on nine tragedies and theoretical essays on tragedy and Shakespearean tragedy in particular. Clifford Leech, ed., *Shakespeare: The Tragedies: A Collection of Critical Essays* (U of Chicago P, 1965), reprints eighteen essays by critics ranging from Dryden to contemporary critics, with an introduction by Leech that reviews some of the criticism on Shakespeare's tragedies. *Shakespeare: The Tragedies: Twentieth Century Views, New Perspectives* (Prentice-Hall, 1984), edited by Robert B. Heilman, reprints sixteen essays and excerpts from books by a number of prominent critics.

A. C. Bradley's *Shakespearean Tragedy* (Macmillan, 1904), perhaps the most influential work on the tragedies and one of the most influential pieces of Shakespearean criticism, has been reprinted more than twenty times, attesting to its eminence. Bradley presents an intensive analysis of *Ham., Oth., Lr.,* and *Mac.,* emphasizing the characters and attempting to define their psychology. In the opening chapters, Bradley discusses the "substance" and "construction" of Shakespearean tragedy. For Bradley, the center of tragedy lies in action issuing from character or in character resulting in action. Calamities and catastrophes follow inevitably from the deeds of men, and the main source of these deeds is character. In a discussion of the nature of the tragic hero, the author observes that the hero's tragic trait, which is also his greatness, becomes fatal to him.

All of *Ham.* turns on the peculiar character of the hero, whose main difficulty is internal. Bradley denies Coleridge's notion that this is a tragedy of reflection; instead, the cause derives from an abnormal state of mind, a state of profound melancholy that grows out of Hamlet's moral shock. This emotional conciliation of melancholy explains most of his actions, which Bradley examines in detail. The sparing of Claudius in the prayer scene constitutes the turning point in the play, from which all the disasters follow. Bradley finds Claudius interesting, both psychologically and dramatically. *Oth.,* the most painfully exciting and most terrible of all the tragedies, focuses on Othello, the most romantic figure among Shakespeare's heroes. His mind simple, he is by nature full of vehement passion; when he trusts, he trusts absolutely. Contrary to Coleridge, Bradley has no trouble finding sufficient motivation in Iago. Iago possesses remarkable powers of intellect and will, and his desire to satisfy the sense of power drives him on.

For Bradley, *Lr.* is Shakespeare's greatest achievement but not his best play. He finds, for example, the blinding of Gloucester to be a blot on the play as a stage play. But the chief fault comes from the play's double action, the Lear and Gloucester stories, though Bradley admits that this technique helps give the play its universal quality. Bradley's own dramatic sense calls for a happy ending; the suffering has been enough. He believes that Lear's final accents and gestures should express an "unbearable joy." In *Mac.*, the most vehement, most concentrated of the tragedies, Bradley finds the witches an influence, but nothing more. Ambition fires Macbeth and Lady Macbeth. After the murder of Duncan, Macbeth exhibits the most remarkable psychological development of a character in Shakespeare. Curiously, Macbeth never loses our sympathy. Lady Macbeth's greatness lies in her courage and will.

The acceptance of Bradley's views has waxed and waned in the history of criticism during this century. These matters have been documented by Katherine Cooke in *A. C. Bradley and His Influence in Twentieth-Century Shakespeare Criticism* (Clarendon, 1972). This book offers a biography of Bradley, covers his critical theories and other critics' attacks on him, and assesses his contribution. On the whole, Cooke believes that Bradley enjoys high regard and that critics read him for the right reasons, devoid of the envy of his success that afflicted earlier decades.

A self-confessed disciple of Bradley's, H. B. Charlton, in *Shakespearian Tragedy* (Cambridge UP, 1948), emphasizes the means by which Shakespearean tragedy achieves its effect of inevitability. In the greatest tragedies, human nature shapes morality by some ultimate and mysterious impulse; Shakespearean tragedy celebrates, then, the apotheosis of the human spirit. Hamlet creates his ideal world and then mistakes it for a true intellectual projection of the real one, thus becoming largely incapable of action. Othello's downfall forms the core of the tragedy; his tragic world emerges from the disastrous meeting point of two cultural and spiritual traditions. Iago's malignity propels him from within. In spite of all his premonitions of agony, Macbeth's ambition overcomes his moral scruples. He murders Duncan, and retribution begins. By its very process of primitive simplicity, *Lr.* universalizes the tragedy that it represents, involving all humanity in the tragic conflict of life.

In *Shakespeare's Tragic Practice* (Clarendon, 1979), Bertrand Evans follows the approach of his 1960 book on Shakespeare's comedies. He studies Shakespeare's habit of creating and exploiting discrepant or unequal awareness as a means of producing various dramatic effects. He focuses on the dramatist's use of awareness-unawareness gaps in the tragedies, especially the dramatic effects created by the protagonist's unawareness of the tragic outcome. In the comedies, the opposition of our awareness to the participants' awareness typically results in incidental, passing effects that have little to do with determining the outcome; but in the later tragedies, the unawareness of the protagonist becomes an integral part of the movement toward catastrophe.

In *William Shakespeare: The Tragedies* (Twayne, 1985), Paul A. Jorgensen studies ten tragedies from *Tit.* to *Cor.*, advancing the argument that the tragic experience in Shakespeare derives not from death or fear of death but from "felt sorrow"—how the hero suffers. Titus changes from a man of rigorous honor to one who can feel. In *Rom.*, separation and stoniness of heart function as major agents of evil. In *JC*, Brutus suffers feelingly, learns from his tragic ordeal, and ultimately improves as a human being. Hamlet must struggle to make of man more than a beast; and in so doing, he must constantly endeavor not to become a dehumanized creature. Othello experiences an ordeal in jealousy, a dehumanizing experience. *Lr.* epitomizes Jorgensen's main point because it constantly tests the human heart, striving to rescue "threatened humanity" through "known and feeling sorrow." Macbeth experiences a torture of the mind, which humanizes him, but *Tim.* shows a man turned to stone. *Ant.* must be seen as the disgrace and defeat of a Herculean hero. In *Cor.*, Shakespeare focuses primarily on nobility and nobleness of heart, a civilized or civilizing human tendency. Finally, Jorgensen suggests that Shakespeare's tragedies remain open-ended because of the many questions that they pose.

Several critical studies deal with groupings of the tragedies according to their date of composition. Nicholas Brooke, in *Shakespeare's Early Tragedies* (Methuen, 1968), examines *Tit.*, *R3*, *Rom.*, *R2*, *JC*, and *Ham.* The book makes no particular attempt to trace development or to outline a common theme; instead, it focuses on the style of the individual plays. In *Tit.*, the central theme underscores that passion causes men to deteriorate into beasts. Brooke emphasizes the poetic stylization as the unifying element of the play. Concentration on the moral history tends to divert attention from the centrality of Richard III's disturbing vitality. In *R3*, Shakespeare admits a skepticism

and in so doing discovers the tragic dilemma of his own orthodoxy. *Rom.* emphasizes a formal structure but also continually
questions and penetrates it. Shakespeare establishes the equation of love and death as part of the youth of Romeo and Juliet; this forms the center of the play's general insistence on
paradox. In *R2*, the king's tragedy comes from his humanity;
his sufferings relate only marginally to his faults. The structure
of *JC* provides a dual vision, pointing to nobility but also to
sham, the ludicrous. In *Ham.*, the rhetorical high style of
ghost, heaven, and hell, where events are significant in an established scale of values, opposes the vivid presence of a mortal
world, where ideas of heaven and hell explain nothing. Shakespeare makes Hamlet's behavior and utterance oscillate between these polarities yet lets him be convincingly one man.

Understandably, much critical attention has focused on the
middle period of the tragedies, the mature plays of *Ham.*, *Lr.*,
Oth., and *Mac.* An early study by Lily B. Campbell, *Shakespeare's Tragic Heroes: Slaves of Passion* (Cambridge UP, 1930),
presents an extensive background of Renaissance philosophy
and psychology. The four major tragedies serve as mirrors of
passion. In *Ham.*, Shakespeare undertook to answer the fundamental question of how men accept sorrow when it comes to
them; the play is thus a tragedy of grief. *Oth.* becomes a study
in jealousy and how it affects those of different races. *Lr.* is a
tragedy of wrath, planned as a tragedy of old age. In such a
study of passion, *Mac.* is a study in fear, set against a background of its opposite. Throughout, the passion of the characters is more important than the action.

A radically different but also somewhat historical approach is
Carol Carlisle's *Shakespeare from the Greenroom: Actors' Criticisms
of Four Major Tragedies* (U of North Carolina P, 1969). This
book brings together widely diffuse information and illustrates
actors' major accomplishments as critics. Carlisle includes actors from several decades (an appendix gives brief biographical
sketches). Each chapter consists of three major divisions of the
criticism: the play, the characters, and from criticism to theater.
A valuable introduction and conclusion evaluate the contributions of the actors and establish the context of their criticism.
The book represents an impressive array of research and explores an area too often overlooked.

In *Shakespeare's Mature Tragedies* (Princeton UP, 1973), Bernard McElroy argues that complementary viewpoints (opposites) define the common foundation of all four tragic worlds. He examines the relationship between the world of the play and the subjective, perceived world of the hero. The experience of the tragic hero forms the central focus of Shakespearean tragedy. McElroy finds five principal qualities that the mature tragic heroes share: a tendency to universalize, an extraordinary sense of self-awareness, a consciousness of themselves not only as individuals but also as part of a broad structure, an ethical sense that sees hypocrisy and misrepresentation of truth as abominable crimes, and a vulnerability that allows their view of reality and of themselves to be undermined at the level of its basic assumptions. Qualities of Hamlet's world include perilousness, elusiveness, and widespread decay. Rage defines Hamlet's most consistent and conspicuous reaction to his world. The tragic conflict derives from what others tell him and what he wants to do. Two principal spheres in *Oth.*—Venice and Cyprus—reveal a play primarily about suffering, but especially about suffering in ever-deepening isolation. The action hinges on belief. Iago believes what his own psychic needs dispose him to believe. Othello stakes everything on a belief in love that can transcend all differences but then discovers that he cannot sustain that faith once it is called into question. *Lr.*, a paradigm of the waning medieval hierarchy confronting the onset of pragmatic materialism, offers worlds of basic primal energy, violently opposed extremes, and constantly shifting identities—greatest in Lear himself. His death suggests the human capacity to hope when nothing remains to hope for. Above all, *Mac.*, a tragedy about self-loathing, about self-horror that leads to spiritual paralysis, depicts a world in which nature seems dead and wicked dreams abuse sleep.

Willard Farnham's *Shakespeare's Tragic Frontier: The World of His Final Tragedies* (U of California P, 1950) concerns the last tragedies—*Mac.*, *Tim.*, *Ant.*, and *Cor.* Deeply tainted rare spirits occupy the center of Shakespeare's last tragic world, a world so paradoxical that it risks overwhelming the tragedy. The heroes of the final world are deeply flawed: Timon's seeming love is really a form of selfishness; Macbeth gives himself to evil in order to gain worldly position; Antony knows the threat that

Cleopatra poses to his honor, yet he embraces her; Coriolanus, so blinded by regard for himself, commits treason. But each of the heroes shows a paradoxical nobility. Farnham relates all this to the Jacobean world as exhibited in its poetry and drama. In summary, *Tim.* emphasizes the beast theme, *Mac.* is a morality play written in terms of Jacobean tragedy, Antony and Cleopatra provide finished studies in paradoxical nobility, and Coriolanus becomes a tragic figure as the paradox of his pride brings about his downfall.

Several critical studies group the Roman plays in order to examine the common ground among them. J. C. Maxwell, in his essay "Shakespeare's Roman Plays: 1900–1956," *Shakespeare Survey* 10 (1957): 1–11, reviews some of the criticism. An anthology of criticism, *Discussions of Shakespeare's Roman Plays* (Heath, 1964), edited by Maurice Charney, includes fourteen essays from Coleridge onward.

The first full-length study of the Roman plays is M. W. MacCallum, *Shakespeare's Roman Plays and Their Background* (Macmillan, 1967; original, 1910). This imposing work, strong on the use of sources, has as its chief critical approach the characters, with detailed analyses (modeled somewhat on Bradley). But the book pays almost no attention to the plays as plays. A long introduction explores other Roman plays of the sixteenth century, Shakespeare's treatment of history, and the source ancestry of these Roman plays. MacCallum discusses in considerable detail the three plays, focusing on both Shakespeare's use of his sources and an analysis of the principal characters.

More analytical, G. Wilson Knight, in *The Imperial Theme* (Oxford UP, 1931), examines the Roman plays. The whole of *JC* bristles with erotic perception; the vision remains optimistic, vivid, startling. All the people are lovers—an emotional, fiery, but not exactly sexual love. The theme of *Cor.* illustrates the intrinsic fault in any ambition, indeed, any value, that is not a multiple of love. The bare style of the play has little brilliance or color. In Knight's view, *Ant.*, probably Shakespeare's subtlest and greatest play, blends the finite and infinite throughout. The play as a whole presents a visionary and idealistic optimism, though it contains plenty of realistic matters and tragic pathos. Knight explores what he calls the "transcendental humanism" of *Ant.* Ultimately, Antony and Cleopatra find not death but life, the high metaphysics of love that melts life and death into a final oneness.

In *Shakespeare: The Roman Plays* (Stanford UP, 1963), Derek Traversi explores the dramatic development from *JC,* the most obvious and familiar of the Roman plays, to *Cor.,* if not the greatest of Shakespeare's tragedies then the most balanced and complete of all his political conceptions. The dramatic growth revealed in the Roman plays corresponds to the growth of Shakespeare's tragic vision. This long, extremely detailed (frequently scene by scene) analysis finds in *Ant.* a world in which ripe universal intuitions of empire turn persistently toward decay. Here two themes interplay—political and metaphysical—making the play one of the culminating achievements of Shakespeare's genius. Unlike in most of the other tragedies, death becomes an instrument of release. Irony offers the key to the peculiar effect of *Cor.*

In *Shakespeare's Roman Plays: The Function of Imagery in the Drama* (Harvard UP, 1961), Maurice Charney examines style in the Roman plays. The book considers the Roman plays as poetry of the theater, principally through their verbal and nonverbal imagery. All this leads to a close examination of the plays themselves. An introductory chapter discusses the function of imagery, and a second one analyzes style in the plays. Separate chapters interpret the imagery of *JC, Ant.,* and *Cor.* In *JC,* the style is most notable in the sharply limited vocabulary of the play and the correspondingly limited imagery, principally the storm and its portents—blood and fire. Contrastingly, *Ant.* contains rich imagery and stylistic effects. The imagery tends to be implicit, meanings suggested rather than stated, leading to an elliptical style that is complex and hyperbolic. The imagery of dimension and scope powerfully expresses the world theme, essentially the movement toward decay and devaluation of the world. Within this imagery, the worlds of Egypt and Rome remain in symbolic contrast. The style of *Cor.* contrasts especially with that of *Ant.* by being curiously cold, aloof, and objective. The imagery centers on food, disease, and animals, and these images help establish the peculiarly satirical quality of the play.

J. L. Simmons takes quite a different approach in *Shakespeare's Pagan World: The Roman Tragedies* (UP of Virginia, 1973). Simmons argues that the three Roman tragedies essentially differ from *Ham.*, *Lr.*, *Oth.*, and *Mac.* and that the most important element in their integral relationship derives from the historically pagan environment out of which each tragedy arises. Brutus, Caesar, Antony, and Coriolanus have limited insight into their own tragedies largely because of the ultimate darkness of Rome; they have no moment of recognition or even the possibility of it. Exiled from Rome, the Roman heroes must, in the falling action of their tragedies, confront their city; there is no world elsewhere. Ironically, although Rome finally destroys, it gives what immortality it can to the tragic heroes.

Simmons begins his study with *Cor.*, which he regards as the clearest and final statement of Shakespeare's idea of the Roman tragedy, with its focus on a protagonist whose moral vision constitutes the moral vision of Rome. Coriolanus and Rome finally become incompatible because of the conflict that man must endure in his allegiance to two worlds, the real and the ideal. Simmons argues that both Brutus and Caesar in *JC* scarcely know themselves. Brutus's ambiguities mirror the reverse image of the enigmatic Caesar. Throughout, Brutus beholds himself only in the eyes of Rome. Paradox and irony lie at the heart of *Ant.*, for the play evokes ideals that are finally incapable of realization but that nonetheless ennoble even as they lead to destruction. In death, Antony embraces both what he was, the noblest Roman, and what he has, the Egyptian, but with no reconciliation. Simmons believes that Cleopatra will put together the fragments of Antony's vision. Simmons argues persuasively throughout the book that the pagan setting limits the characters, preventing the possibility of reconciliation for them. No real means of grace or hope of glory exists.

To illustrate Shakespeare's sensitivity to the differences between the Roman Republic and the Roman Empire, Paul A. Cantor, in *Shakespeare's Rome: Republic and Empire* (Cornell UP, 1976), concentrates on *Cor.* and *Ant.* Cantor argues that Shakespeare intended these two plays as companion pieces. The initial chapter seeks to define ''Romanness'' in Shakespeare—what it meant to be Roman, as Shakespeare understood the matter. For example, the austerity of *Cor.* counters the indulgence of *Ant.*, qualities defined by their reflection of the Roman world. Heroic virtue and the sense of serving a cause larger than oneself are qualities associated with the Roman Republic. Civic religion gets much attention in *Cor.*, and the city bestows lavish honors upon public service. Paradoxically, the plebeians must accept the senate's right to rule; yet they bitterly dispute the way it rules. Politics in Rome makes Coriolanus face troubling issues about himself, such as his dependence on the city. This conflicts with his goal of having the self-sufficiency of a god. Paradoxically, Coriolanus's banishment prevents him from ever becoming free of Rome. In contrast to the Republic, the Empire sets Eros free with a new power, evident in *Ant.*, a play that intertwines love and politics. The problem of fidelity, central in the politics of the Empire, becomes the central problem of the play. But the love of Antony and Cleopatra, a curious mixture of deep passion and profound insecurity, leads to their deaths, reinforcing the paradoxical nature of their love. Indeed, love becomes a kind of tyranny. Either Rome—the Republic or the Empire—is potentially tragic in the disparity between human aspiration and the reality it encounters. The Republic seems to offer nobility, but only at the price of wisdom and self-knowledge; the Empire offers freedom in private life, but only at the price of a lasting and meaningful public context for nobility.

Opening his book with a review of Elizabethan classicism, Robert S. Miola, in *Shakespeare's Rome* (Cambridge UP, 1983), traces Shakespeare's preoccupation with things Roman from *Luc.* to *Cym.* Miola takes an organic approach to the problem of coherence in Shakespeare's Rome, identifying internal similarities in the poem and plays while recognizing differences. Miola argues that Shakespeare viewed ancient Rome as a place apart and that his vision of the city and people evolved dynamically. These Roman works connect through an intricate network of images, ideas, gestures, and scenes. At the center of the vision stands the city of Rome, defined variously. *Luc.*, Miola suggests, balances itself between tragedy and history as it progresses through disorder, loss, and sorrow to the costly expiation of evil and the chastened emergence of a new order. The poem also provides a glimpse of many themes that occupy Shakespeare's attention in the Roman plays. The clash between private interest and public duty reverberates in *Tit.*, destroying the life of the individual, the unity of the family, and the order in the city. In *JC,* Rome shapes the lives of its inhabitants, who struggle to act according to Roman heroic traditions.

Places in and outside Rome take on symbolic precision and importance for the first time in Shakespeare's Roman canon. *Ant.* examines the struggle of Romans with Rome, portrayed as a physical locality and an imagined ideal. This play world shows politic bargaining often prevailing over military might. Rome in *Ant.* is also a kingdom divided against itself in bloody civil war. Least Roman of all Shakespearean women, Cleopatra is, paradoxically, most Roman as well. In *Cor.,* Shakespeare exposes the paradoxes inherent in the civilized community. Coriolanus's exit from Rome, like his entrance, serves as a complex symbol of his ambivalent relationship with the city. Unlike other critics, Miola includes a discussion of *Cym.,* whose Roman elements, he suggests, color the entire play and appear unexpectedly at various places. The play reflects in part Shakespeare's increasingly critical scrutiny of Rome.

The Roman plays illustrate the central values of service to the state, constancy, fortitude, valor, friendship, love of family, and respect for the gods, according to Vivian Thomas in *Shakespeare's Roman Worlds* (Routledge, 1989). These plays create an intense sense of a social universe, an awareness of the values, attitudes, and aspirations of the different Romes of the plays. Thomas argues that Shakespeare's reading of Plutarch's *Lives* constituted a watershed in his career; accordingly, interpretations of the plays concentrate on the dramatist's use of his source. *Tit.* is seminal because it points in two directions: concern for human values and their fusion into a social ethos, and conflict between good and evil. Rome in *JC* exists as a place of fervid political conflict with an acute awareness of the past, but its history and destiny are still being shaped. Brutus creates a self-image as the preserver of Roman democracy. Antony does not convey any commitment to Roman values; he is more a political opportunist. Shakespeare alters his source in *Ant.,* making Antony more attractive than the historical figure and suppressing Octavia's outstanding qualities. The play concentrates on issues of political calculation and the process of creating history and myth. Dissension governs the picture inside the Rome of *Cor.* In contrast to Plutarch, Shakespeare locates the source of tragedy in the ethos of the society; constancy now becomes a fatal flaw because the world belongs to the temporizer. Coriolanus dies not because he is irascible but because he is pure. Similar attempts to define Rome appear in Charles Wells, *The Wide Arch: Roman Values in Shakespeare* (St. Martin's, 1993). Wells adds *Cym.*, which he sees as a synthesis of values that both Rome and Britain stood for.

Other critical studies cover a varying range of tragedies and focus principally on matters of technique or definition of Shakespearean tragedy. For example, William Rosen's *Shakespeare and the Craft of Tragedy* (Harvard UP, 1960) focuses on dramatic technique, specifically studying *Lr.*, *Mac.*, *Ant.*, and *Cor.* Rosen examines how Shakespeare establishes an audience's point of view toward the protagonist. Rapport between audience and protagonist, evident in *Lr.* and *Mac.*, largely disappears in *Ant.* and *Cor.* We come to see the world through Lear's eyes and thus accept his point of view. In *Mac.*, Shakespeare molds audience response by establishing a certain point of view toward Macbeth, a vexing problem because of the villainous nature of the protagonist. We constantly change our point of view in *Ant.*, hence the often contradictory interpretations of the play. *Cor.* scrutinizes the problem of human integrity, its conception and worth, and how it may be destroyed, reinforced in the manipulation of our attitude toward Coriolanus.

In *"King Lear," "Macbeth," Indefinition, and Tragedy* (Yale UP, 1983), Stephen Booth argues that indefinition, incompleteness, and boundlessness characterize the tragic experience. In tragedy, both the characters and the audience constantly seek definition, but definition cannot be attained. Indefinition does, however, generate an illusory sense of pattern and therefore of wholeness and identity. But this sense of pattern only underscores further that all categorization, limitation, and definition are arbitrary and unreliable constructs. The greatness of *Lr.* derives precisely from the play's confrontation with inconclusiveness, making it a trial of our endurance. Booth also cites the example of *LLL,* a comedy that toys with tragedy and indefinition. Finally, Booth turns to *Mac.* to argue that this play puts us through an actual experience of our finite minds' incapacity to apprehend the infinite universe. The tragedy of

Mac., Booth affirms, occurs not in the character Macbeth but in the audience. The audience joins its mind to Macbeth both in his sensitive awareness of evil and his practice of it: "To be audience to *Mac.* is virtually to be Macbeth." Booth also notes that we confuse the form of a play that we call tragedy with the tragic experience, which cannot be defined or categorized. Tragedy thus becomes our attempt to cope with indefinition by giving it form.

John Lawlor explores the use of paradox in *The Tragic Sense in Shakespeare* (Chatto & Windus, 1960), where he examines primarily *Ham.*, *Mac.*, *Lr.*, and *Oth.* Paradox, the foundation and center of the tragic experience, places overburdened human creatures between mighty opposites as they try to work out their salvation or damnation. Lawlor uses the *R2–H5* tetralogy to demonstrate the appearance-versus-reality conflict. *Ham.* poses the question of whether human beings are the patients, never the agents, of their destiny. The tragic conflict centers on the protagonist, who, averse to the deed required of him, seeks the cause of his aversion but fails to know it. The conflict in *Oth.* occurs between accident and design, evil being the design played out in the accidents of domestic and military life. Perhaps the greatest "accident" is the one that brings together Iago and Othello. Against the background of the supernatural in *Mac.*, the perspectives of human action remain. The conflict in *Lr.* centers on the truth of imagination and the idea of justice. As Lawlor suggests, the illusion that Cordelia lives matches the illusion that reality can respond to our contrivings and that repentance will undo the process of time.

For Irving Ribner, Shakespeare grows in moral vision as a tragic dramatist, a point he develops in *Patterns in Shakespearean Tragedy* (Barnes & Noble, 1960). Ribner touches on all the tragedies and also includes *R2*, *R3*, and *Jn.* He senses an evolution or development in Shakespeare's treatment of the tragic stories. The tragic hero, through the process of his destruction, may learn the nature of evil and thus attain a spiritual victory in spite of death. *Tit.*, *R3*, and *Rom.* show the basic forms that Shakespeare uses: *Tit.*, the tragedy of the virtuous man's fall through deception; *R3*, the rise and fall of the deliberately evil man; and *Rom.*, the ordinary man's growth to maturity. Better than before, Shakespeare in *JC* embodies intellectual statement in dramatic character; in character conflict, he exposes the implications of clashing ideologies.

Ham. provides the emotional equivalent of a Christian view of human life. Hamlet's life journey may be viewed as the affirmation of a purposive cosmic order. Shakespeare in *Oth.* gives dramatic form to a Christian view of mankind's encounter with evil, the destructive power of that evil, and yet the ability to attain salvation in spite of it. All the elements of *Lr.* derive from the theme of regeneration that affirms justice in the world. Ribner greatly deemphasizes the characters as characters and sees them instead as performing symbolic functions. *Tim.* and *Mac.* concentrate on the operation of evil within the pattern of order. *Ant.* and *Cor.* illustrate the destructive power of evil and the magnificence of evil. This book represents a wide divergence from Bradley's approach, because the total effect makes the characters simple pawns in some larger structure of symbolism and order.

Ruth Nevo's approach in *Tragic Form in Shakespeare* (Princeton UP, 1972) counters Ribner's moralistic analysis. Nevo argues that within a given play, the phases of the tragic progress can be distinguished. Such a process helps not only in understanding the plays but also in apprehending the nature of the tragic idea. Shakespearean tragedy, according to Nevo, has an unfolding five-phase sequence: Act I or phase 1 (not always the same) forms the predicament; II, "psychomachia"; III, peripeteia; IV, perspectives of irony and pathos; and V, catastrophe.

Nevo's discussion of the plays proceeds on this analysis of form, attempting to strip critical interpretation of its frequently moralistic, didactic bias. Brutus's career in *JC* follows the Shakespearean trajectory. The play stands on the threshold of the great tragedies, but the form remains largely empty of substance. Contrivance, conspiracy, concealment, and dissimulation in *Ham.* reach their crisis in the sequence that runs from the nunnery scene through the play scene to the killing of Polonius; this sequence articulates the peripeteia, or reversal. Iago's role in *Oth.* consistently expands to the culminating vision of the archdevil's taking possession of Othello's soul in Act III. The simultaneity of Othello's anagnorisis and the catastrophe of the play gives his final speech its power. In Act III of

Mac., we watch a more profound disintegration of the tragic protagonist than in any of the other tragedies. Love's inability to redeem burdens *Lr.* Act III (peripeteia) exhibits Lear's total reversal of his status and situation; Act IV offers the antiphonal dialectic of comfort and despair; Act V gives us Shakespeare's quintessential tragic outcome. Cleopatra takes over the tragic role after Antony's death and carries the burden of the final phase of catastrophe. The psychomachia of Act II offers Coriolanus's first dilemma: he must choose integrity or mastery, since he cannot have them both. Reversal and anagnorisis come in the final turns of the catastrophe, giving rise to pure tragic poignance.

Matthew N. Proser, in *The Heroic Image in Five Shakespearean Tragedies* (Princeton UP, 1965), argues that tragedy ensues partly because of the discrepancy between the main character's self-conception and his full humanity as displayed in action, action often shaped by his heroic self-image. Proser examines *JC, Mac., Oth., Cor,* and *Ant.* Brutus visualizes himself as a sacrificial priest, the savior or liberator of Rome. *Mac.* emphasizes Macbeth's "manliness"; action is everything, verifies everything. In both *Oth.* and *Cor.,* Shakespeare takes a soldier-hero and places him in a situation with which his military training cannot help him cope. At the end, Antony must rise to the image of lost nobility in order to recoup everything in one pure and self-defining gesture. The conclusion constitutes the heroic moment that each of the tragic heroes has faced. Throughout the book, Proser places much emphasis on the language of these plays.

In *The Music of the Close: The Final Scenes of Shakespeare's Tragedies* (UP of Kentucky, 1978), Walter C. Foreman, Jr., focuses on the final scenes of *Ham., Lr., Oth.,* and *Ant.* According to Foreman, each ending experiments, offering complex and fascinating variations on the tragic ending. The plays depict a process of moving from one order to another, usually going through a good deal of disorder. This disorder can be mental, sexual, familial, political or military, elemental or cosmic, or metaphysical. The disorder leads to disaster and a new order. The new order, however, is ironic because the world—dull and bounded—at the end of the plays seems diminished without the tragic figures. Shakespeare thus explores the separation of the tragic figures from the surviving community. *Ham.*, more than any of the other tragedies, gains structure by a mutual, personal, increasingly recognized antagonism between Claudius and Hamlet, an antagonism that Hamlet sees as an inevitable duel. *Lr.* also depicts a tragedy of human insularity rather than of human malice. *Oth.* has a fast and striking end, but *Ant.* closes inconsequently.

Audience response forms the focus of E. A. J. Honigmann's *Shakespeare: Seven Tragedies: The Dramatist's Manipulation of Response* (Macmillan, 1976). Honigmann argues that Shakespeare uses a variety of techniques to guide, control, and manipulate audience response to the plays. The intended effect in *JC* evokes a divided response to Brutus. *Ham.* invites the audience to judge Hamlet's judgment. *Oth.* provokes audience response by focusing on secret motives that are never quite fully revealed. In *Lr.*, the audience has to adjust constantly to the vagaries of Lear's mind, an adjustment that affects our response to the entire play. In *Mac.*, Shakespeare carefully controls the flow of information to encourage a sympathetic response to the victim–villain hero. *Ant.* invites an ambiguous and uncertain response to the hero; *Cor.*, contradictory ones.

John Holloway, in *The Story of the Night: Studies in Shakespeare's Major Tragedies* (Routledge & Kegan Paul, 1961), surveys *Ham.*, *Oth.*, *Lr.*, *Mac.*, *Ant.*, *Cor*, and *Tim.* In his introduction, Holloway examines different critical approaches and their implications and indicates his general dissatisfaction with the kind of Shakespeare they suggest. Holloway finds in the plays a developing pattern: the movement toward ritual sacrifice. The protagonist moves from being the cynosure of his society to being estranged from it, a process of alienation. What happens to him may suggest the expulsion of a scapegoat, the sacrifice of a victim, or both. The issue in *Ham.* centers not on what kind of man he is but on what he does. As the play proceeds into decay, an incessant play and thrust of frenzied intrigue, of plot and counterplot, remain. Othello's whole nature transforms into a coherent sequence. Macbeth's act of revolt is an ultimate revolt. *Lr.* in part rehearses the terrible potentiality of Nature, the process of descent into chaos. *Ant.* exhibits the quintessence of vacillation in the world of politics and the world of love. The gradual isolation that the protagonists experience in these plays becomes overt transformation into an outcast in *Cor.* and *Tim.* Holloway's anthropological method sheds light on the fate of the tragic protagonists.

In *Passion Lends Them Power: A Study of Shakespeare's Love Tragedies* (Manchester UP, 1976), Derick R. C. Marsh studies the problems of love primarily in *Rom.*, *Oth.*, and *Ant.* In all three plays, the lovers reject the world's way of judging their situations and follow the demands of their love, even to death. Marsh starts, however, with the comedies, which show an awareness of the dangers and disasters inherent in any love situation. *LLL* focuses on the folly of attempting to shun love. *MND,* in its qualification of the love experience, has tragic undertones. *AWW* shows that individual love is not always enough. The problem comedies put the problems of love in further relief, exploring the relation between love and sexuality and one other element: justice in *MM,* forgiveness in *AWW,* and the collapse of a whole society in *Tro.* Marsh argues that *Rom.* becomes the tragedy of love's intensity, concerned with the nature of first love and intense sexual attraction. Othello's love, the central value in his life, replaces all other values and makes him vulnerable. *Ant.,* a tragedy of love's triumph, depicts Antony and Cleopatra in their growing awareness of the irrelevance of all concerns except love. Concentration on their love leaves them exposed to the worldly danger that their political importance has attracted. Finally, Marsh turns to love motifs as they echo in the Romances, especially *Cym.* and *WT.* These works look forward to a kind of future denied to the tragic heroes.

G. Wilson Knight, in *The Wheel of Fire,* rev. ed. (Methuen, 1949; original, 1930), writes mainly about the tragedies, though he includes some theoretical essays and one each on *MM* and *Tro.* Knight's introductory essay, "On the Principles of Shakespeare Interpretation," outlines his rationale and approach. As elsewhere, here Knight is metaphysical, religious, and greatly concerned with the meaning of the plays' imagery. *Ham.* focuses on the central reality of pain. Hamlet's outstanding peculiarity in the action of the play may be regarded as a symptom of the sickness in his soul, which saps his will. From the first scene to the last, the shadow of death hangs over this play, for Hamlet's disease is mental and spiritual death. Knight sees the style of *Oth.* as detached, clear and stately, solid and precise, generally barren of direct metaphysical content. This style necessitates an approach to the characters as separate persons rather than the more generalized "atmosphere." Knight also works out a comparison between Brutus and Macbeth, with the symbolism in both plays centering on storm, blood, and animals. *Mac.,* Shakespeare's most profound and mature vision of evil, focuses on fear as the dominant emotion. In an essay on *Lr.,* Knight explores the "comedy of the grotesque." The dualism in the play waits to be resolved either by tragedy or by comedy. The Fool sees the potentiality for comedy in Lear's behavior. The Gloucester-Edgar scene at Dover reinforces the grotesque. In a second essay on the play, Knight seeks to define the *Lr.* universe and explores the problem of human and universal justice. The author finds *Tim.* to be a parable or allegory about perfected humanity's search to build its soul's paradise on this earth. Timon becomes the archetype and norm of all tragedy.

Roy W. Battenhouse takes a Christian perspective on the tragedies in *Shakespearean Tragedy: Its Art and Its Christian Premises* (Indiana UP, 1969). He discusses mainly *Rom., Ant., Ham., Lr..* and *Cor.,* with some attention to *Oth.* Battenhouse tries to steer between the thoroughgoing, sometimes excessive apologists and the denigrators. The discussion, firmly grounded in biblical knowledge and knowledge of theologians, especially Augustine, argues that Shakespeare writes in a Christian context regardless of his personal beliefs (or lack thereof). The author suggests that knowledge of Shakespeare's background in medieval Christian lore can be of particular help in better understanding the tragedies. Like Judas's, Othello's tragedy involves not merely his mistakes but also the deeper sin of rejecting grace by neglecting the "mercy" of Desdemona. The recognition of Othello's overall likeness to Judas makes his underlying psychology fully coherent. The action of Romeo's visit to the tomb functions as a kind of upside-down analogy to the Easter story. Christian art reshapes the pagan story in *Ant.* The triumph in death turns out to be both glamorous and hollow. Hamlet's strategy for setting the world right perversely imitates the method of atonement in the Christian story. Lear's lack of charity and Gloucester's lack of faith suit them for their respective roles. Battenhouse sees Volumnia in *Cor.* as the woman of Revelation, the mistress of the beast. For Battenhouse, then, Christian tragedy reveals that beneath all other causes for tragedy is mankind's mislocation of its chief end in the process of a passionate quest for bliss. Christian tragedy ends with a recognition of the divine Providence.

Other books on the tragedies also explore the Christian basis of Shakespeare's drama. Harold S. Wilson, in *On the Design of Shakespearian Tragedy* (U of Toronto P, 1957), separates ten tragedies according to those that exhibit Christian assumptions and those that do not. Those that exhibit the order of faith are *Rom.*, *Ham.*, *Oth.*, and *Mac.*; those that exhibit the order of nature are *JC*, *Cor.*, *Tro.*, *Tim.*, *Ant.*, and *Lr.* Wilson further groups *Rom.* and *Ham.* as "thesis" and *Oth.* and *Mac.* as "antithesis." The former are less somber, and the role of accident is more prominent in them; whereas in the latter, the agents are willful and self-consciously deliberate. *JC* and *Cor.* are "thesis," and *Tro.* and *Tim.* are "antithesis." The former are positive—studies of great and admirable men—whereas the latter are bitter and negative. But none of these four has a comprehensive tragic scope. That honor belongs to *Ant.* and *Lr.*, which together represent the "synthesis" of Shakespeare's tragic vision and his greatest achievement in tragedy. The value of human love, as comprehended in the love of Antony and Cleopatra and of Cordelia and Lear, ultimately emerges.

Two other books focus on Shakespeare and Christianity. Robert G. Hunter, in *Shakespeare and the Mystery of God's Judgments* (U of Georgia P, 1976), examines the impact that the Protestant Reformation had on Shakespearean tragedy (*R3*, *Ham.*, *Oth.*, *Mac.*, and *Lr.*). *Christian Ritual and the World of Shakespeare's Tragedies* (Bucknell UP, 1976), by Herbert R. Coursen, Jr., examines the Christian dimensions of *R2*, *Ham.*, *Oth.*, *Lr.*, *Mac.*, and *Tmp.* Another closely related book is *Mankynde in Shakespeare* (U of Georgia P, 1976), by Edmund Creeth, which explores the connections between *Mac.*, *Oth.*, and *Lr.* and the morality plays with "Mankynde" as their central character.

Virgil K. Whitaker focuses on the philosophical issues in the plays in *The Mirror up to Nature: The Technique of Shakespeare's Tragedies* (Huntington Library, 1965). Whitaker discusses Elizabethan tragedy to the end of Shakespeare's career and examines critical theory in England. Although Shakespeare reflects these practices and theories, he surpasses others by using contemporary theology and metaphysics to develop the full implications of his tragedy. The author groups *R2, R3, Tit., Rom.,* and *JC* together as early experiments. But only *JC* achieves the tragic view of mankind that characterizes Shakespeare's great plays, because a deliberate moral choice is central. In chapter 4, Whitaker isolates and describes the qualities of Shakespeare's tragic maturity. He sees *Ham.* as apprenticeship and *Lr.* as achievement. Lear's tragic stature comes from his moral strength, with which he fights toward regeneration. *Ant.* and *Cor.* represent a falling off from the earlier creative power, lacking growth in the principal characters.

James P. Driscoll's *Identity in Shakespearean Drama* (Bucknell UP, 1983) explores a variety of archetypes and the Jungian view that the psyche comprises multiple interactive, hierarchical levels. Driscoll isolates four components of identity: real, social, conscious, and ideal. Shakespeare develops his conceptions of identity by defining his characters' conscious, real, and ideal identities. In the history plays, the characters create social identity from conscious identity. *Ham., Oth.,* and *TN* show a struggle between social and real identity to determine conscious identity. Ideal identity becomes a significant motif from *MM* on; tension between the real and ideal identities largely shapes conscious identity. In *Lr.,* Shakespeare explores archetypal wholeness in its full complexity and raises large psychological, philosophical, and theological questions. In *Tmp.,* Prospero transcends Lear's nervous striving to secure ego identity and attains serene faith in the greater self.

Michael Goldman's *Acting and Action in Shakespearean Tragedy* (Princeton UP, 1985) is an abstract, philosophical exploration of the relationship between acting and action in *Ham., Oth., Mac., Ant.,* and *Cor.* Specifically, Goldman distinguishes three types of action: the actions that the characters perform, the action of the audience's mind in responding to the events it watches, and the actions by which the actors create and sustain their roles. This book examines the complex structure of these actions.

Directly concerned with the relationship between Shakespeare's tragedies and his society, Paul N. Siegel, in *Shakespear-ean Tragedy and the Elizabethan Compromise* (New York UP, 1957), suggests that the social compromise between the aris-tocracy and the bourgeoisie eventually broke down, bringing with it questions and doubts of all kinds, which are reflected in Shakespeare's tragedies. Siegel relates the new social and philo-sophical world to the tragedies, examining in detail *Ham.*, *Oth.*, *Lr.*, and *Mac.* He argues that Shakespeare's method is, like that of the Christian humanists, ethical rather than theo-logical. The tragedies thus explore the imperilment of the uni-versal order by evil passions. Siegel draws biblical parallels and analogues for some of the plays: for example, Desdemona is the symbolic equivalent of Christ; Duncan and Malcolm are analo-gous to Christ; Macbeth is analogous to Adam, and Lady Mac-beth to Eve. Lear achieves redemption since he cannot be saved on this earth.

In a particularly challenging book on the tragedies, Howard Felperin, in *Shakespearean Representation: Mimesis and Modernity in Elizabethan Tragedy* (Princeton UP, 1977), analyzes the mo-dernity of Shakespeare, which derives in part from the mimetic process. Mimesis arises in Shakespeare not from direct imita-tion of nature but from re-presentation, with a difference, of inherited models or constructs of nature or life. In a character-istic movement, Shakespeare's tragedies contain and at the same time depart from an archaic content: miracle play, re-venge play, or historical morality. Shakespeare, Felperin dem-onstrates, invalidates older models even as he includes them; he supersedes them in the very act of subsuming them. This results in a troubled awareness of the simultaneous resem-blance and discrepancy between the play and its older models. *Ham.* at once repeats and surpasses the morality-revenge tradi-tion, which constitutes its archaic core. Similarly, *Lr.*, *Ant.*, and *Mac.* also subsume archaic structures. For *Mac.*, however, the inherited core is not the morality tradition, as in the other plays, but the tyrant plays of the biblical cycles. For Felperin, the tragedies have "structures which can never quite reunite with their own dramatic models nor leave those models defini-tively behind" (87). Felperin argues that the critic's task is at once archeological, historical, and interpretive; therefore, inter-pretation cannot be isolated from literary history. The last chapter of the book focuses on the works of four of Shakespeare's contemporaries.

Susan Snyder's *Comic Matrix of Shakespeare's Tragedies: "Romeo and Juliet," "Hamlet," "Othello," and "King Lear"* (Princeton UP, 1979) argues that Shakespeare mastered the comic mode before the tragic one and that comedy became for him a point of reference and departure for writing the tragedies. The two modes, the tragic and the comic, interact in complex ways in the tragedies: at first the two are polar opposites, then two sides of the same coin, and finally elements in a single compound. *Rom.* starts out as a comedy, but the well-developed comic movement diverts into tragedy by mischance. In this sense, Snyder argues, this play becomes rather than is tragic. *Oth.* is postcomic because it begins where the comedies usually end. The rather neat comic pattern, glossing over the vulnerabilities and ambiguities in Othello's and Desdemona's love and disposing too opportunely of the implacable forces represented by Iago, sets up a point of departure for what follows: the look beyond and beneath comedy. In contrast, *Ham.* transmutes the comic celebration of multiplicity into an existential nightmare of competing perceptions of reality. In *Lr.,* Shakespeare sets comic order side by side with comic chaos; out of the resulting dislocation, he develops his tragic effect. This perceptive study of the major tragedies demonstrates "how literary convention can operate to shape and enrich a work that is moving in a direction opposite to that convention" (16).

Similarly, Evelyn Gajowski, in *The Art of Loving: Female Subjectivity and Male Discursive Traditions in Shakespeare's Tragedies* (U of Delaware P, 1991), maintains that *Rom., Oth.,* and *Ant.* explore the intersections between comedy and tragedy, genre and gender. With clear gender implications, the love tragedies enclose the comic pattern of the love story in the context of tragic action and retain comedy's psychosocial movement toward social relationship and communal integration. Male protagonists move into the realm of emotional or affective experience, vacillating in emotional commitment, but female characters remain constant in their emotional commitments. As a result, the conflict between female constancy and male inconstancy becomes a tension between comic and tragic impulses.

Another book that calls attention to the relationship between comedy and tragedy is Michael Long's *The Unnatural Scene* (Methuen, 1976), a work much indebted to Nietzsche and Schopenhauer. Long attempts to isolate the "thought-model" for the tragedies, arguing that Shakespeare was concerned with the simultaneity of the personal and the social. Tragedy cannot be understood as an isolated event in the life of the protagonist; it is a social trauma. This dependency between the personal and the social appears in the isolation of Brutus in *JC,* in the crises of the hero's character and the crises of Rome and Romanness in *Cor.,* and in the psychological weakness of Vienna in *MM. Tro.* combines the tragic and the comic by exploring the underview of human societies and civilized consciousness. *Ham.* focuses on the "philistine mind," presenting the traumatic experience of a man who has been thrust out of restricting civilization into the kinetic world. *Lr.* explores the tragic dynamics of a cultured and sophisticated man's relationship with the wild world of nature. Finally, in their lyric romanticism, *Mac.* and *Ant.* center on a romantic apprehension of the Apollonian and the Dionysian, respectively. These two opposites complement each other.

David Scott Kastan also explores generic relationships in *Shakespeare and the Shapes of Time* (UP of New England, 1982), focusing on the tragedies, histories, and Romances. For Kastan, dramatic structures intimately connect with different conceptions of the experience in and of time. From the *H6* plays on, Shakespeare reveals an interest in two temporal modes, linear and cyclical. The history plays, which emphasize linear time, have a linear and open-ended shape; the tragedies, however, are linear but closed, moving toward a decisive ending. In the Romances, Shakespeare uses a form that transcends and transfigures the tragic experience by adopting a suprahistorical perspective from the vantage point of the timeless.

Exploring the icon-iconoclastic tensions in Shakespeare's drama, James R. Siemon, in *Shakespearean Iconoclasm* (U of California P, 1985), focuses on *H5, JC, Ham.,* and *Lr.,* with a few final comments on *WT.* This book offers a fresh appraisal of the significance of visual images in the plays, underscoring the discrepancy (iconoclasm) that often exists between the characters and their images. Thus, certain features of Shakespeare's drama can be understood as refracting the struggles over imagery and likeness that vexed post-Reformation England. Siemon devotes considerable effort to discussing the iconoclastic movement in the sixteenth-century church.

In *H5*, the iconic image of Henry wars with the context of incongruity and dissonance. The use of the iconic in *JC* becomes suspect and alerts us to the elements of figuration at work even in the language. Far from being an icon of Roman nobility, Brutus after the assassination turns out to have much in common with the opposition. Acts of mutilation in *Ham.* reveal the arbitrariness of what had seemed certain. Hamlet's mutilating treatment of Ophelia concentrates in the nunnery scene; here, sign appears set against sign. Throughout the play, one discerns that all representation amounts to violent usurpation, whether the play-within-the-play, the final duel scene, or the larger play itself. The final image in *Lr.*, that of Lear and Cordelia, does not offer a final meaningful emblem of the play's suffering; it sums up the last struggle of a conflict between action and emblem apparent throughout the play. By initially dividing the kingdom, Lear not only destroys a symbol of kingship but also portions royalty itself. Edgar helps make the Dover Cliff incident profoundly iconoclastic because he creates a grotesque emblem to subdue his father.

Robert N. Watson, in *Shakespeare and the Hazards of Ambition* (Harvard UP, 1984), argues that the theme of the hazards of ambition unites a number of plays into a coherent pattern of moral symbolism. The hero attempts to shed his lineal or inherited identity in order to embrace a new identity; but in doing so, he finds himself excluded from the regenerative system he has disdained. In psychoanalytic terms, Watson demonstrates that the hero who assumes a new, artificial identity must struggle to reject the father. In the history plays (*R3, R2, H4,* and *H5*), Shakespeare establishes the Oedipal basis for ambition. *R3*, for example, depicts the protagonist's attempts to forge a new identity by staging a series of rebirths; as a result, Richard's identity becomes something monstrous and artificial. *Mac.* explores Oedipal desire and rejection, implicating the audience in the protagonist's crime. The play exploits the audience's guilt-ridden urges against authority and reality. Coriolanus aspires to replace his hereditary identity with an ideal martial one, hoping to become a "divine warrior, made of steel, honor and wrath." *Cor.* becomes a tragically ambivalent morality play, with its hero torn between the diabolical debasement of bodily pleasures and the godlike exaltation of pure virtue. Leontes in *WT* experiences the hazards of ambition; but unlike the other plays, *WT* allows Leontes safe passage back to regenerative nature.

Jan Kott's *Shakespeare Our Contemporary* (Doubleday, 1966) embraces all the genres and has been highly influential in some theatrical productions, particularly *Lr.* Each generation, Kott argues, must interpret Shakespeare through its own perspective. He sees a "grand mechanism" functioning in history, not divine Providence. In *R2*, Shakespeare deposes the idea of kingly power, and in *R3*, he shows the crumbling of an entire moral order. Kott sees *Ham.* in its political context as a drama of imposed situations. *Tro.* becomes a modern play, a sneering political pamphlet. History in *Mac.*, however, is a nightmare, another metaphor to depict the struggle for power and the crown. Kott underscores the absurd nature of *Lr.*, making connections to Samuel Beckett's drama. The grotesque, in Kott's view, takes over the themes of tragedy and poses the same fundamental questions. All that remains in the play is the earth, empty and bleeding. The play explores no less than the decay and fall of the world. Kott also examines the darkness of some of the comedies, such as *MND*, which he finds to be the most erotic of Shakespeare's plays, containing a cruel and animal dream. He argues that the ending of *Tmp.*, the most disturbing in Shakespeare's drama, renders suspect the ideas of reconciliation and forgiveness. The play contains a profound divergence between the greatness of the human mind and the ruthlessness of history and frailty of the moral order.

Michael Hall, in *The Structure of Love: Representational Patterns and Shakespeare's Love Tragedies* (UP of Virginia, 1989), examines the structure of romantic love and sexual relationships in *Rom.*, *Oth.*, *Tro.*, and *Ant.* He argues that the Elizabethans conceptualized sexual relationships in terms of seven major systems—the ascetic, seduction, rape, epic, Petrarchan, emasculating, and etherealized—which form the basis for conceptualizing and representing sexual relationships in the sixteenth century. Our own modern systems of representing sexual relationships, though grounded in Elizabethan and earlier systems, have expanded into substantially new types; but the old types still live. Shakespeare takes advantage of the inherent contradictions in these systems and turns them into an interior reality for his characters, which differs from the exterior reality that constitutes these systems. *Rom.* rejects the ascetic view of love; *Oth.* manipulates the structural interplay between the Petrarchan and ascetic; *Tro.* suggests that the epic and Petrarchan views are defective; and *Ant.* never discredits the various views of love, providing no perspective from which to define the characters and actions. Although *Tro.* elicits an association with love, it prevents sympathy for or even an understanding of the characters. Its hero Troilus and its spokesmen Thersites and Pandarus are the play's least heroic and believable characters. In *Ant.,* Shakespeare wants us to accept that Antony and Cleopatra's relationship can be a contradiction of itself and that love can be simultaneously decadent and ideal.

Arthur Kirsch, in *The Passions of Shakespeare's Tragic Heroes* (UP of Virginia, 1990), examines the timelessness of Shakespeare's genius in dramatizing human feelings and actions, arguing that Shakespeare subscribes to a notion of temperance. The tragic heroes struggle with their passions. Kirsch argues against new historicist and cultural materialist approaches and contends that *Ham., Oth., Mac.,* and *Lr.* depict enduring truths of our spiritual and emotional lives; hence their vitality in the classroom and the theater. The last chapter, "Shakespeare's Humanism," criticizes Jonathan Dollimore and Stephen Greenblatt for taking Montaigne out of context. Social and cultural phenomena are not as important as the heroes' interior drama of suffering and fundamental passions.

Kristian Smidt, in *Unconformities in Shakespeare's Tragedies* (St. Martin's, 1990), the third volume of the unconformities series, focuses on *Tit., Rom., JC, Ham., Tro., Oth., Lr., Mac., Ant., Cor.,* and *Tim.* The unconformities include a clash between the portrayal of individual character and realistic behavior and the allegorical dimension in *Tit.,* a diptych structure in *JC,* a divided thematic structure in the mother-son relationship in *Ham.,* and unfinished revisions in *Oth.* Formal, thematic, and stylistic irregularities suggest "faults" in the geological and aesthetic sense, but these generally have a positive effect because they add a sense of depth and complexity to the plays.

David Young, in *The Action to the Word: Structure and Style in Shakespearean Tragedy* (Yale UP, 1990), traces a tension between dramatic action and expressive language, movement and speech, and gesture and word in *Ham., Oth., Lr.,* and *Mac.* *Ham.* presents a conflict between its dilatory or amplifying style and a "thrifty structure," which dilates the text but slows the action. In *Oth.,* the art of storytelling and narrative mastery represents one of the play's "curves of action and meaning." Iago learns to master narrative techniques. Through his asides, soliloquies, and direct addresses, the audience shares his perspective and becomes his uneasy and unwilling accomplice. *Lr.* stretches the tension between expansiveness and intimacy, reaching psychological intensity, stretching boundaries, and testing the actors, the theatrical medium, and the genre. *Mac.* interchanges and mingles the metaphoric and literal levels, infusing magic and magical meaning in its structure and style.

From a history-of-ideas approach, Thomas McAlindon explores Shakespeare's use of contrariety, duality, and polarity in *Shakespeare's Tragic Cosmos* (Cambridge UP, 1991). In *Rom., JC, Ham., Oth., Lr., Mac.,* and *Ant.,* Shakespeare adopts a perverse model of reality in which nature, history, society, and self consist of dynamic systems of interacting opposites. Grounded in this world, the tragic hero experiences psychic and interpersonal chaos when the bond that unites him to his world is violently shattered. As a consequence, the tragedies probe fundamental contradictions in human nature and in the cosmic context of our lives. This argument assumes a notion of transhistoric subjectivity and the concept of unchanging laws that are encoded in universal nature.

Kent Cartwright takes a performance-oriented perspective in *Shakespearean Tragedy and Its Double: The Rhythms of Audience Response* (Penn State UP, 1991) and argues that five tragedies—*Rom., Ham., Oth., Lr.,* and *Ant.*—orchestrate meaning by inviting engaged or detached audience responses that involve the spectator's surrender of self-awareness or heightened self-consciousness. *Rom.* engages the audience with its artificiality and carnival-like undertone, diverting our attention from the excesses of the lovers so that we can accept their passion sympathetically. *Ham.* invites identification, decontextualization, and wonder. *Oth.* has a divided spirit—heroic and antiheroic, engaged and detached. Secondary characters such as Cordelia, Kent, and Edgar become response regulators and set the moral coordinates in *Lr.;* Kent becomes the principal respondent to both Lear himself and the play. Spectatorship and acting unify the action of *Ant.*, in which the spectators, not the characters, develop.

David Margolies, in *Monsters of the Deep: Social Dissolution in Shakespeare's Tragedies* (Manchester UP, 1992), analyzes *Lr.*, *Ham.*, *Mac.*, *Ant.*, *Cor.*, and *Tim.* as metaphors of social disintegration. Each tragedy presents a contradictory society at a further stage of decline. *Ham.*, a play with fundamental structural problems, examines social degeneration. *Lr.* does not focus on the contradiction between form and content but rather allows the plot to carry the meaning, producing a world that resembles that of the audience. In *Mac.*, the hero seems aware of the conflict between his social feelings and his antisocial actions. *Ant.* presents a world that fails to recognize social virtues, making heroism impossible. As a result, Antony cannot find a place in this world. Coriolanus, unable to recognize the social dimension of his life, allows his individualism to destroy him. In *Tim.*, human bonds have nearly disappeared. In contrast, *Oth.* does not explore social disintegration; rather, it centers on a conflict of content and form, emerging as Shakespeare's "problem tragedy."

Nicholas Grene, in *Shakespeare's Tragic Imagination* (St. Martin's, 1992), examines Shakespeare's imaginative development from history plays to tragedies and discusses patterns of thematic similarities in nine tragedies from *JC* to *Cor.* These plays reflect an interest in the connection between power and legitimating authority and the gender roles in heroic endeavors. *Ham*, *Lr.*, and *Mac.* present a metaphysical, primal, or archetypal connection between the roles of king and country. *Oth.*, though classified as a domestic tragedy, opens out into a visionary world. In contrast, *JC, Tro., Ant.,* and *Cor.* lack a spiritual or visionary dimension. They combine a secular, relativistic world with a sense of historical determinism. In the classical tragedies, a ruthless and pragmatic order replaces an idealistic one. A sense of the secular predominates in tragedies with classical sources, and the sacred prevails in the nonclassical tragedies.

SONNETS

Criticism of the Sonnets has been plagued by many attempts to identify the persons the Sonnets presumably address. Many have also insisted that the Sonnets reflect Shakespeare's personal experience. Others have wondered about the sexuality expressed in the poems. Altogether, a large segment of criticism has moved from the poetry to the biography of the poet. Those who argue that the poems tell a ''story'' have been countered by those who argue that they do not. Shakespeare has been seen in the tradition of the sixteenth-century poets who produced lengthy sonnet sequences. Much of the criticism has centered on an analysis of the themes of the Sonnets. Debate has been going on for some time about the order of the poems, and attempts have been made to create a new order.

A brief review of criticism can be found in A. Nejgebauer, ''Twentieth-Century Studies in Shakespeare's Songs, Sonnets, and Poems,'' *Shakespeare Survey* 15 (1962): 10–18. Barbara Herrnstein, ed., *Discussions of Shakespeare's Sonnets* (Heath, 1964), includes seventeen essays primarily from the twentieth century. Essays, explications of specific Sonnets, a bibliography, and the texts of the Sonnets themselves appear in Gerald Willen and Victor B. Reed, eds., *A Casebook on Shakespeare's Sonnets* (Crowell, 1964). A bibliography that may be of some help is Tetsumaro Hayashi, *Shakespeare's Sonnets: A Record of Twentieth-Century Criticism* (Scarecrow, 1972). It contains three categories: primary sources and editions; secondary sources, books, and articles; and background sources.

Hyder Edward Rollins's important edition, *The Sonnets,* 2 vols. (Lippincott, 1944), forms part of the new variorum edition. The first volume presents the text of the Sonnets, textual notes, and commentary; the second volume covers a wide range of subjects, including text, authenticity of the 1609 text, date of composition, arrangement, question of autobiography, the friend, the dark lady, and the rival poet.

The arrangement of the Sonnets preoccupies Brents Stirling in *The Shakespeare Sonnet Order: Poems and Groups* (U of California P, 1968). The book is difficult to summarize because the argument depends on intricate details, relating one Sonnet to another. Nevertheless, this sophisticated, complicated, detailed argument opts for an order different from that of the original 1609 Quarto text. Stirling's new arrangement derives from internal evidence of style and subject matter rather than from external, historical matter. In effect, he presents a new "edition" of the poems in the order and sequence that he proposes. Chapter 1 describes the problems inherent in confronting the order of the Sonnets, chapter 2 offers the new arrangement and commentary about the sequence, and chapter 3 presents sixty pages of verification. Although the Sonnets can be praised for their narrative art, they tell no definable continued story. Stirling also suggests that they have no demonstrable reference to "true" or historical happenings. Needless to say, Stirling's new order has not been universally accepted, nor have other proposals for a new arrangement; but he presents a compelling case.

Edward Hubler's *The Sense of Shakespeare's Sonnets* (Princeton UP, 1952) offers a thematic approach to the poems. Hubler does not attempt to identify the young man or the dark lady. In fact, he consciously resists taking the step from poetry to biography and instead focuses on what the Sonnets say. He discusses a number of techniques that Shakespeare uses—wordplay, puns, structural devices, the couplet (which Hubler thinks often fails). He groups thematic discussion around a chapter on the dark-lady poems (Sonnets 127–152), sections on the young man's beauty, problems of mutability and immortality, "the economy of the closed heart," the knowledge of good and evil, friendship, and fortune. In an appendix, Hubler confronts the issue of homosexuality in the poems and the authorship question of the plays.

G. Wilson Knight, in *The Mutual Flame* (Macmillan, 1955), reviews the various critical and factual problems connected with the Sonnets. He finds many of these problems, such as the problem of identities, unsolvable. Nevertheless, he proceeds to identify Shakespeare the person with the poet in the Sonnets. He views the poems as a semidramatic expression of a clearly defined process of integration, pointing toward the realization of a high state of being. The main attention concentrates on the poet's love for the fair youth. Knight also considers symbolism and finds the rose, king, sun, and gold to be the main symbols related to the theme. He has an extended commentary on the problems of time, death, and eternity in the poems. In a chapter entitled "The Expansion," Knight relates the Sonnets to Shakespeare's dramatic works in a thought-provoking manner.

J. B. Leishman, in *Themes and Variations in Shakespeare's Sonnets* (Hutchinson, 1961), offers primarily a comparative study of Shakespeare's poems and the poetry of other writers according to both style and theme. Basically, he observes the resemblance and differences between Shakespeare and other poets. He takes the poems rather literally, suggesting that they tell a story and that the young man is William Herbert. Leishman considers the Sonnets on love as the defier of time, and he argues that Shakespeare desires to transcend rather than refashion himself. In love and friendship, Shakespeare finds a compensation for the evils of life.

In *The Master-Mistress: A Study of Shakespeare's Sonnets* (Chatto & Windus, 1968), James Winny presents a response to the various theories about the Sonnets and a thematic approach to them. The first chapter offers a good summing up of critical and historical theories. Winny denies the validity of the search for the identity of the young man or the dark lady. The Sonnets do not constitute that kind of story; they are fictional, but not in the sense of a coherent narrative. They are certainly not autobiographical, because they do not correspond to anything that we know about Shakespeare's life. Therefore, he should not be precisely identified with the persona of the Sonnets. Winny explores the kind of story the Sonnets contain: vaguely related groupings of events and ideas. The dark-lady section has even less of a narrative thread because the poet is more absorbed in ideas. Two major themes emerge: truth and falsehood, and increase and procreation. Winny emphasizes the dualism of the poems, arguing that the dualistic associations that the poet forms constitute the heart of the sequence.

Making no attempt to pursue a central thesis, Hilton Landry, in *Interpretations in Shakespeare's Sonnets* (U of California P, 1963), essentially presents a series of essays on selected Sonnets. He does, however, argue against the conventional grouping of the Sonnets: 1–126 (young man), and 127–154 (dark lady). Landry sees no evidence to support this arrangement, which only encourages the fallacy of "story" in the poems. In his discussion, Landry places the Sonnets in their surrounding poetic context. He offers extensive commentary on the following: Sonnet 94 as a bridge between 87–93 and 95–96—the octave looks back and the sestet looks forward; 69–70 and 53–54, which address the disparity between physical appearance and moral reality; 33–35, 40–42, and 57–58, which all suggest a "civil war," first involving the young friend (33–35), then aspects of a sexual triangle (40–42), and finally a master-slave relationship, with the speaker in the unhappy role of the slave of love (57–58); 66, 121, and 129, which suggest a strongly negative feeling, chiefly moral indignation; and 123–125, which define in some essential way the quality of the speaker's love for the person addressed in Sonnet 125.

Murray Krieger's *A Window to Criticism: Shakespeare's "Sonnets" and Modern Poetics* (Princeton UP, 1964), a highly sophisticated, aesthetic, theoretical book, uses the Sonnets to construct an aesthetic theory. Krieger finds in the Sonnets a key to the nature of metaphor, poetry, and poetics as well. He focuses on the mirror-window metaphorical system. The mirror of narcissism and the magical mirror of love appear in the poems; love breaks the enclosure of self-love. The world of self-love in some of the Sonnets becomes the world of worms (symbolically); it may also be a political world. The final chapter examines the religious dimension, discussing the miracle of love's eschatology and incarnation. Beginning students may find this book somewhat beyond their reach.

Philip Martin, in *Shakespeare's Sonnets: Self, Love and Art* (Cambridge UP, 1972), does not examine the traditional problems of the Sonnets, finding those issues largely irrelevant. Instead, he argues that Shakespeare's feeling for selfhood underlies the whole body of the Sonnets, evident in his concern with poetry, mutability, and, above all, love. This concern for selfhood is uncommon in the love poetry of the age. In the first two chapters, Martin examines what he calls the "sin of self-love," principally the Sonnets on the youth and on the poet himself. Elsewhere, Martin explores the whole convention of writing sonnets, trying to determine why so many poets in the sixteenth century attempted the form. In one chapter, Martin places John Donne and Shakespeare alongside each other for a comparison of their love poetry in order to demonstrate their awareness and use of love conventions and also their criticism of them. The final chapter discusses the immortality of love, an immortality that seems to have its own existence that is not dependent on the poetry.

In the stimulating book *An Essay on Shakespeare's Sonnets* (Yale UP, 1969), Stephen Booth analyzes how and why we respond to the Sonnets as we do. He notes that the 1609 sequence seems to need interpretation or reorganization, not because of its disorder but because of its obvious order. Booth demonstrates the various kinds of structural patterns in the Sonnets and the effect of their interaction. He reveals a multiplicity of structures, such as formal, logical, syntactical patterns and false starts and changes of direction. In all their details, the Sonnets set a reader's mind in motion, demanding intellectual energy as they are read. This effect (the actual experience of passing from word to word for fourteen lines) becomes unusual and valuable.

In a chapter on multiple patterns, Booth discusses rhetorical structure, phonetic structure, patterns of diction, and multiplicity. Like patterns of syntactical units, sound patterns can also evoke a sense of order. He argues later that the style re-creates the experience of paradox, of coping with things in more than one frame of reference not *for* but *in* the reader. The couplet ties off one set of loose ends and brings the reader's mind back to conceiving of experience in a single system, what Booth calls the "comfort of the couplet." Shakespeare's enlargement of the number and kinds of patterns makes his Sonnets seem full to bursting, not only with the quantity of different actions but also with the energy generated from their conflict. An index of Sonnets discussed helps the reader track down information on particular Sonnets. Sonnets 60, 73, and 94 get especially prolonged attention.

In a challenging edition that follows his critical study, Stephen Booth, in *Shakespeare's Sonnets* (Yale UP, 1977), presents a modern text side by side with a facsimile of the 1609 Quarto edition of the Sonnets. As in his study of the Sonnets, Booth tries in this edition to present the experience that a Renaissance reader might have had moving from line to line and poem to poem. Booth's preface explains (sometimes in witty detail) how he proceeds in the edition and his editorial principles. In the commentary notes that follow the presentation of the texts of the Sonnets, Booth seeks to answer how the Sonnets work and to provide the usual glosses on what the words mean. Some of the commentary is extensive, as in the case of that for Sonnet 116, prompting thoughtful reflection about these poems.

Questions of authorship, biographical intention, topical allusion, and the order of the Sonnets continue to dominate the criticism. Kenneth Muir, in *Shakespeare's Sonnets* (George Allen & Unwin, 1979), and Paul Ramsey, in *The Fickle Glass: A Study of Shakespeare's Sonnets* (AMS, 1979), review in detail some of these questions. S. C. Campbell's *Only Begotten Sonnets: A Reconstruction of Shakespeare's Sonnet Sequence* (Bell & Hyman, 1978) analyzes what he considers to be the defective order in the Quarto text and offers a more coherent order. In *Shakespeare's Dramatic Meditations* (Clarendon, 1976)—a more technical and difficult study based on a comparative analysis of word frequency, structural patterns, and themes—Giorgio Melchiori focuses on Sonnets 20, 94, 121, and 146, which best articulate Shakespeare's thoughts and feelings.

The Sonnets continue to elicit diametrically opposed views. Katharine M. Wilson, in *Shakespeare's Sugared Sonnets* (George Allen & Unwin, 1974), attempts to demonstrate that the Sonnets are not serious but parodic. The ones on the dark lady begin with a parody of Sidney's poem and create a travesty of the additional sonnet lady. The poems to the young man are also parodies of prevailing sonnet attitudes: "To say to a man what is commonly said to a woman is itself to parody" (320). Finally, in an appendix entitled "Shakespeare Not Homosexual," Wilson sets out to prove that Shakespeare was not interested in boys. Robert Giroux, in *The Book Known as Q: A Consideration of Shakespeare's Sonnets* (Atheneum, 1982), approaches the Sonnets from the point of view of a publisher. Giroux argues that Shakespeare was probably embarrassed, if not horrified, by the publication so late in his career of his privately circulated, very personal poems. Joseph Pequigney, in *Such Is My Love: A Study of Shakespeare's Sonnets* (U of Chicago P, 1985), offers an unconventional, homoerotic reading of the Sonnets. He argues that the first 126 poems depict an amorous sexual relationship between the poet and the youth, a relationship that complies with Freud's views on homosexuality. The Sonnets, according to Pequigney, form not only a masterly, coherent sequence but also a masterpiece of homoerotic poetry.

In *The Reader and Shakespeare's Young Man Sonnets* (Macmillan, 1981), Gerald Hammond offers a reader-response study of the Sonnets. He argues that except for the final twenty-six poems, the ones addressed to the young man offer an organized, coherent, and developing sequence of poems. The Sonnets contain a narrative, but what makes them truly sequential is the reader's developing experience of the nature of love poetry. This interesting, original book posits the existence of a character called "the reader" who, through the poems, learns how to read sonnets and what to read into them.

An important, challenging book with an intricate argument, Joel Fineman's *Shakespeare's Perjured Eye: The Invention of Poetic Subjectivity in the Sonnets* (U of California P, 1986) follows a poststructuralist strategy and therefore appeals especially to those interested in contemporary critical theory. Fineman argues that in the Sonnets, Shakespeare creates a genuinely new poetic subjectivity, a new poetics, and a new first-person poetic posture out of outmoded forms. Focusing on differences, paradoxes, and oppositions, Fineman examines, among other things, the relation between the tradition of visionary language of praise and the representation of the poetic persona, the relation between the Sonnets addressed to the youth and those addressed to the dark lady, and the larger implications of his argument for Shakespeare's dramatic works.

STUDIES OF GROUPS AND MOVEMENTS

THE HISTORY OF CRITICISM

Students may be involved with research that includes study of the history of Shakespearean criticism; if so, several works can be helpful. Surveys of some of the issues can be found in three essays: Kenneth Muir, "Fifty Years of Shakespearean Criticism: 1900–1950," *Shakespeare Survey* 4 (1951): 1–25; Hardin Craig, "Trends of Shakespeare Scholarship," *Shakespeare Survey* 2 (1949): 107–14; and M. C. Bradbrook, "Fifty Years of the

Criticism of Shakespeare's Style,'' *Shakespeare Survey* 7 (1954): 111.

In *Shakespeare: The Critical Heritage*, 6 vols. (Routledge & Kegan Paul, 1974–1981), Brian Vickers provides excerpts from Shakespearean criticism from 1623 through 1801, plus useful introductions. The time periods covered are as follows: volume 1, 1623–1692; volume 2, 1693–1733; volume 3, 1733–1752; volume 4, 1753–1765; volume 5, 1765–1774; and volume 6, 1774–1801.

One of the standard works available on the history of criticism is Augustus Ralli, *A History of Shakespearean Criticism*, 2 vols. (Oxford UP, 1932). This monumental compilation of criticism ranges from the beginning to 1925. It covers criticism in England, Germany, and France (interestingly, the only American critic deemed worthy of noting was Stoll). Ralli summarizes and evaluates scores of critics, arranged by nationality, for specific time periods. The discussion proceeds critic by critic. The author also provides a summary at the end of each section. Students may find the book cumbersome to use and the author's style inflated.

Easier to use is Frank Kermode's *Four Centuries of Shakespearean Criticism* (Avon, 1965), an anthology of criticism ranging from Francis Meres's (1598) to items published in the early 1960s. The material centers on general criticism, comedies, histories, tragedies, and essays on the four major tragedies.

Paul N. Siegel's *His Infinite Variety: Major Shakespearean Criticism since Johnson* (Lippincott, 1964) makes its selections on the basis of value rather than historical significance. Topics include general characteristics, history plays, romantic comedies, satiric comedies, tragedies, and tragicomic romances. Siegel also includes an extensive bibliography.

F. E. Halliday, in *Shakespeare and His Critics*, rev. ed. (Duckworth, 1958), presents a forty-page historical survey of the major figures and movements in Shakespearean criticism and then gives examples of criticism from 1592 to 1955, moving from play to play and including the nondramatic poetry.

A major book by Arthur M. Eastman, *A Short History of Shakespearean Criticism* (Random House, 1968), analyzes developments in criticism in a 400-page review of major critics. The first chapter concentrates on the first 150 years; subsequent chapters survey such critics as Johnson, Schlegel, Coleridge, Lamb, Hazlitt, Dowden, Shaw, Bradley, Stoll, Knight, Spurgeon, Tillyard, Harbage, Granville-Barker, and Northrop Frye. Eastman includes generous quotations from their criticism, although one might quarrel with his selection.

Norman Rabkin's *Approaches to Shakespeare* (McGraw-Hill, 1964) offers information on different types of criticism and contains a collection of twenty previously published essays that represent different approaches to Shakespeare, such as textual, stage production, biography, imagery, and Christian.

Patrick Murray, in *The Shakespearean Scene: Some Twentieth-Century Perspectives* (Longmans, 1969), analyzes several of the twentieth-century critical approaches to Shakespeare. He discusses the idea of character—its importance, the nature of Shakespeare's characters, and the psychological treatment of the characters. He also focuses on dramatic imagery—how this approach ties in with themes and character. Murray comments on the religious quality and offers specific analysis of *Lr., Ham.,* and *MM*. From the historical perspective, Murray cites the awareness of Elizabethan times and dramatic conventions. The book concentrates on the theory of a particular type of criticism, its assumptions, its contributions, and its weaknesses, offering evidence from the practitioners.

The importance of Coleridge as a critic has already been emphasized; the standard edition appears in Thomas M. Raysor, ed., *Coleridge's Shakespearean Criticism,* 2 vols. (Constable, 1930). Raysor presents a lengthy introduction and then a text of the criticism from lectures, reports on lectures, and parts of essays. This edition has come under question, however—at least the text for the lectures of 1811–1812. R. A. Foakes, in *Coleridge on Shakespeare: The Text of the Lectures of 1811–12* (UP of Virginia for the Folger Shakespeare Library, 1971), reedited J. P. Collier's diary, which includes transcripts of Coleridge's lectures. The variations from the accepted text of Raysor raise new problems about the reliability and accuracy of the Coleridge text as it has come down to us. Students will appreciate the selection of Coleridge's writings available in the book edited by Terence Hawkes, *Coleridge's Writings on Shakespeare* (Capricorn, 1959).

A narrative account of Shakespeare's reputation appears in

Louis Marder's *His Exits and His Entrances: The Story of Shakespeare's Reputation* (Lippincott, 1963). This book offers a wide range of information, including discussion of the idolatry of Shakespeare, frauds and forgeries, Stratford and Stratford festivals, Shakespeare as a subject in the schools, Shakespeare's popularity in American theater, and, briefly, Shakespeare's reputation in other parts of the world: Germany, Scandinavia, Russia, and the Orient. A useful sourcebook on reputation is *The Shakespeare Allusion Book: A Collection of Allusions to Shakespeare from 1591 to 1700* (Oxford UP, 1932), compiled by C. M. Ingleby, L. Toulmin Smith, and F. J. Furnivall; revised by John Munro (1909), with a new preface by E. K. Chambers. This work emanated from one of the nineteenth-century Shakespeare societies. Volume 1 includes an extensive introduction and the chronological listing of allusions from 1591 to 1649; volume 2 covers 1650 to 1700.

Shakespeare Criticism (Gale, 1984–) provides significant passages of published criticism in twenty-three volumes (this is an ongoing project). Some volumes reprint whole essays; some focus on performance history of individual plays. Students should consult the cumulative topic indexes as an efficient means of using these volumes.

Gary Taylor, in *Reinventing Shakespeare: A Cultural History from the Restoration to the Present* (Oxford UP, 1989), uses key, pivotal years to trace a slightly irreverent history of Shakespeare's reputation. He notes, for example, that during much of the seventeenth century, most critics considered Shakespeare's plays to be inferior to those of John Fletcher and Ben Jonson. Reaction to *Ham.* became the test case of the Restoration's taste and judgment. Events of 1709, including Nicholas Rowe's edition of Shakespeare, transformed the public perception of Shakespeare in the eighteenth century. Edmond Malone's 1790 edition signaled a new shift, opening the way for romantic response to Shakespeare. The founding of the New Shakespere Society in 1874 by F. J. Furnivall epitomized the Victorian image of an evolving Shakespeare. Taylor also emphasizes the importance of Edward Dowden and his impact on Shakespearean interpretation in the United States. The early twentieth century exhibited a growing conviction that Shakespeare addressed his best work to a cultural elite. Additional chapters document the accomplishments of twentieth-century scholars and critics, with particular attention given to the contribution of women. Throughout, the book underscores that Shakespeare's reputation functions as part of larger social and cultural movements. In the final chapter, Taylor attacks an idea that may have seemed self-evident: "Shakespeare cannot claim any unique command of theatrical resources, longevity or reach of reputation, depth or range of style, universality or comprehensiveness" (395).

Brian Vickers assesses contemporary critical approaches to Shakespeare in *Appropriating Shakespeare: Contemporary Critical Quarrels* (Yale UP, 1993). After the first two chapters, in which Vickers explores language and literary theory as the basis for his evaluation, he devotes five chapters to current schools of criticism: deconstruction, new historicism, psychocriticism, feminism, and Christians and Marxists. For Vickers, the turning point came in the late 1960s, with the critical upheaval emerging from Paris. The great change has resulted in a division of the field of criticism, with competing groups now vying for attention in their attempt to appropriate Shakespeare. Basically, Vickers complains that these approaches distort Shakespeare's text to make it fit critical theories. Unconcerned with what actually happens in a play, deconstructionists, Vickers argues, reduce drama to language and characters to mere signs; they cannot cope with the fundamental nature of drama as the interaction between characters. Focusing largely on the work of Stephen Greenblatt, Vickers accuses new historicists of disregarding the integrity of the literary text, bending evidence to suit one-sided interpretations, and foisting modern cultural and political attitudes onto Renaissance texts. Vickers challenges feminists to absorb self-critical developments in feminist theory and acquire greater knowledge of social conditions in the Renaissance. These various approaches, Vickers believes, have led to a politicization of critical discourse, thereby losing sight of the fundamental task of interpreting Shakespeare.

Concentrating on nineteenth- and twentieth-century criticism, Hugh Grady, in *The Modernist Shakespeare: Critical Texts in a Material World* (Clarendon, 1991), documents the transference of discourse on Shakespeare to a new bureaucratic setting (modern university) and to a new class of authors (academic professionals). Modernization, mediated through the specific process of professionalization, intervened and transformed the nature of literary studies. The creation of the modern research-oriented university in the late nineteenth century became seminal for later developments in criticism. Grady singles out American E. E. Stoll as illustrative of the new professional consciousness in literary studies at the turn of the century. Romantic criticism and disintegration of Shakespeare became the enemies. The modernizing of Shakespeare gave way to a new critical paradigm: modernism, whose seminal figure is G. Wilson Knight. For Knight, the modernist Shakespeare arises in reaction against the positivist modernizers; he interprets Shakespeare's plays as modernist artworks. Grady devotes considerable attention to New Critics and their shaping influence on all literary criticism, including Shakespearean. E. M. W. Tillyard's astounding rise in prominence and now the revisionist attack against him demonstrate that literary criticism is, according to Grady, an "overdetermined discourse shaped by politics, aesthetics, and institutional discipline." Tillyard's work exists as a complex synthesis of both modernist and anti-modernist impulses brought together in an uneasy fusion. The final chapter of this book focuses on the "postmodern" Shakespeare as defined by contemporary critical trends—deconstruction, new historicism, cultural materialism, and feminist criticism.

SHAKESPEARE'S LANGUAGE

Considerable attention has focused on matters of Shakespeare's language, especially in modern criticism. (See also the items on language included in the section on reference books earlier in this chapter.) One dimension of language study emphasizes dramatic imagery. One of the most influential books is Caroline Spurgeon's *Shakespeare's Imagery and What It Tells Us* (Cambridge UP, 1935). This pioneering study is statistical and quantitative, complete with charts and graphs. Regrettably, a large part of the book compiles information that portrays Shakespeare the man rather than Shakespeare the artist. Spurgeon sums up his likes and dislikes and sees him as basically Christ-like. Although she understands the importance of imagery for our perception of the drama, she does not seem to know quite what to do with it. She perceives themes of iterative imagery and classifies them. Clearly she pointed a new direction in Shakespearean criticism; many others have built on her study.

Working independently at the same time, Wolfgang Clemen published in 1936 a book in German, later revised and translated as *The Development of Shakespeare's Imagery* (Methuen, 1951). Clemen describes the development of the language of imagery and its functions. He detects a pattern of evolution and growth in Shakespeare's use of imagery as the dramatist little by little discovered the possibilities that imagery offered him. Clemen focuses on imagery of the early and middle period, in the great tragedies, and in the Romances. Shakespeare reaches a certain level of skill, as in the tragedies, and then variations of style occur. Clemen argues that growth in the use of imagery corresponds to increased dramatic skill; thus, Shakespeare fully integrates later images into the plays.

Studying Shakespeare's use of rhetoric, Sister Miriam Joseph, in *Shakespeare's Use of the Arts of Language* (Columbia UP, 1947), presents a sophisticated, scholarly study of the formal art of rhetoric in the Renaissance and the evidence in Shakespeare's plays and poems of his knowledge and use of various compositional devices. The author surveys the theory of composition and of reading in Shakespeare's England, then explores Shakespeare's use of the theory—grammar, rhetoric, and logic. Shakespeare's formal devices contribute to the power and richness of his language, as well as account for some of its peculiarities.

A different language approach appears in Hilda M. Hulme's *Explorations in Shakespeare's Language* (Longmans, 1962). This linguistic study examines in part the traditions that contributed to Shakespeare's language: for example, proverbs, Latin, and bawdy. The author also discusses Shakespeare's spelling habits and variants in pronunciation, examining evidence from contemporary Stratford. Hulme explores the meanings of some of the words and phrases in the plays and provides a helpful index.

Several books make practical application of language studies. Ifor Evans, in *The Language of Shakespeare's Plays* (Methuen, 1959; original, 1952), offers no all-encompassing thesis but presents individual essays covering almost the entire canon, beginning with an analysis of language in *LLL*. Generally, in the early comedies, Shakespeare had no overriding loyalty to the story if wit and invention tempted him. But the histories necessitated a new kind of discipline. Evans finds that nowhere are Shakespeare's intentions in language more complex and his success more complete than in *Lr.*

M. M. Mahood's rich book *Shakespeare's Wordplay* (Methuen, 1957) explores Shakespeare's language through the device of the pun, but the book also examines many subtleties in Shakespeare's use of words. Mahood discusses in some depth *Rom., R2, Ham., Mac., WT,* and the Sonnets. Wordplay is one of the most effective means of achieving the ironic interchange between character and creator. The Sonnets reveal examples of a consciously used, hard-worked device of wordplay as well as more unintentional, involuntary examples. In the final chapter, the author surveys Shakespeare's attitude toward language, his world of words.

In a relatively brief book, *Redeeming Shakespeare's Words* (U of California P, 1962), Paul A. Jorgensen explores the fullest possible explication of words that are either thematic or significant in certain plays: for example, the use of "honesty" in *Oth.,* "noble" in *Cor.,* "redeeming time" in *H4.* Jorgensen also discusses *Ado* and *Ham.*

Brian Vickers, in *The Artistry of Shakespeare's Prose* (Methuen, 1968), traces and analyzes the dramatist's use of prose throughout the canon, with the quantity of prose peaking in *Wiv.* Prose, largely the vehicle of comedy and the comic parts of the histories, becomes in the tragedies one of Shakespeare's greatest achievements, Vickers suggests. Investigation of the prose style centers on imagery, linguistic structure, and rhetorical structure. In order to analyze Shakespeare's development in the use of prose, Vickers proceeds chronologically through the canon. Thus, for example, *MND* can be seen as an improvement over *LLL* by its consistency and economy. Shylock's prose, Vickers observes, is the great innovation in *MV.* Vickers devotes much attention to Falstaff. The prose of *TN* belongs largely to the lower orders of society and to the upper-class representatives when they come in contact with the servants. Iago dominates the prose in *Oth.* and uses it as a medium for dissembling and mounting his intrigue against Othello. Increasingly, the tragedies' prose fulfills its function for clowns and madmen—witness the Fool and Lear in *Lr.*

Madeleine Doran, in *Shakespeare's Dramatic Language* (U of Wisconsin P, 1976), concentrates on the tragedies as she explores connections between language and dramatic style. The opening chapter outlines the essential elements of style, and discrete essays on six tragedies follow. Doran notes, for example, that in Hamlet's style, the range and intensity provide a key vitality. In *Oth.*, she examines conditional and subjunctive statements as indicators of character and action. The interplay of association and negation gives dramatic life and sensibility to the plot; here, syntax informs the larger dramatic structure. In a grammatical and rhetorical analysis of *Lr.*, Doran explores the uses of command, question, and assertion. Subsequent chapters analyze the importance of proper names in *JC,* the language of hyperbole in *Ant.*, and the language of contention in *Cor.*

Jane Donawerth's historical study of language, *Shakespeare and the Sixteenth-Century Study of Language* (U of Illinois P, 1984), examines the language texts that Shakespeare could have known and the use he makes of them. The book's initial chapters provide information about what was known about language study in the sixteenth century, limiting the investigation to topics relevant to Shakespeare's art. Shakespeare uses language controversies in his plays. Donawerth analyzes in detail the language of five plays: *LLL, Jn., MV, AWW,* and *Ham.* She notes, for example, the controlling conception of language in *LLL:* an ordered system of rational symbols through which the speakers generate meaning. Ideas about language in this play help distinguish the major groups of characters. Ideas about language in *AWW* derive mainly from the humanists' distinction between words and things. In *Ham.*, men and women define themselves by their attitudes toward language, demonstrating Shakespeare's consummate ability to use language.

George T. Wright, in *Shakespeare's Metrical Art* (U of California P, 1988), sets out to describe the poetic metrical system that Shakespeare uses, with an emphasis on the iambic pentameter line. This system provides Shakespeare and his characters with expressive gestures and powers. Wright develops a historical perspective, going back to Chaucer. Shakespeare's verse never loses its connections with the rhythms of spoken English; his iambic verse accommodates a wide range of metrical variations. Shakespeare can suit the syntax and meter of almost any important passage to its occasion—to the character, the emotion, the dramatic situation. According to Wright, the iambic pentameter line and all its departures and deviations imply a worldview of continuing reciprocal engagement and mutual responsibility. This rich book offers valuable insights into Shakespeare's technical achievement.

TEXTUAL CRITICISM

If a student wants to investigate the somewhat complicated area of textual studies, several books can prove useful. Philip Gaskell's *A New Introduction to Bibliography* (Clarendon, 1972), which updates and revises the much earlier *An Introduction to Bibliography* (1928) by R. B. McKerrow, provides information about the whole process of book production of the Renaissance period. Gaskell covers such topics as book production, printing type, composition, paper, imposition, presswork, binding, patterns of production, and the English book trade to 1800. He also discusses textual bibliography and includes an extensive reference bibliography.

A helpful guide to the increasing number of textual studies is T. H. Howard-Hill's *Shakespearean Bibliography and Textual Criticism: A Bibliography* (Clarendon, 1971). In this 180-page bibliography, Howard-Hill first defines the limits and explains the arrangement of the bibliography, which has three broad categories: general bibliographies of and guides to Shakespearean literature, works (collected works, collections and libraries, quartos, folios), and textual studies (handwriting, individual texts arranged alphabetically). The entries proceed chronologically from earliest to latest.

A valuable summing up of the world of textual criticism can be found in F. P. Wilson, *Shakespeare and the New Bibliography* (Clarendon, 1970), revised and edited by Helen Gardner. This book, originally written in the 1940s, provides an excellent analysis of where textual criticism stood up to that point, updated by Gardner. It records a history of the years in which the distinctive problems involved in the handling of printed texts first gained definition. The book also serves as a valuable introduction for anyone embarking on a study of the problems of establishing Shakespeare's text. It covers such topics as the beginnings to 1909, publication of plays, printing of plays, dramatic manuscripts, copy for the quartos and folios, and principles of textual criticism.

Fredson Bowers's collection of essays in *On Editing Shakespeare* (UP of Virginia, 1966) probes the following topics: the texts and their manuscripts, the function of textual criticism and bibliography, the method for creating a critical edition, what Shakespeare wrote, today's Shakespeare texts, and tomorrow's. The final chapter comments on past editions back to the Globe text of 1864 and on what remains to be done. Bowers assigns prime importance to the need for a complete old-spelling edition of Shakespeare.

W. W. Greg's *The Shakespeare First Folio: Its Bibliographical and Textual History* (Clarendon, 1955) has become a standard book on the subject. It presents an authoritative summing up of what was known in the mid-1950s about the textual problems of the Folio. Greg initially discusses how the Folio as a collection of Shakespeare's plays came about; he also explores questions of copyright. The bulk of the book surveys the many kinds of editorial problems apparent in the Folio. To do so, Greg systematically goes through the canon play by play and discusses scholarly opinion on the nature of the text. Greg also considers those plays that had earlier quarto texts and their relationship to the Folio. A final chapter, now superseded by Hinman's work, focuses on the printing of the Folio. This book, written by one of the leading authorities in the field of textual criticism, is a handy and indispensable reference for checking on the nature of the texts.

Alice Walker also examines some of these problems in *Textual Problems of the First Folio* (Cambridge UP, 1953). She analyzes what lies behind the Folio texts of *R3, Lr., Tro., 2H4, Ham.,* and *Oth.* She argues that once we recognize conflation and contamination in these Folio texts, it becomes much easier to determine the character of the manuscripts that lie behind them. The book seeks to determine what occurred between

Shakespeare's manuscript and the Folio texts of these six plays and the editorial implications.

A demanding but important book is Charlton Hinman's *The Printing and Proof-reading of the First Folio of Shakespeare*, 2 vols. (Clarendon, 1963). This highly technical survey explores the process involved in the printing of the Folio—the nature of the Jaggard print shop, edition size and speed of production, standard printing-house procedures, and so on. Hinman makes an extensive study of the type used in the Folio and what it reveals. In his analysis of the compositors who set the type, Hinman identifies five different compositors by their characteristic habits, indicating which portions of the text they set. Volume 2 offers a detailed analysis of the printing in the Folio and presents a review.

E. A. J. Honigmann's *The Stability of Shakespeare's Text* (Edward Arnold, 1965) runs somewhat counter to the general drift of the textual critics. The real subject of the book is the "instability" of Shakespeare's texts. Honigmann raises the unsettling prospect that variants of the same substantive text may represent not errors but Shakespeare's different versions. Such a theory goes somewhat against the "new bibliography" school, at which Honigmann takes several good swats. He finds more reason for skepticism about the nature and condition of Shakespeare's texts than for the optimism that generally emanates from the new bibliographers. Honigmann has a keen distrust of their "facts." His final chapter examines editorial policy in light of his argument.

In what were initially lectures, Stanley Wells examines the problems facing an editor of Shakespeare today in *Re-Editing Shakespeare for the Modern Reader* (Clarendon, 1984). Many of these insights come from Wells's involvement with the Oxford Shakespeare edition. He outlines the arguments about old versus modern spelling, argues the case for emending Shakespeare's text, and discusses editorial treatment of stage directions. Many examples support the discussion. Wells closes with a detailed analysis of Act I of *Tit.*, illustrating how editorial theories work in practice. One basic assumption underlies the critical principles for editing: that the texts remain open to different kinds of editorial treatment according to the varying needs of those who read them.

THEATRICAL CRITICISM

"Theatrical" can cover a wide range of studies, including details of the Elizabethan theater, acting companies, specific actors, the repertory, buildings and their physical qualities, the nature of Elizabethan acting, the place of the theater in Elizabethan culture, developments in the staging and construction of the dramas, and stage history from earliest to latest productions.

A convenient and helpful bibliography is Philip C. Kolin and R. O. Wyatt, "A Bibliography of Scholarship on the Elizabethan Stage since Chambers," *Research Opportunities in Renaissance Drama* 15–16 (1972–1973): 33–59. This list of some 360 items covers the scholarship since 1923 on the physical characteristics of the Elizabethan stage. A review article is Allardyce Nicoll's "Studies in the Elizabethan Stage since 1900," *Shakespeare Survey* 1 (1948): 1–16. M. St. Clare Byrne's "Fifty Years of Shakespearean Production: 1898–1948," *Shakespeare Survey* 2 (1949): 1–20, reviews production. A valuable collection of essays on the theater is G. E. Bentley, *The Seventeenth-Century Stage: A Collection of Critical Essays* (U of Chicago P, 1968). It includes documents of the early seventeenth century and modern discussions of theaters and productions, mostly in the reigns of James I and Charles I; additional essays deal with actors and acting of the period.

An impressive mass of material appears in the authoritative work by E. K. Chambers, *The Elizabethan Stage*, 4 vols. (Clarendon, 1923). Not a narrative that one would read straight through, this study contains vast amounts of material arranged as follows: volume 1, the court and control of the stage; volume 2, the companies (boy companies, adult companies, international companies), actors, and public and private playhouses; volume 3, staging at court and in the theaters and plays and playwrights; volume 4, anonymous work (plays, masques, entertainments) and appendixes and indexes. Here one might find all the information, for example, on a particular actor or the facts about a particular play. Chambers's cutoff date is 1616.

Equally impressive and thorough is the continuation of Chambers by G. E. Bentley, *The Jacobean and Caroline Stage*, 7 vols. (Clarendon, 1941–1968). This work also provides a source of primary records and other materials pertinent to the stage, covering the period 1616–1642. The subjects are arranged as follows: volume 1, acting companies; volume 2, players; volumes 3–5, plays and playwrights; volume 6, private theaters, public theaters, and theaters at court; and volume 7, appendixes to volume 6 and a general index to volumes 1–7. Building on this research, Bentley has also written two books that pursue some theater topics in detail: *The Profession of Dramatist in Shakespeare's Time, 1590–1642* (Princeton UP, 1971) and *The Profession of Player in Shakespeare's Time, 1590–1642* (Princeton UP, 1984).

An important study on the development of theatrical production and related matters is Glynne Wickham's *Early English Stages: 1300 to 1660*, 4 vols. (Routledge & Kegan Paul; Columbia UP, 1959–1981). Concerned with theatrical history and matters of staging, Wickham devotes volume 1 principally to medieval stagecraft: the open-air entertainments (miracle plays, pageant theaters), indoor entertainments (morals, interludes), and medieval dramatic theory and practice. In volume 2, part 1, Wickham notes how medieval dramatic tradition carried on into the Renaissance; he also examines state control of drama. He emphasizes the emblematic tradition (nonrealistic) in the playhouses of the Renaissance. In volume 2, part 2, Wickham discusses the Privy Council order of 1597 for the destruction of London's playhouses and how actors circumvented it. Mainly he concentrates on the playhouses, the recognized theaters, some of the inns with a theatrical tradition, and stage conventions. More than most theater historians, Wickham emphasizes the role of festivals, pageants, and entertainments in the development of a dramatic tradition. Volume 2, part 2 (pp. 3–8), offers a good summary of where Wickham's argument stands. The 1981 volume explores drama and occasion, emblems of occasion, and English comedy and tragedy from their origins to 1576.

M. C. Bradbrook, in *The Rise of the Common Player: A Study of Actor and Society in Shakespeare's England* (Chatto & Windus, 1962), examines both social and dramatic history. Part 1 gives the social history of the public theaters and of the acting companies that played there. Part 2 focuses on typical individuals such as Richard Tarlton, the first great star of the English stage, and Edward Alleyn, the greatest tragic actor of his time. Bradbrook also discusses the household players and the rise and fall of choristers' theaters in London, 1574–1606. In the final part, the author illustrates the general dramatic sports of the age and the common life that gave rise to many occasions for dramatic entertainment. Bradbrook also considers performances at the universities. Thus the book traces the rise of actors from positions of insecurity and no social standing to places of considerable prominence.

Robert Weimann argues the importance of the popular dramatic tradition in *Shakespeare and the Popular Tradition in the Theater*, edited by Robert Schwartz (Johns Hopkins UP, 1978). He explores various traditions from medieval times to Shakespeare's own era and emphasizes the structure and function of the popular tradition rather than its influence. Only when we view Elizabethan society, theater, and language as interrelated does the structure of Shakespeare's dramatic art emerge as fully functional. Shakespeare's theater helped create the specific character and transitional nature of his society, informed by the power of popular dramatic traditions. The dramatic integration of varied social values and cultural elements makes the structure of the plays balanced and the poetic perspective of experience satisfying. Through many references to the plays, Weimann illustrates how Shakespeare appropriates attributes of the popular tradition. Certainly this theater history charts an unusual course in criticism by emphasizing the function of theater in society.

Andrew Gurr's *The Shakespearean Stage, 1574–1642*, 3d ed. (Cambridge UP, 1992; original, 1970) explores five topics: the companies, the players, the playhouses, staging, and audiences. His work derives from materials compiled by Chambers and Bentley, but the book is more than a redaction of their work. By providing this background, Gurr hopes to minimize our misunderstandings about the theater and related matters in the period 1574–1642—that is, from the first royal patent granted to a group of actors to the closing of the theaters by Parliament in 1642. We learn, for example, about the composition of the acting companies, how many there were, the nature of their repertory, the kinds of buildings they performed in, the economics of the theater, and techniques of staging. This well-documented book makes a contribution to scholarship, and students will find it especially valuable.

Understandably, a number of studies exist on the nature of the playhouse itself. One must remember that all these theories are largely conjectural because little hard evidence survives. One of the first studies that became widely accepted is John Cranford Adams, *The Globe Playhouse: Its Design and Equipment*, 2d ed. (Barnes & Noble, 1961; original, 1942). The book aims to reconstruct as fully as possible the design and equipment of the Globe. Such a study prepares the way for a fuller understanding of Shakespeare's plays. Adams's study follows two assumptions: that the requirements of Elizabethan plays reflect design and available equipment, and that all the evidence should be taken into account—pictorial, stage directions, and so on. Adams presents an extensive discussion about the location of the Globe and the playhouse frame, auditorium, platform stage, tiring-house, and superstructure. His approach has been challenged, especially the notion of the inner stage and the third-level upper stage, but most models of the Globe adhere to Adams's theory. Irwin Smith essentially follows Adams in *Shakespeare's Globe Playhouse* (Scribner's, 1956). He discusses the same topics as Adams does, but includes fifteen scale drawings of the reconstruction of the Globe.

C. Walter Hodges counters some of the earlier views of the theater in *The Globe Restored: A Study of the Elizabethan Theatre*, 2d ed. (Oxford UP, 1968; original, 1953). Hodges argues that we must recognize the uncertainties involved in attempting to reconstruct the Globe. He discusses the problems involved, such as the scaffold (platform stage) and the nature of the tiring-house. The Globe ought to be rebuilt only for the purpose of reestablishing, as the proscenium theater cannot, the intimate, vital relationship between actor and audience.

In a searching analysis of evidence of many kinds, John Orrell, in *The Quest for Shakespeare's Globe* (Cambridge UP, 1983), seeks to understand the physical dimensions of the Globe Theater. Examining pictorial evidence, Orrell applies mathematical formulas to determine the accuracy of drawings of London, such as the seventeenth-century ones by Visscher and Hollar. The theater that emerges from this study is a larger, less intimate house than once thought likely, capable of holding 3,000 spectators and requiring a wide range of abilities from its actors. Orrell moves from the evidence of the contract for building the Fortune Theater to its implications for the Globe. He wonders about the sound in the Globe and about the significance of its site placement. (Discoveries in the late 1980s offer a means of challenging the previously determined physical nature of the Globe and Rose Theaters.)

Other studies specifically examine the relationship of the stage to the actual production of Elizabethan plays. In *Shakespeare at the Globe, 1599–1609* (Macmillan, 1962), Bernard Beckerman analyzes staging demands at the Globe. Topics covered include repertory, dramaturgy (climax, finale, scene structure, dramatic unity), stage (parts, design), acting (influences on acting style), and staging (stage illustration). The book focuses only on plays produced at the Globe during the first decade of its existence. Beckerman argues against the conventional idea of the "inner stage" and finds little evidence to support it as a permanent feature of the tiring-house facade. He believes that the actual production of a play relied less on specific parts of the Globe stage than previously thought. The style in staging inhered in the dramatic form, not in the stage structure.

J. L. Styan, in *Shakespeare's Stagecraft* (Cambridge UP, 1967), explores the theater equipment (stage, staging and acting conventions), Shakespeare's visual craft (the actor and his movement, grouping on the open stage and full stage), and Shakespeare's aural craft (speaking the speech, orchestration of speech). Although Shakespeare's text gives the actor precise instructions about how to do certain things, it also allows for flexibility and some improvisation.

Examining Shakespeare's theatrical techniques, Jean E. Howard argues in *Shakespeare's Art of Orchestration: Stage Technique and Audience Response* (U of Illinois P, 1984) that Shakespeare carefully controls and shapes what an audience hears, sees, and experiences and that this verbal and visual orchestration becomes central to the effectiveness and meaning of the plays. Howard identifies a group of techniques by which Shakespeare implicitly prepared his plays for effective stage presentation: aural, visual, and kinetic effects. Evidence suggests that Shakespeare thought a good deal about potential response from audiences. Howard analyzes Shakespeare's management of verbal diversity, the technique of counterpoint, the note of silence, the orchestration of bodies, and the effect of orchestration on the play's theatrical structure and the audience's total experience. In the chapter on silence, for example, Howard explores the varying functions of silence, from denoting closure of an action to creating tension. Her examples range across a number of plays, including *Ham., Oth., Lr.,* and *Ant.* A full discussion of *TN* closes the book; this play illustrates the intimate relationship between Shakespeare's stage technique and meaning for the audience.

Concentrating on visual language in the plays, David Bevington, in *Action Is Eloquence: Shakespeare's Language of Gesture* (Harvard UP, 1984), examines Shakespeare's attitude toward stage gesture and image. He perceives a duality: the power of these gestures and the potentially misleading nature of this visual language. Bevington attempts to develop a contrastive vocabulary of visual signals in a number of plays; he explores costume and hand properties, gesture and expression, theatrical space, and the language of ceremony. A final chapter analyzes *Ham.* Costuming symbolizes an ordered world of hierarchical rank and also celebrates a festive world of release from constraints. Shakespeare's characters find something invaluably normative in the gestural language of emotion. The dramatist also uses the stage space to frame a world of illusion, escape, and rebellion against authority. Drawing on other critics, Bevington argues that universal role-playing in Elizabethan society provided the dramatists with a significant model for their portrayal of characters. Throughout this richly documented book, Bevington pursues his dialectic of seemingly fixed meaning and ambiguous transformation, as seen in the visual language of Shakespeare's theater.

More historically oriented, T. J. King's *Shakespearean Staging, 1599–1642* (Harvard UP, 1971) surveys the theatrical requirements for 276 plays first performed by professional actors in the period 1599–1642, providing a clear picture of how Shakespeare's contemporaries acted the plays. King seeks positive correlations between the external evidence (architecture and pictures of early English stages) and the internal evidence provided by the texts. He specifically evaluates stage requirements: entrances and large properties, above the stage, doors or hangings, below the stage. Appendix A offers a valuable review of major scholarship since 1940.

Harley Granville-Barker's influential *Prefaces to Shakespeare,* 2 vols. (Princeton UP, 1947), examines production problems and techniques for ten plays—three comedies and seven tragedies. In an introductory essay in the first volume, the author raises such matters as Shakespeare's stagecraft, the convention of place, the speaking of the verse, the boy-actress, the soliloquy, and costume. Granville-Barker focuses throughout on how a modern director or producer must solve the staging problems inherent in the text.

B. L. Joseph examines techniques of acting in *Elizabethan Acting,* 2d ed. (Oxford UP, 1964; original, 1951). This brief study covers what we know about acting in the period and Joseph's own inferences from available material. He discusses external action, speech habits, gestures, and development of character. Joseph argues that the actors could seem to be the very persons they represented in performance. The speaking suited both character and style. Appearance and movement served the same two purposes simultaneously: communicate naturally what is within the imaginary character, and become the creative instrument ideally suited to the needs of Elizabethan plays and audiences.

Alfred Harbage, in *Shakespeare's Audience* (Columbia UP, 1941), responds to another part of the theater experience. Harbage explores the available evidence that provides accurate information about the audiences. He discusses the likely size of the audiences at the theaters, the kind of people, and their behavior. He also evaluates the scholarship on this subject. In his view, the audience represented a cross section of the London population, predominantly a working-class audience. At times, Harbage paints a somewhat romantic portrait of the audience, but this is a valuable book for the information gathered about economics and society.

Ann Jennalie Cook responds to Harbage and others in *The Privileged Playgoers of Shakespeare's London, 1576–1642* (Princeton UP, 1981). She counters with a portrait of theater audiences as dominated by members of the privileged class because only they had sufficient money, time, and interest to frequent the theaters regularly. Thus, the playgoers, in Cook's view, came chiefly from the upper levels of the social order. Cook offers an impressive gathering of historical facts and social analysis to establish her case. She reminds us of the privileged society's involvement with drama through education and the system of patronage. Other evidence indicates how much the professional drama slanted its enterprise toward an affluent, educated, leisured clientele. This book offers a necessary corrective to the view of theater audiences as a democratic cross section of the population. Whether privileged playgoers dominated the audience, as Cook claims, remains problematic.

Negotiating between Harbage and Cook, Andrew Gurr, in *Playgoing in Shakespeare's London* (Cambridge UP, 1987), explores historical changes in theatergoing over a seventy-five-year period, beginning in 1567. Evidence about audiences comes from several sources: the physical circumstances of performance in theater buildings, demographics, contemporary comment, and the collective expectations revealed in the plays themselves. Gurr examines each of these in separate chapters. The price of admission offers the strongest material basis for assuming a diverse social composition of the audience. Gurr argues that all social classes attended the theater. Appendix 1 provides an alphabetical listing of all persons for whom we have evidence of their theatergoing; appendix 2 arranges by date and source all contemporary references to playgoing.

In *Shakespeare the Actor and the Purposes of Playing* (U of Chicago P, 1993), Meredith Anne Skura analyzes Shakespeare's texts in the context of performance conditions and the Elizabethan actor's subculture. This book provides not only a reading of the plays but also a reading of the man who wrote them. Skura explores what it might have meant to be an actor in the sixteenth and seventeenth centuries and then moves to the question of how Shakespeare's acting might have shaped his texts. Chapter 3 focuses on *R3* as a way of understanding what it meant to Shakespeare to be a player. The fictive player can be illuminated when read against his life, actors, and Elizabethan theater. Players within plays depend on aristocratic hospitality, as in the "great-house" plays (*Shr., LLL, MND,* and *Ham.*). *Shr.* tells the story of a beggar who has histrionic greatness thrust upon him; in *MND,* Shakespeare creates his most affectionate portrait of the player. Skura examines Falstaff as a self-conscious player and Hamlet as an actor who becomes emotionally involved with his audience. *Tim.* is the last of the great-house plays, complete with its own inner play; but Timon's theater is a false feast. This suggests the actor's ambivalent relation to the audience. In the Sonnets, Shakespeare recreates the actor's stance before an audience as vacillation between grandiose claims and self-abasement.

Although few texts survive, evidence indicates that throughout the middle years of the sixteenth century, the city of London was full of players, presumably performing plays. William Ingram, in *The Business of Playing: The Beginnings of Adult Professional Theater in Elizabethan London* (Cornell UP, 1992), approaches the subject from the point of view of the participants themselves. He therefore has much to say about the lives of John Brayne, James Burbage, Jerome Savage, and others who were instrumental in building the first theaters. Ingram concludes that the future lay with players who had aggressive instincts, performing entrepreneurs who sold their vision of active drama to patrons and investors. After a discussion of the Red Lion, which functioned as a theater as early as 1567, Ingram examines in turn the three theaters built in 1576: the one at Newington Butts, the Theater, and the Curtain. These new theaters brought about a new kind of legitimacy, principally social and economic.

In a book that foregrounds calamities, *Politics, Plague, and Shakespeare's Theater: The Stuart Years* (Cornell UP, 1991), Leeds Barroll examines when and under what circumstances Shakespeare was able to follow his profession in the final years of his career, 1603–1611. Barroll notes that Shakespeare's career was fraught with unexpected difficulties, especially the plague. He argues that Shakespeare stopped writing plays when he knew that they would not immediately be put on stage (in performance or in rehearsal) and that he produced plays at great speed. The major narrative of this book reconsiders the order and tempo of Shakespeare's production between 1603 and 1611, during which time Shakespeare produced only ten plays. Barroll diminishes the value of the royal patent of 1603 that put acting companies under royal patronage; such action had little effect on the basic situation of the common players. Because of the plague, for example in 1603, the court offered the only environment accessible to Shakespeare and his fellow actors. Finding an erratic and uneven rate of production, Barroll argues that *Ant., Lr.,* and *Mac.* may all have appeared in 1606–1607. In any event, Barroll finds a direct correspondence between the rate of composition and the opportunities for playing.

Other books bring the matter of stage history up to more recent times. A standard source is George C. D. Odell's *Shakespeare from Betterton to Irving,* 2 vols. (1920; reprint, Benjamin Blom, 1963), which treats two and a half centuries of staging practices, from 1660 to the beginning of the twentieth century. Volume 1 proceeds through Garrick (1742–1776). This study includes a history of the theaters but emphasizes stage presentation. Arthur Colby Sprague, in *Shakespeare and the Actors: The Stage Business in His Plays (1660–1905)* (Harvard UP, 1945), examines stage history arranged as follows: comedies; histories; *Ham., Oth.,* and *Mac.;* and the other tragedies.

J. C. Trewin, in *Shakespeare on the English Stage, 1900–1964* (Barrie & Rockliff, 1964), presents a selective survey of Shakespearean productions in the British theater since 1900. Trewin outlines theories and experiments, changes and chances. The appendixes list all Shakespearean productions for West End, 1900–1964; Old Vic, 1914–1964; and Stratford, 1879–1964. The book contains a generous selection of photographs of productions and actors.

What is the appropriate setting for Shakespeare's plays? This fundamental question for scene designers occupies Dennis Kennedy in *Looking at Shakespeare: A Visual History of Twentieth-Century Performance* (Cambridge UP, 1993). This book focuses on the relationship between scenography and international performances of Shakespeare in the modern and postmodern eras. It covers Europe and the United States, investigating how the visual relates to Shakespeare on the stage and attempting to understand the complex cultural uses of Shakespeare in this century. Kennedy establishes a clear relationship between what a production looks like and what its spectators accept as its statement and value. The book has 172 illustrations and traces dozens of productions, noting important historical changes, such as the establishment in the 1920s of the theater in Birmingham under the guidance of Barry Jackson and the Cambridge Festival Theater under the direction of Terence Gray. Kennedy suggests that the creation of the Shakespeare Festival in Stratford, Ontario, under Tyrone Guthrie in the 1950s produced the most important development in Shakespeare scenography, partly because of its open stage. Kennedy explores the contributions of such directors as Orson Welles, Peter Hall, Granville-Barker, and Peter Brook.

FILM AND TELEVISION

Twentieth-century productions of Shakespeare in films and on television have made major contributions. Millions of people now have the opportunity to see performances without ever going to a theater. *Shakespeare Survey* 39 (1987) concentrates on Shakespeare in film and on television. In *Shakespeare and the Film* (J. M. Dent, 1971; rev. ed., A. S. Barnes, 1979), Roger Manvell describes and discusses the principal sound films that have been adapted from Shakespeare's plays and comments on the modification of the plays to make them effective films. Separate chapters examine Laurence Olivier, Orson Welles, Russian adaptations, adaptations of *JC,* Italians and Shakespeare, and theater into film. The book includes many illustrations. Although revised and updated for the 1979 paperback edition, Manvell's book does not discuss any film appearing after 1971.

In an opening chapter of *Shakespeare on Film* (Indiana UP, 1977), Jack J. Jorgens explores the problems that beset any filmmaker trying to move from the text to the screen. The filmmaker must balance "horizontal" movements (good plots, developing characters) with powerful "vertical" moments (resonant images, penetrating meditations, complex poetic patterns). Camera angles, choice of music, use of sound effects, visual spectacle, and how the verse should be spoken are all matters that the filmmaker must resolve. The remainder of Jorgens's book examines some major Shakespeare films; for example, one can gain an assessment of the success and limitations of Franco Zeffirelli's *Rom.,* the most commercially successful Shakespeare film. Peter Hall, Laurence Olivier, Orson

Welles, Roman Polanski, and Grigori Kozintsev are among the prominent filmmakers whose work Jorgens analyzes.

The essence of cinematic expression derives from the moving image, in contrast to the stage's emphasis on the projection of the spoken word. So argues Anthony Davies in *Filming Shakespeare's Plays* (Cambridge UP, 1988). Davies concentrates on three Olivier films, three by Welles, Peter Brook's *Lr.*, and Kurosawa's *Throne of Blood*. Olivier's *H5* offers a cinematic treatise on the difference between cinema and theater as media for the expression of drama. Its spatial fabric engages both an emotional identification and an intellectual alertness without an ostentatious intrusion of style. The spatial strategy of Olivier's *Ham.* is more organically integrated and more subtly eloquent than the versatility of spatial resources in his *H5*. His *R3* invites our complicity in Richard's voyeurism. Welles's *Mac.* becomes a turning point in the development of Shakespearean cinematic adaptation; it communicates its thematic substance primarily through spatial strategy. Davies sees Brook's *Lr.* as a drastic innovation; it broke cinematic tradition by rebelling against romanticism. The film makes Shakespeare's play a revelation of the grotesque. Kurosawa's spatial strategy corresponds closely to Welles's. Students should also consult the collection of essays, *Shakespeare and the Moving Image: The Plays on Film and Television* (Cambridge UP, 1994), edited by Davies and Stanley Wells.

Taking a different approach to Shakespeare films, John Collick, in *Shakespeare, Cinema and Society* (Manchester UP, 1989), works on the assumption that a film is the sum of a number of discourses culled from various areas of production. Therefore, we should locate the film within the economic and political structures of a society. Collick ranges from British silent films to Kozintsev and Kurosawa. He notes, for example, that the BBC television productions of the plays bear striking resemblance to the British silent films in terms of aim, form, and content. Throughout, Collick examines the artist's relationship to the state and how the resulting films are culturally bound. The 1935 *MND*, for example, produced by Warner Brothers and directed by Max Reinhardt, is not so much the reproduction of a text as a specific point in cultural production where varied concepts and methodologies converge.

Peter S. Donaldson, in *Shakespearean Films/Shakespearean Directors* (Unwin Hyman, 1990), brings together film theory, psychoanalysis, and biographical materials to examine films of Olivier, Welles, Kurosawa, and Zeffirelli, as well as Liz White's *Oth.* and Jean-Luc Godard's *Lr.* Donaldson provides a close and detailed reading of seven films. He sees Olivier's *Ham.* as a tragedy of narcissistic self-enclosure and Zeffirelli's *Rom.* as antipatriarchal and homoerotic. Godard's film, only partly based on Shakespeare's play, embraces fatherhood as a metaphor for the relation between authors and texts, artists and disciples, cultural traditions and their influence. The all-black milieu of White's *Oth.* transforms the treatment of race in a film never commercially released.

Lorne M. Buchman focuses on cinematic technique in *Still in Movement: Shakespeare on Screen* (Oxford UP, 1991). He explores how films organize the material of Shakespeare's plays in order to activate a particular imaginative response. Buchman pays particular attention to Kozintsev and Welles but also looks at Brook, Olivier, and Polanski, with a primary focus on cinematic space. Welles's *Oth.* illustrates how the director creates temporality through cinematic technique. Buchman insists that films make an important contribution to the critical histories of the plays.

Samuel Crowl, in *Shakespeare Observed: Studies in Performance on Stage and Screen* (Ohio UP, 1992), examines films by Polanski, Welles, Peter Hall, and Kenneth Branagh, as well as theater productions by Adrian Noble, Hall, Branagh, and Michael Bogdanov. Basically, Crowl argues for the natural resonance that exists between performance criticism and the central issues raised by postmodern literary criticism. He notes, for example, Polanski's use of Jan Kott's criticism in the film *Mac.* Here we find a fruitful dialogue with modern Shakespearean criticism, with an emphasis on the instability of power. Welles's *Chimes at Midnight* participates in the ongoing critical debate about Falstaff; Welles's *Oth.* anticipates the convoluted turns of postmodern literary theory. Hall's *MND* is the finest realization of a Shakespearean comedy on film. Branagh's *H5* likewise illustrates an intertextual dialogue among stage, film, and criticism.

H. R. Coursen's *Shakespearean Performance as Interpretation* (U of Delaware P, 1992) concentrates on film and television productions, although he also discusses some stage performances. He takes into account three variables that are crucial to performance as interpretation: space, script, and the subjectivity of the individual spectator. Coursen analyzes, for example, the three television versions of *Lr.* for their treatment of Edmund and of the Lear-Cordelia story. He suggests that the BBC television production of *Ham.* provides the best version of the play outside the theater itself. The book closes with a chapter on *Tmp.* and television.

FEMINISM AND GENDER STUDIES

In 1980, an important collection of essays in feminist criticism appeared, entitled *The Woman's Part: Feminist Criticism of Shakespeare,* edited by Carolyn Ruth Swift Lenz, Gayle Greene, and Carol Thomas Neely (U of Illinois P, 1980). Seventeen essays by different critics examine a wide range of topics and plays. The introduction by the editors offers a fine summary of where feminist criticism was by the beginning of the 1980s. The editors suggest that the authors of these essays liberate Shakespeare's women from the stereotypes to which they have too often been confined; they examine women's relations to each other, analyze the nature and effects of patriarchal structure, and explore the influence of genre on the portrayal of women. These valuable essays conclude with a bibliography on "Women and Men in Shakespeare." Students should also consult *Women's Studies* 9:1 (1981) and 9:2 (1982); both of these special issues have as their topic feminist criticism of Shakespeare and include an assessment and categorization of that subject.

Philip C. Kolin, in *Shakespeare and Feminist Criticism: An Annotated Bibliography and Commentary* (Garland, 1991), first evaluates the contribution of feminist criticism and then presents an extensive annotated bibliography, arranged alphabetically by author and year of publication. Kolin's starting point is Dusinberre's 1975 book; he ends with contributions for 1988. Helpful indexes assist in tracking down discussions of particular plays or subjects.

Believing the drama from 1590 to 1625 to be essentially feminist in sympathy, Juliet Dusinberre, in *Shakespeare and the Na-*

ture of Women (Macmillan, 1975), argues for the powerful influence of Puritanism in shaping new ideas about the position of women in society. Dusinberre sees this influence throughout the drama. She therefore asserts that Shakespeare's feminism lies in his skepticism about the nature of women; that is, Shakespeare questions accepted ideas about women. Dusinberre explores such major topics as chastity, equality, and femininity and masculinity, with some examination of the authority of women and their education. Dusinberre does not focus on individual plays but connects appropriate parts of plays with the ideas being analyzed. She argues that the Elizabethan and Jacobean periods bred the conditions of a feminist movement, sparked by the breakdown of old ideas in religion and politics and the spirit of independence fostered by the Puritans. This important book helps define a number of issues confronted by other feminist critics.

Lisa Jardine, in *Still Harping on Daughters: Women and Drama in the Age of Shakespeare* (Harvester, 1983), sets out to counter an emerging orthodoxy in feminist studies. Specifically, she takes aim at Dusinberre's optimistic assessment of women's situation in the Shakespearean era. To some extent, this book, like Dusinberre's a historical study, tries to sketch the actual position of women, with some attention to the fictional women in drama and elsewhere. Jardine argues that the steady interest in women in drama does not reflect newly improved social conditions and greater possibilities for women; rather, it reveals patriarchy's unexpressed worry about the great social changes that were occurring in this period. In one chapter in particular, Jardine analyzes the presumed liberating possibilities for women: Protestantism, humanist education, and marital partnership. She finds a bleaker picture than did Dusinberre, believing that little change had actually occurred in attitudes about women. Jardine's study helps make clear the difficulties of learning precisely what position women occupied in Renaissance society.

In her *Women in Shakespeare* (Harrap, 1980), Judith Cook surveys most of Shakespeare's female characters, with some emphasis on how actresses have portrayed them on the stage. Similarly, Angela Pitt, in *Shakespeare's Women* (David & Charles, 1981), ranges through the canon, commenting on the female characters. Neither book has an all-encompassing thesis, but both have excellent illustrations. Pitt has a final chapter on Shakespeare's women on stage.

In her study of the plight of women in a patriarchal society, Irene G. Dash, in *Wooing, Wedding, and Power: Women in Shakespeare's Plays* (Columbia UP, 1981), focuses on *LLL* and *Shr.* (courtship); *Rom., Oth.,* and *WT* (sexuality); and the *H6–R3* tetralogy and *Ant.* (power). Dash observes, for example, that *Shr.* questions accepted premises and offers a remarkably mature affirmation of the potential for understanding between a man and a woman. Dash's study obliges critics to abandon some stereotypical notions about the position of women in the plays, thereby opening the plays to a fresh examination and showing the multifaceted portraits of women.

Concerned with the process of maturation, social integration, self-knowledge, and various rites of passage, Marjorie Garber, in *Coming of Age in Shakespeare* (Methuen, 1981), ranges across Shakespeare's canon, exploring the characters' processes of achieving maturity. Garber moves from the experience of childhood to matters of death and dying. In between, she explores other rites of passage, such as sexual development, language acquisition, and marriage. Shakespeare reminds us, Garber argues, that the players are merely men and women like ourselves, with similar stresses in development and maturation.

Marilyn French's *Shakespeare's Division of Experience* (Summit, 1981), a feminist approach to the plays, spans the entire canon. According to French, two gender principles govern all experience and literature: masculine and feminine. The extreme of the masculine side is the ability to kill; that of the feminine side, the ability to give birth. The masculine principle pursues power in the world and is associated with prowess and ownership, physical courage, authority, and legitimacy. By contrast, the feminine principle embraces the acceptance of simple continuities and identifies itself with nature.

French argues that Shakespeare's comedies are feminine (circular structure) and the tragedies, masculine (linear structure). Shakespeare's history plays are primarily masculine because they focus on power in the world. In the last plays, the feminine principle seems to triumph. Analyzing the plays, French explores such issues as power, marriage, money, emotion, and chaste constancy in the comedies and early histories. For example, French suggests that *Shr.* concludes with a harmonious synthesis of unabused masculine and inlaw feminine principles; but it also celebrates the outlaw aspect, defiance and rebellion. In *Lr.*, French finds Edmund, Goneril, and Regan to be "masculine" and argues that Lear himself moves from masculinity to femininity. *Ant.*, unique in the canon, presents in a positive way the outlaw feminine principle embodied in a powerful female. The Romances reassert the feminine principle; in these last plays, powerful males learn by suffering the limits of worldly power.

Locating feminism in the critic rather than in the author or his work, Linda Bamber, in *Comic Women, Tragic Men: A Study of Gender and Genre in Shakespeare* (Stanford UP, 1982), concentrates on the connection between gender and Shakespeare's different genres. She examines in detail *Ant., Ham., Mac., Cor.,* several comedies and histories, and *Tmp.* Bamber designates the feminine principle as "Other"; therefore, according to her, Shakespeare portrays the Self in tragedy and the Other in comedy—hence tragic men and comic women. In every genre, the possibilities of the masculine Self and the nature of the feminine serve as functions of one another. Whether or not consistently a feminist, Shakespeare as author responds to the centrality of the feminine in his work. One dimension of Cleopatra's character, for example, views her as the Other against Antony's representation of the Self. In contrast, *Mac.* and *Cor.* offer no clear example of Other, because the principal female characters are not Other to the heroes. In Shakespeare's comedies—and only in his comedies—we see the feminine Other face to face; therefore, our response to the comic heroine is direct and unmediated by her father, lover, or husband. The confidence that permeates the world of the comedies derives from genre and grows out of the avoidance of a choice between serious meaning and frivolousness. Bamber traces an evolutionary development of women in the histories from second-class citizens in the world of men toward a separate identity in a movement toward tragedy. Bamber sees *Tmp.* as postsexual: Prospero is not only bereft of the Other; he is also free of the Other. He renounces sexuality and takes control of everything.

Focusing on selected plays that span Shakespeare's canon,

Marianne Novy, in *Love's Argument: Gender Relations in Shakespeare* (U of North Carolina P, 1984), examines the conflicts between mutuality and patriarchy and between emotion and control. Both conflicts involve the politics of gender. In the comedies and Romances, Shakespeare creates images of gender relations that keep elements of both patriarchy and mutuality in suspension; the Romances in particular portray female resilience. Comedies, such as *Ado, AYL,* and *TN,* illustrate the mutual dependence in male-female relationships, a dependence reinforced by imagery, structure, and characterization. In these comedies, Novy argues, women's gestures of submission often balance similar gestures from the men. She explores the theme of patriarchy and play in *Shr.,* observing that Kate's behavior is a dramatically heightened version of the kind of compromise that keeps a society going.

Women in the tragedies occupy a problematic position because often confined to serving as audience to the heroes—*Ant.* being an exception. Men in the tragedies often have to define their masculinity by violence. *Rom.* and *Tro.* show women set in a society that deems them weak. In *Oth.,* the combination of patriarchy and mutuality breaks down and cannot be restored. In loving Desdemona, Othello ventures outside the man's world of war and thus becomes vulnerable. *Lr.,* Novy suggests, implies criticism of the prerogatives of the father and explores some behavior that patriarchy fosters. In contrast to the tragedies, the Romances illustrate the inadequacy of the traditional masculine stereotype. The power of generation informs all the Romances, and the men uncharacteristically respond to this force of procreation. In a final chapter, Novy examines how Shakespeare's use of gender and cross-gender imagery changes significantly from the comedies through the tragedies to the Romances.

Using psychoanalytic theory, Coppélia Kahn, in *Man's Estate: Masculine Identity in Shakespeare* (U of California P, 1981), sets out to define the dilemmas of masculine selfhood as seen in two major problems: men's relationship to women, and the problem of patriarchy, which paradoxically gives men power over women and thus makes them vulnerable to women. Kahn proceeds chronologically, not through the Shakespeare canon but through the ages of man from adolescence to fatherhood.

Thus she ranges from *Ven.* through the history plays, to problems of marriage in *Rom.* and *Shr.*, to psychosocial meanings of
cuckoldry in *Ham.*, through incomplete men such as Macbeth
and Coriolanus, and finally to the masculine quest for selfhood
in the context of the family and the life cycle, epitomized in
WT. Shakespeare, Kahn argues, questions matters of sexual
identity, not providing neat answers but rather documenting
and illustrating the struggle. Kahn's illuminating analysis underscores the importance of the artist's definition of masculinity.

By examining in detail *AYL, H5, Ham., Oth., Lr., Ant.,* and
WT, Peter Erickson's *Patriarchal Structures in Shakespeare's
Drama* (U of California P, 1985) documents the pervasive social and political structure of patriarchy and its implications for
the position of women. Erickson observes that male characters
in the early plays powerfully resist women; a gradual shift toward a possible accommodation with women eventually occurs, accompanied by struggle and anguish. This shift results in
part from the need to marry and establish families. The *Ham.-
Oth.-Lr.* sequence is crucial for demonstrating the lessening of
male bonding and a corresponding increase in attention to the
male hero's bond with women. In *Ant.*, boundaries blur, and
WT enacts the disruption and revival of patriarchy. This valuable book offers the fullest treatment of the dominant social
structure in the fictional and real worlds of Shakespeare.

Carol Thomas Neely, in *Broken Nuptials in Shakespeare's Plays*
(Yale UP, 1985), explores in detail how marriage, achieved or
broken, influences the themes and structures of the plays, particularly *Ado, AWW, Oth., Ant.,* and *WT.* Taken together,
these plays encompass the whole process of wooing, wedding,
and repenting; they also embody the conflicts attendant on
marriage by the incorporation of broken nuptials. Neely briefly
sketches marital patterns and customs in the Renaissance and
fully explores the intricately interwoven contexts that define
the meaning of women's actions in the plays. Throughout the
comedies, broken nuptials counterpoint the festive wedding
ceremonies. Neely shows how *Ado* extends earlier uses of the
broken-nuptial motif and anticipates its darker configurations
in the problem comedies and tragedies. Neely notes, for example, that male power in *Ado* remains tame and diffused. In the

problem plays, women fulfill a different function: they temper
the skepticism and cynicism of the plays. Sexuality in these
plays, for example *AWW,* frequently dissociates itself from
marriage and procreation, as manifested in seduction, prostitu-
tion, aggressive lust, promiscuity, and adultery. The conclusion of *AWW* shows marriage not as a happy ending but as an
open-ended beginning. *Oth.* illustrates the idealization and
degradation of sexuality, the disintegration of male authority
and loss of female power, and the association of sexual consummation with death. Neely discusses the interaction between
gender and genre in *Ant.,* with its generic boundaries expanded. In *Ant.,* marriage loses its comic purpose of rejuvena-
tion and its tragic status as a catalyst to self-knowledge and self-
destruction. Neely analyzes the problem of incest and issue
throughout the Romances, focusing on *WT.* She sees birth as
the central miracle of *WT,* a birth that leads to a restoration
achieved by the rich presence and compelling actions of
women.

In *Shakespeare's Restorations of the Father* (Rutgers UP, 1983),
David Sundelson explores the nature and consequences of patriarchy in certain plays that present the central Shakespearean
pattern: not just the fall of fathers, but also their restoration;
not only death and absence, but also revival and return. Sundelson also seeks to determine what makes the father's restoration so necessary. He concentrates on history plays (*R2–H4*),
MV, MM, and *Tmp.* Appearance, disappearance, reappear-
ance: this rhythm recurs throughout Shakespeare's work con-
cerning fathers. Closeness without kinship and familiarity but
not family pervade *H5.* Whereas history is for Shakespeare an
almost exclusively male affair, the comedies focus on women
and the exploration of their nature. But in *MV,* fathers may be
absent or feeble, defeated by law or by circumstance, or simply
dead; still, their power is difficult to escape. Ferdinand will
marry Miranda in *Tmp.;* but the central attachment, Sundelson
argues, remains between father and daughter.

Sarup Singh, in *Family Relationships in Shakespeare and the Restoration Comedy of Manners* (Oxford UP, 1983), offers a general
portrait of actual family structures as well as fictional ones, examining, for example, the changing patriarchal structure in the
Renaissance. One distinguishing feature of Shakespeare's plays,

Singh observes, is the open rebellion of daughters against fathers, fathers who are not willing to tolerate disobedience. Prospero's relationship with Miranda is exceptional. Generally, Shakespeare recognizes the urges of youth and the traditional role of old age, even as he reflects the inherent tensions in a patriarchal society. Examining Shakespeare's comedies, Singh concludes that Shakespeare endeavored to reconcile love and marriage. This book further explores how later seventeenth-century drama corresponds to or differs from Shakespeare's treatment of family relationships.

Diane Elizabeth Dreher, in *Domination and Defiance: Fathers and Daughters in Shakespeare* (UP of Kentucky, 1986), explores the complex relationship between fathers and daughters in Shakespeare in terms of psychological tensions and the changing concepts of marriage and family during the dramatist's time. One chapter examines the historical background of family relationships in the Renaissance. Dreher also discusses the psychological perspective of these familial bonds. Essentially, Dreher argues that the conflicting tensions in Shakespeare's father-daughter relationships resolve in comedy, explode in tragedy, and transform in romance. For examples of dominated daughters, Dreher turns to Ophelia, Hero, and Desdemona. Some daughters resist and defy their fathers, such as Hermia, Imogen, Jessica, and Cordelia, leaving behind traditional filial obedience. The plays uphold intelligence and assertiveness as admirable qualities in women, and Dreher examines such qualities in a chapter on androgynous daughters—Portia, Viola, and Rosalind, for example. Shakespeare's final plays emphasize the fathers' need for balance and integration, and the daughters serve a symbolic function in helping to bring about desired harmony.

In *The Matter of Difference: Materialist Feminist Criticism of Shakespeare* (Cornell UP, 1991), editor Valerie Wayne brings together essays that explore the possibilities for materialist feminism's engagement with history and literature. In part, these essays arose out of conflict with new historicists; therefore, the essays criticize new historicism for its apolitical effects. But the essays also criticize feminism for its tendency to idealize women. With twelve different contributors, this collection covers Shakespearean comedy and tragedy and English culture.

It closes with Catherine Belsey's assessment of materialist feminist criticism.

Karen Newman, in *Fashioning Femininity and English Renaissance Drama* (U of Chicago P, 1991), examines *Shr., Oth.,* and *H5* and analyzes other non-Shakespearean plays. She answers such questions as: how was femininity fashioned and deployed in early modern England? What is the relationship of gender to power and the state? She assumes that gender was a significant way of figuring social relations in the period. The Induction in *Shr.,* Newman argues, subverts relations of power and gender by the metatheatrical foregrounding of such roles and relations as culturally constructed. Kate's threat to male authority derives from her language, which serves as an index of identity. Her final speech displays the fundamental contradiction between women as sexually desirable silent objects and women of words who may disrupt their place. In *Oth.,* both Desdemona and Othello deviate from the norms of the sex-race system. The play identifies femininity with the monstrous, an identification that makes miscegenation doubly fearful. Henry systematically denies his French queen's difference and fashions her into an English wife in *H5*. The play reinforces gender hierarchies. Newman also discusses the historical significance of marriage, witchcraft, and sartorial extravagance.

The struggle for male identity permeates Janet Adelman's *Suffocating Mothers: Fantasies of Maternal Origin in Shakespeare's Plays, "Hamlet" to "The Tempest"* (Routledge, 1991). Adelman argues that masculine selfhood embedded in maternal origin is the stuff of tragedy. The mother occluded in early plays returns with a vengeance in *Ham.,* and the plays from *Ham.* on all follow her return. Female sexuality, largely absent in the comedies, invades *Ham.* in Gertrude and utterly contaminates sexual relationships; this decay has its point of origin in Hamlet's mother's body. For Hamlet, assuming masculine identity means taking on the qualities of the father's name by killing off a false father. Hamlet's main psychological task becomes to remake his mother. In *Tro.,* Troilus inherits the world of broken marriage, in which his desire for Cressida must find a place. The transfer of blame from male to female that is just below the surface in *Ham.* becomes the surface in *Tro.* But in *Oth.,* the source of corruption resides not in the unstable female body but in the diseased male imagination. Desdemona's apparent betrayal enables Othello's return in fantasy to the male identity he had lost by succumbing to her maternal identity; his death enacts this resumption of his masculinity. Through separation and recombination, *AWW* and *MM* consider both the recoil from sexual union and the desperate remedies that might make marriage possible again.

According to Adelman, Lear appears simultaneously as the father who abdicates and the son who must suffer the consequences; this gives rise to infantile fantasies. His confrontation leads him back to the mother who was ostensibly occluded by the play. Much of the play's power comes from its confrontation with the landscape of maternal deprivation. The Lear plot scrutinizes and criticizes the scapegoating logic of the Gloucester plot, which makes only the female the agent of darkness. In her death, Cordelia pays the price for acquiring the power of the displaced and occluded mother. The threat of maternal power in *Mac.* and the crisis it presents for individual manhood emerge in response to paternal absence. The play becomes a representation of primitive fears about male identity, about those looming female presences who threaten to control one's actions and mind. *Ant.* reveals Shakespeare's most strenuous attempt to redefine the relationship of masculinity to the maternal and hence redefine tragic masculinity itself. The Romances present Shakespeare's final attempt to reinstate the ideal parental couple lost at the beginning of *Ham.* In the plays of paternal recovery, the mother must be demonized and banished before the father's authority can be restored. But what Shakespeare broke asunder in *Ham.* cannot be fully joined, even in the last plays.

Jeanne Addison Roberts, in *The Shakespearean Wild: Geography, Genus, and Gender* (U of Nebraska P, 1991), argues that Shakespeare's plays mark an attempt to combine the male cultural center with the wilds of female, animal, and barbarian. The frontiers of culture impinge on the female wild (often associated with the malign and benign forces of the green world); the animal wild; and the barbarian wild, populated by marginal figures such as the Moor and the Jew. The plays reveal projections of suppressed fears and fantasies that haunt the cultural constructs of the male psyche. Roberts first examines natural landscapes, such as those in *Tit.*, which associate the female with the forest. *AYL* demystifies the forest wild. The boundaries between humans and animals sometimes collapse, as in *Lr.* Chapter 3 analyzes the problems that males encounter in confronting the female wild in *Err., Ado,* and *TNK*. Fragmentation of the female engenders both reluctance and delay in the male need for a spouse and precipitates violence in the cultural community, as in *Ado*. In several plays, Shakespeare invents older female figures, such as Paulina in *WT,* who transforms the tale from tragedy to romance.

POSTSTRUCTURALISM AND NEW HISTORICISM

Two movements in criticism have had an increasing impact on Shakespeare studies: poststructuralism and new historicism (both discussed in chapter 1, the first under Analyses of Language and Imagery and the second under Historical Criticism). A collection of essays that brings together discussions of several plays from new and different critical perspectives is *Shakespeare and the Question of Theory,* edited by Patricia Parker and Geoffrey Hartman (Methuen, 1985). The three principal critical areas are language (including deconstruction), feminism, and new historicism (with a dash of psychology). The editors also add several essays on *Ham.* They seek to raise for debate a whole range of central issues that reflect current critical thinking. The British equivalent of the Parker-Hartman volume is *Alternative Shakespeares* (Methuen, 1985), edited by John Drakakis. This collection of essays seeks to accelerate the break with established canons of Shakespearean criticism; it offers a variety of essays on deconstruction, new historicism, Marxism, feminism, cultural materialism, and psychoanalytic criticism. *Shakespeare and Deconstruction,* edited by David M. Bergeron and G. Douglas Atkins (Peter Lang, 1988), examines this mode of criticism, ranging across the canon. Joel Fineman's book on the Sonnets, reviewed earlier in this chapter, is another example of poststructuralist criticism.

Norman Rabkin, in *Shakespeare and the Problem of Meaning* (U of Chicago P, 1981), explores from a poststructuralist perspective the question of meaning. Rabkin argues that much criticism seems unsatisfactory because it seeks univocal and unequivocal meaning in Shakespeare and ignores the welter of often contradictory responses. Instead, Rabkin suggests, the critic should seek divergent and multivalent responses. According to Rabkin, meaning depends on complementarity—a paradox in which "radically opposed and equally total commitments to the meaning of life coexist in a single harmonious vision" (113). Meaning encompasses both the paradigm that invites us to reduce our experience and the elements that undercut the paradigm. *MV,* for example, asks us to establish a thematic center but simultaneously undermines that center.

Although unequivocal readings deny divergent responses, they can help us understand the complexities of Shakespeare's drama by calling attention to what the critics have left out. Reductive readings of *H5* distort the play's meaning and ignore Shakespeare's recognition of the irreducible complexity of things. *H5* suggests radically opposed, contradictory responses to a historical figure about whom we expect the simplest of views. Similarly, Rabkin examines several eighteenth-century imitations and adaptations of Shakespeare's tragedies and argues that such versions, which can be seen as critical interpretations of Shakespeare's drama, attempt to offer a single meaning. Finally, Rabkin argues that the Romances exhibit a different problem of meaning. Unlike the other plays, they do not tempt us to choose between contradictory responses but rather to accept an overlay of paradoxically contradictory patterns.

Stephen Greenblatt's several essays and his book *Renaissance Self-Fashioning: From More to Shakespeare* (U of Chicago P, 1980) have had major influences on many new historical studies. Although it does not focus exclusively on Shakespeare, this book examines the poetics of culture and sees in Shakespeare the historical pressure of an unresolved and continuing conflict. Greenblatt finds in Shakespeare a condition of subversive submission toward the state. In his *Shakespearean Negotiations: The Circulation of Social Energy in Renaissance England* (U of California P, 1988), Greenblatt examines in four essays the theatrical appropriation of sixteenth-century social practices. He concentrates on *H4, Lr., TN,* and *Tmp.* Issues of gender and sexuality, for example, govern the approach to *TN,* a play that underscores the mobility of desire.

Jonathan Goldberg also explores the relationship of artists to the state in *James I and the Politics of Literature: Jonson, Shakespeare, Donne, and Their Contemporaries* (Johns Hopkins UP, 1983). He argues that language and politics are mutually constitutive, that society shapes and is shaped by the possibilities in its language and discursive practices. Goldberg studies the relationships between authority and its representations in the Jacobean period. For Goldberg, the theater becomes the place where the royal style can be most fully displayed. He focuses on Shakespeare primarily in *MM*. In the Duke, Shakespeare represents his powers as playwright as coincident with the powers of the sovereign, the clearest emblem for the relationship between literature and politics in the Jacobean period. A most helpful analysis of the movement in new historicism is Jean Howard's essay "The New Historicism in Renaissance Studies," *English Literary Renaissance* 16 (1986): 13–43.

In *Radical Tragedy: Religion, Ideology and Power in the Drama of Shakespeare and His Contemporaries*, 2d ed. (Duke UP, 1993; original, U of Chicago P, 1984), Jonathan Dollimore explores the connections between Jacobean tragedy and its social context. Seeking to undermine religious and political orthodoxy, the Jacobean theater submitted institutions and all means of ideological legitimation to skeptical, interrogative, and subversive representations. The theater employs subliteral encoding— namely, parody, dislocation, and structural disjunction—to bypass censorship. Dollimore focuses on a number of non-Shakespearean tragedies in addition to *Tro.*, *Lr.*, *Ant.*, and *Cor.* He discusses political, social, and ideological contradictions in *Tro.*, a play that offers a prototype of the modern decentered subject. *Lr.* is, above all, a play about power, property, and inheritance. Rejecting both the Christian and the humanist interpretations of this play, Dollimore argues that *Lr.* shows man decentered. *Ant.* and *Cor.* both question the martial ideology and expose the contradictions inherent in it. A collection of eleven essays in *Political Shakespeare: New Essays in Cultural Materialism* (Cornell UP, 1985), edited by Jonathan Dollimore and Alan Sinfield, points the way to an interpretation of Shakespeare that emphasizes politics and power—the problems the state has with containment, subversion, and consolidation, and the role of literature in these sociopolitical events. Such an approach ranges across all parts of the canon, not just the history plays.

Concerned with how Shakespeare represents power, Leonard Tennenhouse, in *Power on Display: The Politics of Shakespeare's Genres* (Methuen, 1986), demonstrates how a new historicist approach might reinterpret the drama. Simply put, he argues that the plays participated in the political life of Renaissance England; thus, political imperatives were also aesthetic imperatives. Rather than merely reflecting political life, the theater, Tennenhouse suggests, became a place where political events occurred and where history was produced, giving rise to spectacles of power. *MND* declares that the theater has the power to create the illusion of a community out of the contradictory bodies of authority. The final scene in *Shr.* gives Kate real political power for the first time. *MV* demonstrates the political importance of writing. These early comedies transfer power to the aristocratic female. *TN* presents another variation. Tennenhouse explores how the carnival spirit helps bring about change and reveals a struggle for power.

The author uses both *H8* and *Ham.* to show that the figures who organized materials for the stage also shaped policies of state. This leads Tennenhouse into a discussion of some history plays, including *R2* and *R3*. Indeed, the history plays turn on the use of materials of carnival, and they demonstrate that power rests with those who can seize the symbols and signs that legitimize authority. Analyzing *Lr., Mac., Oth.,* and *Ant.,* Tennenhouse focuses on the determinant components of Jacobean drama: kingship versus kinship, natural versus metaphysical bodies of power, the signs and symbols of state versus the exercise of state power. In the Romances, the paternally organized family provides the occasion not for resistance but for spectacular displays of patriarchal authority. Tennenhouse provides much historical background and examines a number of plays by Shakespeare's contemporaries.

In pursuing the medieval dramatic heritage of Shakespeare's plays in *Shakespeare and the Dramaturgy of Power* (Princeton UP, 1989), John D. Cox embraces a new historicist approach while also criticizing it as he ranges across the canon. He finds that the early comedies have vestiges of medieval drama, even the seemingly unlikely play *Err.* They repeatedly question the centers of power, as in *TGV*. The early histories illustrate the downfall of characters resulting from intense competition for power at court, as in the uncontrolled struggle for power in *3H6*. Shakespeare arrived at his approach by a process of contrasting secular dramatic history with its sacred prototype. The archetypal pattern of *R3* derives from salvation history itself, in which a devilish spoiler destroys the order of an innocent beginning. *H5* enacts the realities of Tudor power. Hal seizes on the conventional model of the morality play as a model of the self used to his political advantage. Cox views *AWW* as an experiment in the dramaturgy of power; the principal problem arises from Helena's recourse to power as a benign trickster. In *MM*, the outlines of Angelo's tyranny are distinctly medieval. Because Lear gains far greater dignity in his humiliation than he had known in his power, Cox calls the play Shakespeare's most powerful comedy of forgiveness. Shakespeare's debt to medieval dramatic heritage can be clearly seen in *WT* and *Tmp*. This cultural residual tradition strongly qualified current ideas of power.

CULTURAL STUDY

What did Shakespeare's contemporaries think about the body, its physiological processes, and their relation to the mind and soul? How were health and different diseases understood? How were the sick treated? Such questions and possible answers occupy F. David Hoeniger in *Medicine and Shakespeare in the English Renaissance* (U of Delaware P, 1992). In Shakespeare's England, only a small number of the sick received treatment by physicians. Hoeniger explores medicine and medical practitioners in the period and the major medical philosophies and systems, including those of Hippocrates, Galen, and Paracelsus. Chapter 13 discusses the diseases referred to in the plays; venereal diseases are cited most often. The final three chapters examine in turn *Mac.*, *AWW*, and *Lr.* (Lear's madness is the subject of the last chapter).

A different approach to the body can be found in Gail Kern Paster's *The Body Embarrassed: Drama and the Disciplines of Shame in Early Modern England* (Cornell UP, 1993), which focuses on the place of physiological theory in the social history of the body. Paster emphasizes the importance of the humoral theory, both physical and psychological. She attempts to isolate different internal and external functions of the humoral body as textually complex signifiers of embarrassment. The focus is the represented body in both non-Shakespearean and Shakespearean drama. Natural behavior becomes thoroughly implicated in a complex structure of class and gender difference, as in *WT* and *TN*. Perdita's key position in *WT* illustrates the traumatic experience of the seventeenth-century child sent away from home soon after birth and returned later. Leontes demonstrates overwhelming oral deprivation. The play as a whole thematizes the measure of affection between parent and child. In a word, this book examines practiced bodily behavior and the professional mimesis of affect.

Using insights from feminism, psychoanalysis, and gay and lesbian critical theory, Valerie Traub's *Desire and Anxiety: Circulations of Sexuality in Shakespearean Drama* (Routledge, 1992) explores the relation between erotic desire and anxiety and their role in the construction of male and female subjects in Shakespeare's drama. This drama marks within itself a struggle over the meaning of desire. Traub discusses such topics as the importance of female chastity, horrors associated with fantasy of the female reproductive body, disgust about erotic relations, and pleasures and anxieties occasioned by homoerotic desire. The gender asymmetry of patriarchal representation complicates the circulation of desire. *Ham., Oth.,* and *WT* illustrate the strategies of containment of female erotic power, in which the erotic warmth of women transforms into cold, static form. Ophelia's chastity, for example, embodies a masculine fantasy of a female essence. Othello associates fear of chaos with sexual activity. Hermione's sexuality must be metaphorically contained and psychically disarmed. The history plays perpetuate repression of the female reproductive body. Hal's rejection of Falstaff temporarily assuages anxieties about homoerotic bonds and about the equation of women and maternity. War and sexuality link strongly in *Tro.*, which offers a particularly telling rendition of the vulnerabilities of the erotic body and the body politic. The homoerotic circulation of desire finds much of its focus in the comedies. The homoeroticism of *AYL* seems playful; that of *TN*, anxious and strained.

The cultural practice of homosexuality informs Bruce R. Smith's *Homosexual Desire in Shakespeare's England: A Cultural Poetics* (U of Chicago P, 1991). Of the discourses about sexuality—medical, legal, moral, and poetic—only the latter confronts desire. Therefore, Smith writes about the connections between homosexual desire and patterns of discourse. He constructs six myths of such desire in Shakespeare and finds connections to social structures. The myth of "Combatants and Comrades" constitutes the foundation of all the myths, and it opens questions about legal restrictions on homosexual behavior. Smith examines this myth at work in *Tro.*, *Oth.*, *Rom.*, and *Cor.* Seen in the terms that Achilles himself provides, the slaughter of Hector becomes an act of sexual consummation. Homoerotic feeling arises out of Iago's self-definition as a man among men, a soldier among soldiers; this all-male world allows no place for women. Psychologically, this myth leaves homosexual desire diffuse and undefined, making it possible to deny any connection between desire and deed. The "Passionate Shepherd" myth evokes the Arcadian world of adolescent sexuality, as in several of the comedies. The myth of the "Secret Sharer" governs the first 126 Sonnets—Shakespeare's attempt to bring structures of ideology and power into the kind of viable alignment with feeling that we find in more conventional love poetry. Poetic discourse provided an outlet for desire in a society that legally condemned homosexual practices. Pursuing similar topics, *Shakespeare Survey* 46 (1994) concentrates on Shakespeare and sexuality.

Enclosure Acts: Sexuality, Property, and Culture in Early Modern England, edited by Richard Burt and John Michael Archer (Cornell UP, 1994), offers a collection of essays informed by feminist and historicist analysis. The enclosure and consolidation of the land extend to a redefinition of sexuality and the body. Shakespeare's history plays and Romances get the main attention. Enclosure functions as a trope for the ways in which sexuality and gender mark the body.

In *Making a Match: Courtship in Shakespeare and His Society* (Princeton UP, 1991), Ann Jennalie Cook reconstructs the system of courtship familiar to Shakespeare and his audience and analyzes how Shakespeare incorporates the attitudes and experiences of wooing into his plays. In these plays, love appears as the primary impetus for such wooing, despite society's frequent pattern of arranged marriages for economic and social reasons. *AWW* offers the longest and most direct exploration of inequality in birth and rank between marriage partners. Shakespeare explores the full social gamut from the union of servants to the wedding of royalty. *Shr.* provides a merciless exposure of the matrimonial market as it confronts the issue of money most directly. *Lr.* shows how the denial of a marriage portion leads to a break with family, custom, and society. Only in *H5* and *Shr.* does Shakespeare give the complete pattern of conventional courtship; *MM* illustrates the dangers in irregular courtship. The impediment of sexual dishonor finds its fullest expression in *Ado*. The dissolution of marriage in *H8* passes through a labyrinth of political, religious, and aesthetic issues. Clearly, the plays do not offer a precise representation of social practice.

Daryl W. Palmer, in *Hospitable Performances: Dramatic Genre and Cultural Practices in Early Modern England* (Purdue UP, 1992), examines the cultural practice of hospitality versus the representation of hospitable practice, primarily in drama. Palmer argues that the representation of hospitality both stabilizes and destabilizes literary genres. In the hospitable surroundings of a theater, playwrights appropriate the idea of hospitality. Palmer suggests that what Shakespeare's romantic comedies tested, England's successful households put into practice. In *MND,* marriage hinges on successful hospitality. *Shr.* offers the best introduction into the place of hospitality, and Duke Senior in *AYL* demonstrates the importance of a host. Shakespeare toys with the ways in which welcoming awakens desire; indeed, hospitality and desire often share the same language. *Lr.* underscores the problematic position of women as hosts. In Goneril's hands, hospitality becomes a trap; convivial entertainment vanishes.

Examining the institutional situation of London's playhouses, Douglas Bruster, in *Drama and the Market in the Age of Shakespeare* (Cambridge UP, 1992), demonstrates how dramatists came to mythologize the elaborate realities of London's material base. Three strategies allowed dramatists to explore and define the character of socioeconomic changes affecting London: linking the sexual and the economic, the urban and the rural, and the ancient and the modern. The theater became the center for production and consumption of an aesthetic product; it also participated in the dawning of institutionalized capitalism in London. City comedy reveals an obsession with the integrity of commodity and the inevitable hazards of ownership. The handkerchief in *Oth.* retains a social significance that depends on English society's growing commercialism. Cressida takes control of her commodity function, even as the Troy myth raises anxiety about London and the possibility of a fall. The material culture of London fed dramatic imaginations as the theater played its role as part of the market.

John Gillies, in *Shakespeare and the Geography of Difference* (Cambridge UP, 1994), argues that Shakespeare wrote in a rich geographical tradition alive with the meaning of human difference. He offers a dramaturgical version of the ancient poetic geographical economy of difference. Gillies explores the poetic interrelatedness of the Elizabethan theater and sixteenth-century cosmography. Shakespeare's geography incorporates the creation of exotic characters whose generic fate includes some annulment of difference. Shakespeare's voyagers tend to form deeply compromising relationships with the exotic, to the point where the two types merge in the same character. Gillies examines *Tit., Ant., MV, Oth.,* and *Tmp.* The exotic character in *Ant.*, for example, appears as insidiously threatening. The untranslatable mystery of Cleopatra's difference constitutes the central issue in the last act. Shakespeare's Venice in *MV* invites barbarous intrusion through the sheer exorbitance of its maritime trading empire, seen most clearly in the opposition between Shylock and Antonio. Gillies suggests that Othello's political and military penetration of the city is recapitulated at the level of Brabantio's house and thence at the level of Desdemona's body. Prospero rehearses three poetic geographic moments, corresponding respectively to the "voyages" of Sycorax, Prospero, and Alonso. The play itself offers a conventionally geographic impression of the exotic.

François Laroque, in *Shakespeare's Festive World: Elizabethan Seasonal Entertainment and the Professional Stage* (Cambridge UP, 1991), demonstrates the interconnections between the plays and the popular, festival world outside them. This includes the interplay of both festival and liturgical calendar correspondences, as in *MND*, or the seasons in *WT.* The festivities of funeral and wedding intervene in *Ham.* *TN* highlights the festival of Epiphany as supporters and opponents of festivity square off against each other. Many of the themes of *Oth.* derive from comedy and popular festivals.

Peter Holbrook's *Literature and Degree in Renaissance England: Nashe, Bourgeois Tragedy, and Shakespeare* (U of Delaware P, 1994) explores the social symbolism of various English Renaissance texts that take social difference as their subject matter. They deliberately manipulate social relations, especially those between gentle and common life. *Shr.* and *MND*, for example, feature theatrical occasions that involve social interplay. The latter play's sensitivity about differences in rank forms the basis for its consciousness of genre and the potential social uses of art. Lear on the heath moves away from an elite to a popular social space; this takes the king deep into the world of the dispossessed. The lower-class plot of the Jailer's Daughter in *TNK* indicates Shakespeare's social and generic mixing.

INTERDISCIPLINARY STUDIES

MUSIC

Scholars have studied the relationship between music and Shakespeare's drama. Some have examined the specific use of song in the plays, whereas others have tried to locate sources of the songs or find the original settings. As a result, we have considerable information about the music in Shakespearean drama. F. W. Sternfeld reviews twentieth-century scholarship on music in his part of the larger essay "Twentieth-Century Studies in Shakespeare's Songs, Sonnets, and Poems," *Shakespeare Survey* 15 (1962): 1–10. Another interesting essay is D. S. Hoffman's "Some Shakespearean Music, 1660–1900," *Shakespeare Survey* 18 (1965): 94–101.

The earliest studies only hinted at what has eventually become known about the music. Edward W. Naylor, in *Shakespeare and Music,* rev. ed. (1931; reprint, Da Capo & Blum, 1965; original, 1896), discusses technical musical terms of the period as well as instruments, musical education, songs and singing, dances, music of the spheres, and the use of musical stage directions. This elementary book has a descriptive rather than analytic approach to the function of music in the drama. On a different order, Richmond S. Noble's *Shakespeare's Use of Song, with the Text of the Principal Songs* (Oxford UP, 1923) presents the word text and extensive information on each song in the plays but includes no music. He credits Shakespeare with most of the songs.

John H. Long's three books have contributed much to our knowledge of music in the drama. His first book, *Shakespeare's Use of Music: A Study of the Music and Its Performance in the Original Production of Seven Comedies* (U of Florida P, 1955), briefly surveys songs and instrumental music in Elizabethan drama and offers discussions of *TGV, LLL, MND, Ado, AYL, MV,* and *TN.* Music as a dramatic device not only intensifies the impact of language but also forwards the action, the portrayal of character, the delineation of settings, and the creation of atmosphere. Long sees three phases in these comedies: music (1) signals the presence of critical or climactic situations; (2) serves as a sedative, countering intense (tragic) moments (*MV, Ado*); and (3) experiments, weighing the advantages of stylistic use of music and its naturalistic use.

In *Shakespeare's Use of Music: The Final Comedies* (U of Florida P, 1961), Long concentrates on *Shr., Wiv., AWW, MM, Per., Cym., WT,* and *Tmp.* Again he seeks to determine the functions of the performed music, the manner of performance, the original musical scores (where possible), and significance. The music in these plays underscores crucial scenes, makes the supernatural perceptible, and synthesizes abstract or psychological ideas.

The final volume, *Shakespeare's Use of Music: The Histories and Tragedies* (U of Florida P, 1971), examines all the history plays except *Jn.,* all the tragedies, and *Tro.* The histories use music primarily in its public, social, and ceremonial vein; hence the music is largely instrumental. Vocal music in the tragedies consists almost entirely of bits of ballads or parts of old popular songs. In contrast, the comedies generally have art songs or complete lute songs. Long argues that the use of music in the tragedies suggests that Shakespeare saw tragedy as an intense vision of inner conflict and mental and physical destruction. All three of Long's books have bibliographies.

A major study that focuses on the tragedies, F. W. Sternfeld's *Music in Shakespearean Tragedy* (Routledge & Kegan Paul, 1963), contains a critical discussion and facsimile reproductions of available songs or likely ones (scores of the original songs). Sternfeld discusses the tradition of vocal and instrumental music in tragedy, including non-Shakespearean drama. Two chapters deal specifically with the complexity of Desdemona's "Willow Song" and with Ophelia's songs. Sternfeld believes that Robert Armin was the principal musician-actor in the dramatic company. Two chapters concentrate extensively on instrumental music, and chapter 10 has a retrospect of scholarship on Shakespeare and music, up to about 1960. This book includes an extensive bibliography and helpful indexes— for example, an index of lyrics and a dictionary catalogue of all the songs in Shakespeare's plays.

Peter J. Seng's *The Vocal Songs in the Plays of Shakespeare* (Harvard UP, 1967) is basically as a reference book that attempts to bring together all the relevant material on the vocal songs in the plays. The material proceeds as follows: (1) headnote giving the source of the text (Folio or Quarto) and the song's location in that text, as well as act, scene, and line number in modern editions; (2) the text of the song exactly reproduced from the earliest authoritative edition; (3) general critical commentary arranged according to date (what critics have said about it); (4) textual commentary (glosses with comments from various scholars as to the meaning); (5) information about music for the song (earliest known source, if any); (6) information about sources for the song or any analogues to the particular song (words, not melody); and (7) observations about the dramatic function in the play. A bibliography of both primary and secondary sources appears at the end.

Several books examine music in the Renaissance in general and may be of interest to researchers. Bruce Pattison, in *Music and Poetry of the English Renaissance* (Methuen, 1948), demonstrates the relationship between the lyric and poetry. He defines the various musical forms—madrigal, air, ballad, and so on. John Stevens provides good background material in *Music and Poetry in the Early Tudor Court* (Methuen, 1961). This book focuses principally on the early sixteenth century; one chapter deals with music in ceremonials, entertainments, and plays.

Gretchen L. Finney's *Musical Backgrounds for English Literature: 1580–1650* (Rutgers UP, 1962) approaches music as a philosophical concept (speculative music). Wilfrid Mellers, in *Harmonious Meeting: A Study of the Relationship between English Music, Poetry, and Theatre, c. 1600–1900* (Dobson, 1965), includes two chapters specifically on Shakespeare: "Music in the Shakespearean Theatre" and "Masque into Poetic Drama," which deals with *Tmp.*

Gary Schmidgall, in *Shakespeare and Opera* (Oxford UP, 1990), concentrates first on matters of style, then dramaturgy, and finally performance as he explores the interconnections between Shakespeare and opera, especially that composed by Verdi. He also notes the operatic qualities of Shakespeare's plays. The book closes with several chapters on individual plays and their manifestations in operatic form.

INTELLECTUAL AND POLITICAL HISTORY

Several types of interdisciplinary studies include investigations into the philosophy of the period and cultural and political history. E. M. W. Tillyard's *The Elizabethan World Picture* (Chatto & Windus, 1943) has become one of the classic summaries of the intellectual milieu. In this brief book, Tillyard outlines common beliefs of the Elizabethan period, demonstrating that the English Renaissance was not so much a reaction against medieval ideas as a subsuming and appropriation of them. Tillyard emphasizes the hierarchical, ordered universe, illustrated from the works of many different kinds of writers and thinkers. The Elizabethans, according to Tillyard, perceived order in three forms: the Chain of Being (a design of order stretching from God through inanimate objects), a series of corresponding planes (macrocosm-microcosm, body politic–macrocosm, and so on), and a cosmic dance. Tillyard's assessment emphasizes this optimistic, ordered world to the exclusion of the new, contrary voices that became prevalent at the end of the sixteenth century.

Theodore Spencer shows something of the other side of the coin in *Shakespeare and the Nature of Man,* 2d ed. (Macmillan, 1961; original, 1942). In the first two chapters, which are especially relevant for intellectual background, Spencer describes the ideal picture of mankind, the optimistic theory of order and hierarchy based on the concept of universal order and law, with humans as the center of such a world. Opposing voices existed; and Spencer traces them to three general areas: new science, Copernicus, and others; new politics, epitomized in Machiavelli; and new morality, apparent in the writings of Montaigne. All these forces question the premise of universal order. The remainder of the book offers interpretations of various plays, viewing them, partly, in light of the Renaissance intellectual conflict as they come to terms with the nature of mankind.

These new matters of conflict receive extensive treatment in Hiram Haydn's *The Counter-Renaissance* (Scribner's, 1950), a lengthy intellectual history of the movement that ran counter to the received, medieval worldview of the ordered, hierarchical world. The counter-Renaissance originated as a protest against the basic principles of the classical Renaissance as well as against those of medieval Scholasticism. All its strands— whether science, morality, or politics—argued for a repeal of universal law. Haydn discusses the various manifestations of this collective movement and assesses the Elizabethan reaction to it; he sees the Elizabethans as much more responsive and attuned than Tillyard does. In the final chapter, Haydn specifically examines Shakespeare, focusing on *Ham.* and *Lr.* He believes that Shakespeare was aware of this countermovement and used a number of its ideas for dramatic purpose.

C. S. Lewis, in *The Discarded Image: An Introduction to Medieval and Renaissance Literature* (Cambridge UP, 1964), defines common philosophical beliefs of the medieval period, their derivation, and their perpetuation into the Renaissance. In his final chapter, Lewis assesses the influence of this model of the ideal world.

Believing Scholasticism and Neoplatonism to be the two dominant Renaissance approaches to philosophy, Walter Clyde Curry discusses both in *Shakespeare's Philosophical Patterns* (Louisiana State UP, 1937). He interprets *Mac.* in light of the former and *Tmp.* in light of the latter. Although he was not a systematic philosopher, Shakespeare seems to have possessed a comfortable and accurate knowledge of the basic principles of the two philosophical systems dealt with here.

Roland M. Frye discusses religious philosophy more explicitly in *Shakespeare and Christian Doctrine* (Princeton UP, 1963). Frye first examines the contrasting critical approaches to Shakespeare: theological analysis (epitomized by G. Wilson Knight) and secular analysis (A. C. Bradley). Part 2 of the book concerns the historical background of sixteenth-century theology in order to give a more precise view of the theological inheritance of Shakespeare. The final part analyzes the dramatist's theological references, arranged by topics. Frye attempts to steer a course between the excesses of either side; he especially takes to task, for excesses in the Christian approach, J. A. Bryant, Jr., *Hippolyta's View: Some Christian Aspects of Shakespeare's Plays* (UP of Kentucky, 1961). Frye's book functions by and large as a sensible corrective.

Lars Engle embraces a view of social interaction as a market economy, a world of contingent values, in *Shakespearean Pragmatism: Market of His Time* (U of Chicago P, 1993). Such dynamic economies replace fixed systems of belief. After extensive discussion of the Sonnets, Engle focuses on *Ham.*, in which Hamlet accepts dramatic pragmatism as a mode of action. The constitution of individual agents in discursive environments becomes the crucial pragmatic issue. Hamlet hopes to reform the agency of others. Engle examines the connection of pragmatism to marriage and friendship, royal succession and legitimation, and literary influence in *MV* and the Henriad. *MV* shows the intersection of four major value systems that interact vigorously in Shakespeare's London and in the theater: religion, hereditary rank, capitalism, and love. This play presents the world of human relations as a market of exchangeable values. The Henry plays turn on relations of debt, homosocial affections, rivalry, and the troubled inheritance of blessings. Economic terms and transactions become particularly striking in these history plays. The final section of the book analyzes the relation of Shakespeare's pragmatism to politics, seen especially in *Tro., Cor.,* and *Ant.* Engle describes *Tro.* as a thought experiment that takes up the problem of generating value without large systems of belief to support it. Coriolanus tries to keep his idea of nobility from being compromised by a market economy; the play serves as a parable of political economy. *Ant.* works pragmatically with large questions about the scope and limits of human agency, examining how to shape the political self in a changing world without firm rules.

The "book of life" and the "theater of the world" constitute the informing metaphors in Robert S. Knapp's *Shakespeare—The Theater and the Book* (Princeton UP, 1989). A fundamental tension permeates the interpreter's discourse: between character or event as sign and as deed, between reading as a form of knowledge and as experiential (re)enactment. Knapp examines the difference between narrative as a fable of connectedness and drama as a display of the face of things. An analysis of medieval drama and Tudor interludes leads Knapp to see new puzzles in cosmic order and personal identity that grew out of the drama and social reality of the sixteenth century. Shakespeare's management of genres displays the logically different possibilities, preserving a real undecidability within the antinomies: theater and book, symbol and function, cognitive and performative, word and deed. Generic impurity distinguishes Shakespeare's plays from others; he seems determined to test the limits of different representational modes. *R2* enacts a conflict between two interdependent yet partly incompatible sorts of authority, but neither Richard at the beginning nor Henry at the end can bring words and deeds of monarchy together. The Hal who becomes Henry V preserves his power by falsifying men's hopes; theatricality gives him power. In Shakespeare's comic universe, only those with an ill will or a stubborn literality need fail to participate consensually in solutions. Devices of the double, conversion, and reinterpretation characterize such plays as *Err., TN,* and *AWW.* Shakespearean tragedy thwarts efforts to apportion blame between a fatal context and an errant self. The Romances emphasize difference itself: between art and nature, between experience and innocence, between belatedness and the imaginary unity it always posits. *WT,* for example, sets up a dissonance between showing and telling.

Several books give students a sound introduction to the political and cultural history of the period. Two volumes in the Oxford History of England series are appropriate. J. B. Black, in *The Reign of Elizabeth, 1558–1603,* rev. ed. (Clarendon Press, 1959; original, 1936), focuses on the political and social history of the Elizabethan period and includes a chapter called

"Literature, Art and Thought"; there is also an extensive bibliography. In a companion volume, *The Early Stuarts, 1603–1660,* 2d ed. (Clarendon, 1959; original, 1937), Godfrey Davies discusses political and constitutional history as well as social and economic history. He also includes separate chapters on the arts and on literature, along with a bibliography.

Two books by A. L. Rowse specifically concern cultural history. *The Elizabethan Renaissance: The Life of the Society* (Macmillan, 1971) contains chapters on the court, the role of the gentry, class and social life, food and sanitation, sex, custom, witchcraft, and astrology. In *The Elizabethan Renaissance: The Cultural Achievement* (Macmillan, 1972), Rowse portrays the cultural life of the age with chapters on drama, language, literature, and society; words and music; architecture and sculpture; painting; domestic arts; science and society; nature and medicine; and mind and spirit (philosophical).

SOURCES

Shakespeare's likely sources or major influences from various literatures and cultures constitute another area of interdisciplinary or intercultural studies. Such an investigation involves not only source hunting but also a consideration of how the dramatist uses these likely sources for dramatic purposes. Certainly one measure of Shakespeare's artistic achievement derives from setting his source alongside the drama to see how they differ.

For students doing research in Shakespeare's sources, the major work of scholarship that must be consulted is the eight-volume *Narrative and Dramatic Sources of Shakespeare* (Routledge & Kegan Paul; Columbia UP, 1957–1975), compiled by Geoffrey Bullough. This monumental work includes an extensive introductory essay on the sources, the texts of the possible or probable sources, and analogues, where appropriate. The volumes proceed as follows: 1, early comedies, poems, and *Rom.*; 2, comedies (1597–1603) through *MM*; 3, earlier English history—*H6, R3,* and *R2*; 4, later English history—*Jn., H4, H5,* and *H8;* 5, Roman plays; 6, other classical plays—*Tit., Tro., Tim.,* and *Per.*; 7, major tragedies—*Ham., Oth., Lr.,* and *Mac.*; 8, the Romances—*Cym., WT,* and *Tmp.* Bullough includes a useful bibliography.

Several books designed primarily for students provide source materials for selected plays. For example, Alice Griffin, ed., *The Sources of Ten Shakespearean Plays* (Crowell, 1966), includes the source texts for *Rom., Shr., 1H4, 2H4, H5, JC, TN, Oth., Mac.,* and *Ant.* The texts use modernized spelling and punctuation. Joseph Satin, ed., *Shakespeare and His Sources* (Houghton Mifflin, 1966), offers modernized texts of the sources for *R3, R2, MV, H4, H5, JC, TN, Ham., Oth., Lr., Mac.,* and *Ant.* Richard Hosley's edition, *Shakespeare's Holinshed* (Putnam's, 1968), focuses on one particular source: the 1587 text of Holinshed's *Chronicles* for all the history plays and *Lr., Cym.,* and *Mac.* Hosley cites not only the page number from Holinshed but also the appropriate section from the plays by act, scene, and line number.

In *Shakespeare's Sources: Comedies and Tragedies* (Methuen, 1957), Kenneth Muir interprets Shakespeare's use of sources. Muir finds no discernible pattern indicating how Shakespeare worked or used his sources throughout the comedies and tragedies; the dramatist seems to have come to each play individually. In all, Muir considers twenty plays and discusses the likely sources, Shakespeare's use of them, parallels, and comparisons.

Believing that the study of the use of sources provides an invaluable clue to Shakespeare's art and thought, Virgil Whitaker, in *Shakespeare's Use of Learning: An Inquiry into the Growth of His Mind and Art* (Huntington Library, 1953), pursues the argument throughout the canon. Whitaker argues that Shakespeare added to his knowledge while he developed as a playwright and that this progress as a dramatist depended to a considerable extent on his increased learning. The attempt to understand the growth of the dramatist's mind focuses on his use of sources. The methodology first examines the plays that have clearly defined sources and then looks for occurrences of allusions to the learning of Shakespeare's day and their importance to the play. Shakespeare's intellectual development apparently led to a fundamental change in his method of building plays from his sources: first he follows the sources rather closely, and then he reshapes them drastically in order to make the action reveal characters that illustrate or conform to philosophic concepts (for example, in *Mac.* and *Lr.*). Whitaker's argument may go a bit far, but this imposing study reminds us again of Shakespeare's apparently immense learning.

A number of scholars have been concerned with the dramatist's dependence on or knowledge of classical literatures and traditions. An edition of one source can be found in T. J. B. Spencer's *Shakespeare's Plutarch* (Penguin, 1964). This text follows the 1595 folio edition of Plutarch's *Lives* as translated by North. Spencer presents here the lives of Julius Caesar, Marcus Brutus, Marcus Antonius, and Martius Coriolanus. The notes at the bottom of the pages make the links to the plays.

J. A. K. Thomson, in *Shakespeare and the Classics* (Allen & Unwin, 1952), argues for the two greatest classical sources—Plutrach's *Lives* and Ovid's *Metamorphoses*—which were familiar to Shakespeare through Elizabethan translations. Thomson sees in Plutarch a model for Shakespeare's tragic form. He discusses the poems and plays individually and their indebtedness to or treatment of a classical story. The lack of an index makes this book somewhat difficult to use.

Arguing that Seneca served as both text and tradition for Shakespeare, Robert S. Miola, in *Shakespeare and Classical Tragedy* (Clarendon, 1992), explores Seneca's place in the tragedies and tragicomedies by focusing on three major qualities: revenge, tyranny, and furor. Seneca's *Phaedra,* for example, not only provides quotations for *Tit.* but also contributes to Shakespeare's sense of locality. Senecan rhetoric and Stoicism inform *Ham.* Macbeth often strikes Senecan poses and speaks Senecan speeches; Lady Macbeth owes a debt to *Medea.* Miola argues for a parallel structural design between *Oth.* and Seneca's *Hercules Furens.* Lear's furor is both error and heroic response to evil, both misconceived passion and righteous anger. Even *MND* exhibits verbal echoes from Seneca and a dramatic parody. Miola closes by commenting on the furor of Leontes and Prospero. He builds in part on the work of Gordon Braden, *Renaissance Tragedy and the Senecan Tradition: Anger's Privilege* (Yale UP, 1985).

Jonathan Bate, in *Shakespeare and Ovid* (Clarendon, 1993), explores Shakespeare's indebtedness to Ovid for the early poems and plays through the final Romances. The narrative poems *Ven.* and *Luc.* demonstrate Shakespeare's recurring use of Ovid through both imitation and amplification. *Tit.* offers a revisionary reading of the Ovidian text, principally the story of Philomel, and an examination of the efficacy of humanist education. Sly's perspective in *Shr.* rests on an exotic, erotic, poetic world of strange transformations and experiences far removed from the audience's everyday world. The philosophy of love and change, the operation of the gods, animal transformation, and symbolic vegetation in *MND* offer a displaced dramatization of Ovid. To go to the Forest of Arden in *AYL* involves going to Ovid in his capacity as a teacher of love. The Phaëthon myth governs much of what happens in *R2*. Metamorphosis takes place in *Lr.* when identity breaks down. The Ovidian traditions at work in *Ant.* are rich and complex. Bate argues that Shakespeare returns to Ovid in full force in the last plays. He is most Ovidian in *Cym.*, where his sustained use of language fuses the characters with the natural world. The stories of Proserpina and Pygmalion permeate *WT,* the latter emphasizing the power of imagination, the magic of the awakening, and the art that outdoes nature. *Tmp.* serves as Shakespeare's last revision of the *Metamorphoses,* providing clear evidence of the dramatist's collaboration with Ovid.

In *Shakespeare and the Uses of Antiquity: An Introductory Essay* (Routledge, 1990), Charles and Michelle Martindale begin by assessing the extent of Shakespeare's classical knowledge, the doctrine of imitation, and the influence of Seneca on English Renaissance drama. They focus primarily on the influence of Ovid, especially in *Tit.*, *MND*, and *WT.* The story of Tereus and Philomela lies behind the action of *Tit.* and helps control it; the "Pyramus and Thisbe" play comes directly from the *Metamorphoses;* and the final scene in *WT* derives from Ovid's story of Pygmalion. *Tro.* is Shakespeare's *Iliad,* his play about the matter of Troy. Shakespeare's reading of Plutarch provides the essential catalyst for the Roman plays.

In *Shakespeare and the Greek Romance: A Study of Origins* (UP of Kentucky, 1970), Carol Gesner investigates the Greek romances, their tradition, and Shakespeare's use of them, culminating in the full-fledged use of Heliodorus and *Apollonius of Tyre* in the final Romances. In *Per., Cym., WT,* and *Tmp.,* we see the ancient genre deliberately used and lifted to new dimensions, turned to a new vision of reality. Gesner argues that Greek romance served as a major fabric of Renaissance narrative and drama and functioned as a source for and an influence on Shakespeare.

An older book in need of revision is Robert K. Root's *Classical Mythology in Shakespeare* (Holt, 1903). After an introduction in which Root assesses Shakespeare's use of mythology, principally drawn from Ovid, the book consists mainly of an alphabetical listing of the mythological characters in Shakespeare. The book includes discussions of these characters, references to them, and likely sources of the stories or qualities being alluded to in plays or poems. Root also lists Shakespeare's works individually, with a brief summary of the mythology involved in each.

Several studies explore in some detail the dramatist's reliance on the Bible. Richmond Noble, in *Shakespeare's Biblical Knowledge* (Society for Christian Knowledge, 1935; Macmillan), considers Shakespeare's general and specific knowledge of the Bible. Noble also discusses the versions of the Bible available to Shakespeare, as well as the Book of Common Prayer. Primarily, the book lists allusions and parallels for each play (except *Per.*), but it also includes a useful list of biblical proper names, identified and cross-referenced to the plays in which they appear. An index of books of the Bible, with all the plays that quote or paraphrase that particular book of the Bible listed by act and scene, also proves helpful.

In three books, Naseeb Shaheen explores Shakespeare's indebtedness to the Bible: *Biblical References in Shakespeare's Tragedies* (U of Delaware P, 1987), *Biblical References in Shakespeare's History Plays* (U of Delaware P, 1989), and *Biblical References in Shakespeare's Comedies* (U of Delaware P, 1993). Each includes an initial chapter that examines the English Bible in Shakespeare's day, observing that the Geneva Bible was the one most often used. The plays also offer abundant evidence that Shakespeare had thorough knowledge of Anglican liturgy, based on the Book of Common Prayer. Each book then proceeds to examine individual plays, scene by scene, for their biblical quotations or references. Appendixes list the biblical citations in Shakespeare arranged by the books of the Bible.

James H. Sims's *Dramatic Uses of Biblical Allusions in Marlowe and Shakespeare* (University of Florida Monographs, Humanities no. 24; U of Florida P, 1966), explores Shakespeare's dramatic use of the Bible. In the comedies, the misuses and mis-understandings of scripture add to the element of ludicrousness and sometimes provide insight into particular characters. Biblical echoes make the audience conscious of the moral and spiritual order of the universe. In the histories and tragedies, Shakespeare underscores theme and foreshadows action by biblical allusion. Sims includes a useful bibliography.

PERIODICALS

Some periodicals relevant for Shakespearean studies have been mentioned earlier in this chapter. In the journals cited, students will find many essays on particular Shakespearean topics as well as other helpful materials. Since 1948, Cambridge University Press has published *Shakespeare Survey*, an annual publication now edited by Stanley Wells. Volumes 11, 21, 31, and 41 contain indexes to the preceding ten volumes. In addition to essays on particular plays or poems, each issue includes reviews of the year's contribution to Shakespearean study, arranged under three topics: critical studies; life, times, and stage; and textual studies—exceptionally valuable reviews of recent studies. *Shakespeare Quarterly*, founded in 1950 by the Shakespeare Association of America, has been published since 1972 by the Folger Shakespeare Library. Its annual bibliography has already been cited. The forerunner of this journal was the *Shakespeare Association Bulletin*, published from 1924 to 1949 (volumes 1–24). The annual publication *Shakespeare Studies*, begun in 1965 and edited by J. Leeds Barroll, contains reports on research, critical essays, and book reviews. Begun in 1982, *Shakespeare Bulletin* emphasizes performance criticism and scholarship; in 1992, it took over the function of the *Shakespeare on Film Newsletter.*

Periodicals not specifically devoted to Shakespeare also contain valuable information. *Studies in Philology* frequently contains essays on Shakespeare; volumes 19–66 (1922–1969) include a Renaissance bibliography, with a section on Shakespeare. Begun in 1961 at Rice University, *Studies in English Literature* devotes one of its four issues (usually the spring issue) to Elizabethan and Jacobean drama, and essays on

Shakespeare frequently appear. The annual review article usually includes Shakespeare items. *Research Opportunities in Renaissance Drama,* begun in 1956 and edited by David M. Bergeron, occasionally has articles, checklists, and other materials relevant to Shakespeare, although it focuses primarily on his fellow dramatists. *Renaissance Drama,* begun in 1964 and now edited by Mary Beth Rose, often includes articles on Shakespeare. Similarly, *Medieval and Renaissance Drama in England,* begun in 1984 and edited by Leeds Barroll, contains work on Shakespeare's contemporaries. Begun in 1971, *English Literary Renaissance,* edited by Arthur Kinney, regularly contains essays on Shakespeare.

BIOGRAPHICAL STUDIES

Students who wish to investigate the life of Shakespeare will find few facts available but a plenitude of theories. Despite the relatively small number of facts about his life, we actually know more about Shakespeare than about most of his contemporaries. Parts of his life, however, remain tantalizingly vague, even after four centuries. Charles Sisson presents a summary of some of the biographical studies in his essay "Studies in the Life and Environment of Shakespeare since 1900," *Shakespeare Survey* 3 (1950): 1–12. G. E. Bentley's *Shakespeare: A Biographical Handbook* (Yale UP, 1961) is a sensible, readable summary of the dramatist's life. Bentley discusses such topics as the nature of Shakespearean biography in the seventeenth and twentieth centuries; legends; anti-Stratfordians; Shakespeare in Stratford and London; Shakespeare as actor, playwright, and nondramatic poet; the printers; and Shakespeare's reputation. Bentley includes a bibliography as well as a list of books and documents from which he quotes.

For more extensive research, students should consult E. K. Chambers's massive *William Shakespeare: A Study of Facts and Problems,* 2 vols. (Clarendon, 1930). Volume 1 contains chapters on Shakespeare's origins, the stage in 1592, and Shakespeare and his company. Volume 2 reprints all the records that Chambers could find pertaining to Shakespeare's life—nearly 200 pages—with Chambers's comments on them; topics covered include the grant of arms, christening, lawsuits, marriage, and epitaphs. Biography is much too narrow a term to describe what these volumes contain, for they provide a collection of materials rather than a straight narrative biography. In a much briefer account, *Sources for a Biography of Shakespeare* (Clarendon, 1946), Chambers discusses the records (court, national, legal, and municipal), allusions, and traditions that provide materials on Shakespeare's life.

One of the early standard biographies is Joseph Quincy Adams, *A Life of William Shakespeare* (Houghton Mifflin, 1923), the first substantial American biography and the first to emphasize the place of the theater in Shakespeare's life. Although frequently reprinted, this biography needs to be checked against more recent ones. A good, reliable biography is F. E. Halliday's *The Life of Shakespeare* (Duckworth, 1961), which breaks down Shakespeare's life into segments of certain years. A more specialized study is Mark Eccles's *Shakespeare in Warwickshire* (U of Wisconsin P, 1961). This intensive study focuses on life in Warwickshire, Shakespeare's home county. Eccles traces family relationships of the Shakespeares and the Ardens, the neighbors in Stratford, the school in Stratford, Anne Hathaway, gentlemen and players in Stratford (dramatic performances), Shakespeare at New Place, and Shakespeare's friends.

The most controversial biographer is renowned historian A. L. Rowse. His first study, *William Shakespeare: A Biography* (Macmillan, 1963), although a substantial biography, adds no new information. Rowse's tone and boastful claims alienate many literary scholars. He believes that only a historian, such as himself, can unravel the mysteries of Shakespeare's life, especially the problems of the Sonnets. He dates the Sonnets 1592–1595 and names the Earl of Southampton as the young man and Marlowe as the rival poet. The only problem that he could not solve at the time was the identity of the dark lady. But historical method or no, Rowse has not solved the "mysteries" of the Sonnets.

In 1973, Rowse came back to the subject with *Shakespeare the Man* (Macmillan, 1973), which bears many striking resemblances to his earlier book. The major contribution is Rowse's "discovery" of the identity of the dark lady. He claims that she is one Emilia Lanier. With characteristic immodesty, Rowse says, "For the first time we can now write a three-dimensional biography of William Shakespeare." Conveniently, this discovery corroborates all his previous theories. Rowse suggests that this new book supersedes all other biographies of Shakespeare. Rowse's much-celebrated historicism aside, he can be quite romantic as he analyzes Shakespeare's life; for example, he sees Prospero as Shakespeare bidding farewell to the stage. Unbelievably, on the last page of the book, we learn of Shakespeare's final memories as he lay dying, with the chapel bell tolling in the background; not surprisingly, Shakespeare remembers Emilia in his final earthly vision. Obviously, no historical records substantiate such a claim.

One of the nagging problems in Shakespearean biography involves that hardy group of denigrators who raise questions about the authorship of his plays, sometimes referred to as the anti-Stratfordians. No doubt the general public is still teased by the possibility that one William Shakespeare did not write the plays generally ascribed to him. No evidence to support such a view exists, but such perversity continues to rear its head. This problem is adequately dealt with in H. N. Gibson's *The Shakespeare Claimants* (Methuen, 1962). Many claimants to Shakespeare's work have been suggested; but Gibson focuses on the four principal ones: Francis Bacon, the Oxford syndicate, Lord Derby, and Marlowe. He finds no convincing argument and certainly no evidence recommending any of these positions. About half of this book examines the evidence common to two or more of the theories. The book includes a brief bibliography. In *The Mysterious William Shakespeare: The Myth and the Reality* (Dodd, Mead, 1984), Charlton Ogburn devotes nearly 800 pages to arguing for authorship by the Earl of Oxford.

Another book that deals with such problems and many more is S. Schoenbaum's *Shakespeare's Lives,* rev. ed. (Clarendon, 1991; original, 1970). This book reviews and analyzes the many Shakespeare biographies, including the "deviations," that is, the Baconians and others. The first forty pages or so review the evidence and materials we have for a life of Shakespeare. The remainder evaluates and describes the biographical ventures, from comments in the seventeenth century through Rowse's 1963 biography and beyond. The book proceeds more or less along historical lines—for example, the Victorians, the twentieth century, and so on. Schoenbaum writes with verve and enthusiasm and demonstrates great learning. Students will find it extremely interesting and easy to use. Another book by Schoenbaum, *William Shakespeare: A Documentary Life* (Clarendon and Scola, 1975), emphasizes facts. One of its unusual features is the inclusion of the Shakespeare records—manuscripts and print—in facsimile, with the facsimiles joined to the text. A certain amount of material is not strictly biographical but is of interest to biographers: sketches of Holy Trinity Church in Stratford, prospects of Stratford, panoramas of London, and so on. In all, the book includes about 220 facsimiles. Students will find this book, produced by an outstanding authority, a delight to look at and to read. Two years later, an abridged version was published, entitled *William Shakespeare: A Compact Documentary Life* (Oxford UP, 1977). Minus many of the illustrations of the larger book, this handy and reliable guide to Shakespeare's life has become the standard one to consult, as it assays the myths and facts of the poet's life.

A sequel to *Documentary Life* is Schoenbaum's *William Shakespeare: Records and Images* (Oxford UP, 1981), which contains 165 facsimiles and illustrations of documents and pictures pertaining to Shakespeare's life and career. Here one can see examples of Shakespeare's handwriting, the Shakespeare forgeries, facsimiles of the Stationers' Register records, and, especially interesting, the various portraits of Shakespeare. This beautifully produced book offers a treasure of photographic reproductions.

E. A. J. Honigmann upsets some notions of biography and chronology in *Shakespeare's Impact on His Contemporaries* (Macmillan, 1982). The author questions assumptions about Shakespeare's life and the dating of his plays. He also assesses Shakespeare's reputation among his contemporaries, especially Ben Jonson. The idea of a sweet and gentle Shakespeare, Honigmann suggests, is partly the fabrication of bardolatry; a very different man, sharp and businesslike, appears in some of the principal life records. The most unambiguous evidence of Shakespeare's preeminence during his lifetime derives from the exceptional number of surreptitious publications based on his plays. Honigmann devotes considerable attention to the relationship between Jonson and Shakespeare and their relative artistic standing. He concludes, contrary to some scholars, that Shakespeare enjoyed the higher reputation. Reassessing the chronology of the early plays, Honigmann pushes them back a few years, some into the late 1580s. He also argues that Jonson was the rival poet in the Sonnets and that *WT* in part responds to Jonson's criticism of Shakespeare's art. Honigmann offers a challenging evaluation of evidence and assumptions about Shakespeare's life and works, much of it passed on unquestioningly by earlier scholars.

Honigmann continues his work in Shakespeare biography with *Shakespeare: The "Lost Years"* (Manchester UP, 1985). Honigmann tries to pin down the whereabouts of Shakespeare before 1592 and concludes that Shakespeare spent time in the early 1580s in Lancashire, in the employ of the Houghtons and then the Heskeths as a schoolmaster. Because these families were Catholic, Honigmann argues that so was Shakespeare, at least during this period of his life, and changed later. Honigmann suggests that Shakespeare got his start as an actor in Lancashire and eventually served Lord Strange and became associated with his acting company. Admittedly a highly speculative book, it must nevertheless be considered seriously by any future biographer. Honigmann's superb detective work often convinces.

Russell Fraser, in *Young Shakespeare* (Columbia UP, 1988), provides an account of the life and art of Shakespeare's first thirty years. He explores such topics as the country; Stratford; Shakespeare's schooling; the condition of London at the end of the sixteenth century; the nature of the theater, including dramatic developments; some of Shakespeare's fellow dramatists, including Marlowe, Kyd, Greene, and Nashe; and the Sonnets and other poems. Throughout, Fraser assesses Shakespeare's dramatic writing, even as he interlaces the biography with quotations from the plays.

In *Shakespeare: The Later Years* (Columbia UP, 1992), Fraser continues his biography, starting in 1594 and ending with Shakespeare's death. He focuses, for example, on the death of Shakespeare's son Hamnet in 1596 and its impact. As in his earlier volume, Fraser assumes that Shakespeare conceals personal matters in his art but that they constitute his principal truth. The plays therefore reflect the cost of experience, and they offer commentary on the dramatist's life. Or, as in the case of *Lr.* and *Tim.,* they offer a picture of the Jacobean court. Shakespeare comes close to us in Prospero, even if *Tmp.* is not his final play.

CHAPTER THREE
The Research Paper

Preparing a research paper on a Shakespearean topic may strike fear in the hearts of many students, but it need not. This book has already provided access to many of the tools that can help in doing research on Shakespeare. After all, research procedures need not seem mysterious, like rituals reserved for the holy few who fathom them. Our daily lives contain many examples of research as we sift through conflicting newspaper accounts or editorials or try to determine which is the better product to buy. The process consists largely of gathering evidence and drawing inferences.

Considering the monumental amount of material published on Shakespeare—and no end is in sight—one can become frustrated just contemplating an investigation. But this book cuts through at least part of the material. Students frequently complain that nothing new to be discovered or said remains. Probably every generation of students reaches this erroneous conclusion, believing that all Shakespearean materials have been discovered and that the final critical word has been uttered. But as surely as we look back to the nineteenth century with some smugness at its apparent naïveté about Shakespearean matters, the next century will doubtless come to regard us as a bit quaint, if not altogether wrong. Students preparing undergraduate research papers need not think that they must say something original about Shakespeare or unearth some previously hidden fact about Shakespeare's life.

Briefly, the research paper is an investigative, formal essay with a thesis or argument. Its style should be concise without being cryptic; it should have adequate documentation without drowning in a sea of pointless notes. The paper and the research process itself constitute in part an exercise in logic and sound thinking. The paper should be persuasive and convincing, as well as creative and imaginative. Unfortunately, research papers often have a bad reputation among students, as if they are something that one must endure and, like most unpleasant experiences, survive. Contrary to common myth, one may need just as much creative energy to produce a successful research paper as to write a poem or short story. It is not altogether perverse to suggest that a research paper can be fun. Certainly, producing such papers may be one of the most valuable learning experiences students have during their formal training.

Doing the research involves both a trustworthy method and maximum efficiency. Some students waste incalculable hours wandering helplessly through the library, not knowing where to turn. Again, this book offers guidance so that students can make efficient use of their efforts. The process of research can be applied to other endeavors and is one of the most useful tools that students can possess. Research consists of more than methodology, though it must contain that; it is also hard work and involves a commitment of time and resources. The final product becomes greater than the sum of its parts. Students should feel some exhilaration at finishing such an assignment, at having grappled with an intellectual problem, resolved it, and given it some coherent shape. Perhaps more than any other academic procedure, writing a research paper forces one to grow and mature as an analytical thinker.

For additional assistance or information, students can consult textbooks on composition and rhetoric for discussions of the research paper and other matters of style. Some colleges have their own style manuals and guides to research. The note and bibliography forms suggested below correspond to those outlined in the manual published by the Modern Language Association of America, *MLA Handbook for Writers of Research Papers,* 3d ed. (1988). Because scholarly journals devoted to literature and some university presses regularly adhere to the *MLA Handbook,* students will profit by learning and following its style. If it is unavailable in college bookstores, it may be purchased from the Materials Center, Modern Language Association, 10 Astor Place, New York, NY 10003.

SELECTING A TOPIC

Grandiose, sweeping topics are often the first to occur to the beginning researcher as he or she sets out. But unless you are developing a book-length study, your ambitions must be scaled down. You naturally start with a large idea; then the twin processes of thinking and research lead to a narrowing of the subject. In some cases, the topic may be decided for you by your instructor; your instructor may suggest general approaches to a research study of Shakespeare, or you may be left to your own devices. Where to start becomes a matter of paramount importance.

To oversimplify, three broad areas exist for research topics in Shakespeare: his life and times, the plays or poems themselves, and textual problems. If you choose the first area, several questions may come to mind. What do we know about Shakespeare's close links to his hometown of Stratford, the place he always returned to despite his popularity and success in London? What do we know about Shakespeare's children or his son-in-law John Hall, a well-known physician in Stratford? Certain parts of Shakespeare's life before he arrived in London remain a mystery. What theories have scholars proposed? Was Shakespeare a wealthy man of property? Who were Shakespeare's companions or fellow dramatists? The nature of the theater itself affords many topics for investigation.

The plays and poems offer almost limitless possibilities. Generally, such broad topics as Shakespeare's tragic vision or the nature of Shakespearean comedy should be avoided, because these require book-length development. But more narrowly focused topics within those broad concepts can work; for example, how *A Midsummer Night's Dream* is a comedy. Different approaches can be followed. Certainly an investigation of how critics have treated a particular play or dramatic character is both manageable and valuable. You might want to examine themes, images, language, or structure. Shakespeare's Sonnets offer a rich area for investigation. Research into what the critics have theorized about the possibly autobiographical nature of the Sonnets could be fascinating, perhaps revealing more about the critics than about Shakespeare.

The textual problems of the early editions of Shakespeare's plays and Sonnets can be especially perplexing and probably should not be approached by beginning students, but advanced Shakespeare students may find some topics manageable. Investigations of textual matters often necessitate a highly specialized knowledge; but you might, for example, undertake a generalized study of how eighteenth- and nineteenth-century editors approached the Shakespearean text, or do research into the most notable early editors. The nature of the Elizabethan print shop, government regulations and censorship, the matter of copyright, the relationship of author to printer—all can be worthwhile topics that shed light on Shakespeare's texts.

In any event, you must select a topic, no matter how vaguely defined it may be at the moment. Whatever the initial choice, it should not be whimsical or altogether arbitrary; it should be grounded in some knowledge, however slight, of the subject. Topics picked out of thin air often yield exactly that. Many of the materials discussed earlier in this book suggest possible topics. At least three criteria should be kept in mind: you must be reasonably sure that ample material exists for your subject (the opposite problem usually applies when working on a Shakespearean topic); an adequate treatment of the topic must fit within the limits of the paper, as determined by either you or your instructor (a five-page paper on style in Shakespeare is preposterous, whereas a similar-length paper on the light and dark imagery in *Romeo and Juliet* may work); and the proposed investigation must be interesting to you. This last point may seem obvious, but it cannot be overemphasized. If you become bored with your topic, the chances are good that your reader will also. In choosing a topic, you basically evolve a working hypothesis that you take with you to your investigation in order to give that effort some shape and direction. The clearer the topic, the more efficient the research can be.

DEVELOPING A TOPIC

Assuming that a topic has been chosen, then what? If you have chosen to work on one of the plays or some of the poems, you must thoroughly familiarize yourself with those works. This is absolutely crucial. Only with a firm grasp of the basic material can you go forward to develop a topic. No matter what topic has been chosen, reading and studying the pertinent material in a reliable edition of Shakespeare will help the pursuit greatly.

As ideas about the topic begin to take shape, jot them down so they won't be lost. Already, the original concept may begin to be modified in some way. Occasionally, students find that the final thesis bears little resemblance to the first idea, and this is not necessarily undesirable. Many things happen along the way in the process of thinking about and investigating a subject. You should approach the project with an open mind. Often the subject seems to choose the researcher rather than the other way around.

You might now venture to the library with a specific and limited purpose: namely, to do additional background reading. A good place to start might be *The Reader's Encyclopedia* and other such collections of information cited earlier in this book. If you are working on a problem in criticism, you might read appropriate parts of Mark Van Doren's *Shakespeare* or Maurice Charney's *All of Shakespeare,* books that provide insight into the plays or Sonnets, even if you do not finally agree with their analyses. This guide offers you access to many other books that pertain to your topic, either generally or specifically. You must gain sufficient familiarity with the critical terrain so that you can wisely pursue your investigation. In a real sense, you begin to get a feel for the subject. Then, and only then, can you proceed in an intelligent and informed way to launch your full-scale work.

PREPARING A WORKING BIBLIOGRAPHY

Preparing a bibliography will, of necessity, send you to the library. Despite the best efforts of teachers, many students unfortunately remain intimidated by the library. A humbling sense of awe at the knowledge contained within is understandable; but it makes just as much sense to view the library as a potential place of enjoyment, pleasure, and learning. Far too many students complete their undergraduate education without having come to terms with the library; in fact, some claim never to have been in it. Some of this regrettable attitude probably has to do with myths perpetuated among generations of students. After all, scholars are supposed to be gray-headed, slightly stooped old men with terrible coughs engendered by dust from the books, who only occasionally emerge into the real world. Such a portrait constitutes a travesty of a researcher. Scholars come in all sizes, ages, shapes, genders, and temperaments. The library is for Shakespeare students what the laboratory is for those in scientific disciplines. Armed with this book, you should feel a degree of confidence.

As you begin to work in the library, record on 4 x 6 index cards or something similar all potential sources, *using one entry per card;* this method provides an efficient way of keeping track of the references. Information on the card should include the author's full name (last name first), the exact title of the book or essay, place of publication, publisher, and date of publication. Record in the upper left-hand corner the library call number. Two examples illustrate the procedure:

book:	PN 2592 B4	Bentley, Gerald Eades. *The Jacobean and Caroline Stage*. 7 vols. Oxford: Clarendon Press, 1941–68.

article or note:	PR 2885 S63	Boswell, Jackson C. "Shylock's Turquoise Ring." *Shakespeare Quarterly* 14 (1963): 481–83.

Cards containing references to sources not actually used in preparing the paper can be discarded; the remaining ones will help prepare the final bibliography or list of Works Cited.

Information for the working bibliography can come from at least four places:

1. Obviously, this book is one place to begin. The books analyzed here on the tragedies, comedies, Romances, histories, Sonnets, and other topics may provide a number of possibilities. But this book makes no attempt to cite the thousands of essays published in scholarly journals, and these will prove to be of great value.

2. You then need to consult the standard bibliographies on Shakespeare (listed in the section on reference sources in chapter 2), especially the annual bibliographies produced by the

MLA and in *Shakespeare Quarterly* (*SQ*). To use the *SQ* bibliography most efficiently, you should consult the indexes in it. Other more generalized bibliographies can also help.

3. The library's card catalogue or on-line computer system will provide titles of books on Shakespeare and confirm whether it has the books already on your list. Most catalogues proceed alphabetically according to author, title, and subject. The subject classification under Shakespeare, if well done, can be of considerable help. The call number indicates where the book can be found on the shelves in the library. Most libraries now use the Library of Congress classification system, but some still follow the Dewey decimal system. You need not try to penetrate the mysteries of either system; all you need to know is that the number tells you where to find the work. Librarians are often great storehouses of knowledge and should be consulted if you need assistance.

4. The books and essays you read also provide valuable references. Their notes and bibliographies will point the way to other materials.

Having canvassed at least these four areas for resources, you are now ready to begin reading and sifting through the materials to determine what you need to help you develop your paper.

TAKING NOTES

All beginning researchers face the temptation to take too many notes—a wholly natural impulse that can be conquered only through experience. But keep in mind that it is better to end up with too much rather than too little. In the long run, it will be easier to discard a few notes than to repeat some of the research effort in order to get sufficient information.

To safeguard against excessive note taking read and reread the material so that you can better judge what is important, what is truly noteworthy. Thus, you should read the entire essay or portion of the book before taking notes; just jot down page numbers of those passages that seem important at first glance. Some students choose to photocopy whole essays or portions of books. Without getting into the issues of possible copyright violations, suffice it to say that photocopying cannot replace careful reading and analyzing of the material to determine whether it contains something worthwhile. A mound of photocopies does not constitute research; it reflects money spent and possible laziness. It may, of course, occasionally reflect time saved, but postponing the process of sifting through the material carefully may not save time in the long run.

When you find something important, you can do one of at least three things in making a note card: (1) quote the comment directly from the printed page and enclose it in quotation marks, inserting ellipsis marks (three spaced periods) for anything deleted; (2) paraphrase the statement; or (3) summarize the argument very briefly, perhaps simply to note that this critic opposes another critic whose view you have already recorded. Different circumstances demand different techniques. As a beginning researcher, you may find it more efficient to use direct quotations; if so, quote accurately.

Notes should be written in ink on 4 x 6 cards or something comparable, one piece of information per card. Recording information in a notebook may ultimately be inefficient because the material cannot be easily filed or shuffled. On the first line of the card on the left, indicate the author of the statement (this assumes that a separate bibliography card will be made); in the middle, a word or phrase to reveal the subject or topic; and on the right, the appropriate page number. Nothing particularly sacred inheres in this system, but it works fairly well; more experienced researchers may devise their own methods. The samples below demonstrate the technique:

Quotation:

Smidt—	Changes in text of *R2*—	p. 89

"Such confusions and omissions—and there are others—reinforce the impression derived from a study of the larger movements of plot and theme that *Richard II* underwent some major changes of design in the course of its shaping. Stage adaptation and condensation would account for some, but certainly not all, of the irregularities."

Paraphrase:

Smidt—	Changes in text of *R2*—	p. 89

Confusions and omissions in the text of *R2* indicate that the play underwent major changes of design, only some of which can be accounted for by stage adaptation and condensation.

Summary:

Smidt—	Changes in text of *R2*—	p. 89

Smidt argues that *R2* underwent many changes of design and that only some of them may be attributed to stage adaptation or condensation.

Taking good notes is as much an art as a science, and your whole project will come to naught if you have inaccurate or irrelevant notes.

OUTLINING THE PAPER

Many students (and others) prepare outlines of their papers after the writing has been completed—usually to satisfy the teacher or a requirement. Given human nature, this will always occur, but it reveals a failure to understand the function of an outline. It also, no doubt, grows out of students' scarred past, when they were required to produce outlines and thus quickly grew to detest them. Admittedly, making outlines for hypothetical subjects should be an exercise reserved for the idle. For an outline to have any efficacy or justification as part of the total writing process, it must be tied to a concrete, immediate need.

Constructing an outline requires no mystical insights. An outline is simply a practical tool in the process of organizing a paper—no more, no less. In many ways, it is the acid test of the whole process of thinking about the subject, investigating, and taking notes. The outline constitutes the skeletal structure for the logical development of the paper. Presumably, you have jotted down ideas along the way, but the evidence collected through research provides the major basis for your conclusions and for the structure of the argument of the paper. If you cannot produce a logical and coherent outline of the subject, then something has gone wrong—either your thinking is fuzzy or your evidence remains inadequate in some way.

You can develop either a sentence outline or a topic outline; use the one that best suits your needs. At a minimum, the outline should contain a statement of your thesis (the argument or main idea) that the paper sets out to develop and a logical organization of the paper, usually set up in the following manner:

> Thesis statement
> Introduction
> I.
>   A.
>   B.
>   1.
>   2.
> II.
>   A.
>   B.
>   C.
> III.
>   A.
>   1.
>   2.
>   B.
> Conclusion

This structure suggests that the paper has three main ideas (represented by Roman numerals I, II, and III), with subcategories under them. A logical development of ideas determines the sequence. Why, for example, does point III come where it does? Does it naturally follow point II? (Obviously, the paper may have any number of developed ideas, largely dependent on the subject and the length of the paper.) The outline should be taken seriously, not because it has some special significance in and of itself but because it serves as a means to an end—the logical organization and presentation of the paper.

WRITING THE PAPER

The ultimate test of research comes in the ability to communicate your findings in some persuasive, comprehensible form, usually in writing. Research has limited value if no one else ever learns the results or understands them. To successfully negotiate the various procedures suggested here and then to fail to produce an effective paper means failure. But to shuffle the note cards, organize the ideas, and then bore people to death by the paper is unforgivable. All the skills of good writing must prevail in the research paper. We should discard the myth that scholarly writing must be dull if it is to be respectable, but you need not go in for stylistic fireworks either. Imaginative writing embraces clarity and forcefulness.

Inexperienced researchers and writers often confront the problem of how to achieve the right balance between reliance on sources and their own ideas. A research paper is not a string of quotations, the proverbial ''scissors-and-paste job'' in which the writer provides only an occasional transitional phrase or connective. Instead, the paper amalgamates the writer's ideas with selected documentation used either for corroboration and support or for refutation. You do not merely report; you must demonstrate a synthesis and analysis of the materials on the subject and present your conclusions in a forceful and effective manner. As in all good writing, you cannot divorce form from content.

Because quotations will be used, several matters of form must be considered. If you are quoting one or two lines of poetry, run them on within the text of the paper and enclose them in quotation marks. Two lines of verse should be separated by a slash, as in ''Down, down I come, like glist'ring Phaeton, / Wanting the manage of unruly jades.'' More than three lines of verse should be set off from the text, indented (usually ten spaces) from the left margin; you then need no quotation marks. Quoted prose passages of fewer than four lines should be run on in the text and enclosed in quotation marks. Longer passages should be set off and indented from the left margin, with no quotation marks. Unless you have been instructed otherwise, all quoted material should be double-spaced. After the edition of the play or poem has been established initially in a note or parenthetical documentation, you can identify other quoted material from the same source by citing in parentheses the act, scene, and line numbers for plays or line numbers for poems. Examples: As Sebastian says, "This is the air; that is the glorious sun" (IV.iii.1). In Sonnet 60, Shakespeare writes, "Like as the waves make towards the pebbled shore, / So do our minutes hasten to their end" (1–2). The first example presupposes that the writer has already indicated that he or she is discussing *Twelfth Night.* Style manuals, such as the *MLA Handbook,* offer additional instruction about matters of form in writing the paper.

Writers and painters of the Renaissance depicted Truth as the daughter of Time, and on a practical level, that seems worth remembering for the research paper. To enable a sensible, intelligent argument grounded in evidence (truth) to emerge in your paper, you must allow sufficient time to bring this about. Nerve-racking, desperate, last-minute efforts seldom achieve satisfactory results. The key to much of this is pace—determining how long you should spend on the various steps along the way. You should allow enough time so that you can write a rough draft of the paper, put it aside for a few days, and then pick it up again. Sometimes a little detachment can reveal startling things about our own flaws and confusion in a paper. The paper prepared by dawn's early light on the due day offers no time for reflection; it barely affords time for the ink to dry.

Your paper should be typed on 8½-by–11-inch paper and be double-spaced throughout. Page numbers go in the upper right-hand corner, half an inch from the top. Generally, leave one-inch margins on all sides, unless given other instructions. Typically, you should not justify the right margin. Do not underline or put in quotation marks the title of your essay.

DOCUMENTATION

Whether quoted directly, paraphrased, or summarized, any material that you borrow from others needs some kind of documentation to indicate where you got your information or ideas. Such procedures reveal the nature and extent of your research and obviously give credit to others. By careful documentation, you provide your readers with access to additional resources beyond your paper. You also acknowledge an indebtedness to a community of scholars and critics.

Two basic systems of documentation prevail at the moment: parenthetical documentation and notes. What follows is a summary of procedures that receive more extensive treatment in the *MLA Handbook*. Please consult it for problems not covered here. Your instructor may also have special requirements for handling documentation. Each system may contain something of the other; in some ways, each is the inverse of the other.

Simply put, parenthetical documentation means that you cite within parentheses in the body of your paper whatever references you need; such references get full bibliographical treatment in a list of Works Cited. The other system uses footnotes or endnotes (gathered at the end of the paper) to identify the specific references you used. This system may include a separate Bibliography or List of Works Consulted if the instructor so requires. The instructor may also express a preference about which system to follow. In any event, you will need to choose one or the other.

PARENTHETICAL DOCUMENTATION SYSTEM

This system always has two parts: parenthetical references within the body of the paper and a separate list of Works Cited, to which you have keyed the references. There may also be explanatory endnotes in this system.

Parenthetical References

Several variations are possible in the parenthetical references, depending on how you refer to the sources. For example:

1. Direct quotation, naming the source and page in parentheses. Your paper would read: "No conventional language of word or gesture seems able to convey the enormity of the family's tragic experience" (Bevington 31). [Bevington refers to the author and his book in the list of Works Cited, and 31 refers to the page number for the direct quotation.]

2. Direct quotation (the same as above), but with the author cited in the sentence. Your paper would read: Bevington says that "no conventional language . . ." (31).
3. Summary of the same quotation. You can either cite the author and page in parentheses at the end of the sentence or name the author in your sentence and put the page number at the end in parentheses.
4. Multivolume work. Give the volume number, colon, and page reference: (Bentley 2:5–6).
5. Two or more works by the same author. The appropriate short title of the work must be used either in the sentence or in parentheses. Your paper would read: Bevington, in his *Action Is Eloquence,* says that . . . (55). Or: Bevington says that . . . (*Action Is Eloquence* 55).
6. Literary works. Your paper would read: Polixenes describes his son to Leontes: "He's all my exercise, my mirth, my matter" (*Winter's Tale* I.ii.166). [If it is already clear that you are discussing *The Winter's Tale,* simply cite act, scene, and line numbers; your list of Works Cited indicates what edition of the play you used.]

These examples cover the probable requirements for documentation in critical research papers; consult the *MLA Handbook* for additional examples.

Works Cited

Having given the necessary documentation within your paper, you need to construct a list of Works Cited—an alphabetical listing of sources referred to in your paper. This double-spaced list comes at the end of your paper, beginning on a separate sheet of paper. Each entry typically has three main parts: author, title, and publication information, with each part set off by a period. The first line of the entry is flush with the left margin; subsequent lines are indented five spaces. The last name of the author comes first.

1. A book by a single author:
   Bevington, David. *Action Is Eloquence: Shakespeare's Language of Gesture.* Cambridge: Harvard UP, 1984.
   [The full title is given, with the subtitle preceded by a co-

lon. The *MLA Handbook* recommends that the abbreviation UP be used for University Press.]
2. Two or more books by the same author:
Frye, Northrop. *Anatomy of Criticism: Four Essays.* Princeton: Princeton UP, 1957.
---. *The Secular Scripture: A Study of the Structure of Romance.* Cambridge: Harvard UP, 1976.
[The three hyphens indicate that this item is by the same author as the immediately preceding item.]
3. A book by two or more persons:
Kay, Carol McGinnis, and Henry E. Jacobs, eds. *Shakespeare's Romances Reconsidered.* Lincoln: U of Nebraska P, 1978.
[Only the first name is reversed; a comma separates the names. If there are more than three authors, name only the first and add "et al.": Edens, Walter, et al., eds. *Teaching Shakespeare.* Princeton: Princeton UP, 1977.]
4. A multivolume work:
Bentley, Gerald Eades. *The Jacobean and Caroline Stage.* 7 vols. Oxford: Clarendon, 1941-1968.
[List the total number of volumes, whether you have used them all or not.]
5. An edition:
Shakespeare, William. *William Shakespeare: The Complete Works.* Gen. ed. Alfred Harbage. Baltimore: Penguin, 1969.
6. An unpublished dissertation:
Smith, Mary Allen. "Shakespeare's View of Tragic Women." Diss. U of Kansas, 1985.
7. An essay within a collection:
Yoch, James J. "Subjecting the Landscape in Pageants and Shakespearean Pastorals." *Pageantry in the Shakespearean Theater.* Ed. David M. Bergeron. Athens: U of Georgia P, 1985. 194-219.
8. A later edition or reprint:
Partridge, Eric. *Shakespeare's Bawdy.* 2d ed. London: Routledge, 1968.
Bradley, A. C. *Shakespearean Tragedy.* 1904. London: Macmillan, 1968.
[In the second example, this is a reprint of the same text,

not a revised or altered edition. Indicate the original date of publication, then cite the copy that you are using.]
9. Essays in periodicals:
Greenblatt, Stephen. "Invisible Bullets: Renaissance Authority and Its Subversion." *Glyph* 8 (1981): 40–61.
[The name of the journal is followed by the volume number, year of publication, and inclusive page numbers.]
10. A signed review:
Bergeron, David M. Rev. of *Art and Power: Renaissance Festivals 1450–1650,* by Roy Strong. *Renaissance Quarterly* 39 (1986): 401–2.

Endnotes

When using the parenthetical documentation system, two reasons exist for also having notes (placed at the end of the paper, beginning on a separate sheet): for additional bibliographical information or for further explanation of points that cannot be fully explored in the paper.

In the body of your paper, the note number (a superscript Arabic number) comes after the final mark of punctuation. Thus, your paper would read: Many critics have debated the staging of medieval drama.[1]

On the notes page, you cite the necessary information:

[1]The following critics have argued for a fixed, single stage on which the plays were performed: . . . .

[The first line is indented five spaces; subsequent lines are flush with the left margin.]

NOTES DOCUMENTATION SYSTEM

Simply stated, the notes system gathers bibliographical information about works being quoted or used in some way at the end of the paper. Thus, your paper would read:

One critic observes: "If similarities in design and execution are an indication of closeness in time *King John* and *Richard II* must be near companions."[1]

Then, on a separate Notes page, the information would appear as follows:

1. A book:
   ¹Kristian Smidt, *Unconformities in Shakespeare's History Plays* (London: Macmillan, 1982) 86.

   [In this system, the author's first name comes first, then the last name, followed by the title, then the publication information set off in parentheses, followed by the page to which you refer. The first line of the note is indented five spaces; subsequent lines are flush with the left margin. Commas replace periods for separating units of information in the notes.]
2. An article in a periodical:
   ²Jeanne Addison Roberts, "The Merry Wives: Suitably Shallow, but Neither Simple nor Slender," *Shakespeare Studies* 6 (1970): 110.

   [Here, 6 indicates the volume of the periodical; the year of publication is in parentheses, followed by a colon, a space, and the page that you cite.]
3. A multivolume work:
   ³Gerald Eades Bentley, *The Jacobean and Caroline Stage,* 7 vols. (Oxford: Clarendon, 1941–1968) 2:115.

   [This includes the total number of volumes. After the publication information, indicate which volume and page(s) are being cited.]
4. An edition:
   ⁴William Shakespeare, *William Shakespeare: The Complete Works,* gen. ed. Alfred Harbage (Baltimore: Penguin, 1969) II.ii.33.

   [If you are quoting from the text, indicate act, scene, and line numbers. Add a sentence indicating that all quotations come from this edition; then cite the remaining quotations parenthetically within your paper. Thus, subsequently, your paper would read: Richard II says: "Arm, arm my name" (III.ii.86).]

If you have already cited a work in a note, use shortened references to it thereafter:

⁵Smidt 75.

If you cite more than one work by the same author, use a shortened form of the title in the note:

[6]Smidt, *Unconformities* 78.

Even in the notes system, feel free to use parenthetical documentation when it would be clear to your reader which work you are citing, as in the reference above to a quotation from *Richard II.*

If one is required, you will have to construct a selected bibliography or a list of works consulted. This comes after the notes, beginning on a separate page and arranged alphabetically. The advantage of such a list is that it gives the reader a fuller picture of your research than may be apparent in your notes. The form of the references in such a bibliography follows that indicated in ''Works Cited,'' above.

PLAGIARISM

In its simplest definition, plagiarism is stealing. With regard to research papers, plagiarism refers to the use of the ideas or words of another person without giving that person credit. Plagiarism may spring from carelessness, ignorance, or dishonesty. Of the last, not much can be said, but students bear the responsibility of being both sufficiently accurate and sufficiently informed so that they do not inadvertently commit plagiarism. Borrowing material from a copyrighted source without giving credit is, of course, illegal.

How can you avoid accidental plagiarism? First, by taking very careful notes. By doing so, you run less risk of confusing the author's words or ideas with your own. In the research paper itself, the problem can be avoided by carefully documenting all borrowed material, unless, of course, it is common factual information. Sometimes students mistakenly believe that if they change a word or two or generally tinker with the author's style they can claim it as their own. Nothing could be farther from the truth, because the original idea still belongs to the author. Obviously, no defense can exist for using direct quotations and not citing the sources. Even ideas gleaned from class lectures and used in a paper ought to be cited, giving credit to the person who voiced the ideas. Again, factual information, such as the date of Shakespeare's birth, need not be documented. Experience will go a long way toward making clear when and how to document; the guidance of instructors and style manuals will also assist.

A MODEL RESEARCH PAPER

An example of a research paper follows, illustrating how one can be put together and demonstrating several matters of form. You may be required to include a title page, an outline, or other materials. This example begins with a title page, followed by the text; it also includes appropriate documentation.

The Tempest and Colonial Discourse

Hershini Bhana
English 332
23 April 1992

Any reading must be made from a particular position, but it is not reducible to that position (not least because texts are not infinitely malleable or interpretable, but often certain constraints and resistances to readings [are] made of them (Barker and Hulme 193–94).

Historicist criticism, writes Louis Montrose, "in its antireflectionism, its shift of emphasis from the formal analysis of verbal artifacts to the ideological analysis of discursive practices, its refusal to observe strict and fixed boundaries between 'literary' and other texts (including the critic's own), this emergent social/political/historical orientation in literary studies is pervasively concerned with writing as a mode of action" (qtd. in Gallagher x). Using this approach, instead of studying various literary texts such as *The Tempest* as objects isolated and independent of time, one emphasizes their interaction with time. The text changes from an artifact to a social practice. Thus operating from the premise that a literary text functions as both a product of human action and a means whereby both readers and critics perform certain kinds of action or social practices, the recent interpretations of Caliban as a metaphor for the colonial experience by people of color gain validity.

Caliban recast stands for the countless victims of European imperialism and colonization. Like Caliban (as the argument goes), colonized peoples have been disinherited, exploited, and subjugated. Like him, they have endured and resisted European enslavement. Such readings of Caliban stem from an anticolonial sentiment tied directly to the burgeoning of both international Black consciousness and more localized nationalist movements. *The Tempest* has been adopted as a founding text in an oppositional lineage—in a tradition of rereading, which in turn serves as a means of getting out from under what George Lamming calls the "ancient mausoleum of [Western] historic achievement" (Nixon 558).

Most of the historicist critics who borrow this motif of Caliban as colonized ignore Shakespeare's sources and intentions. They adopt Caliban for what he represents to the observer and not for what Shakespeare probably had in mind. Few would argue that Shakespeare wanted to represent the African American or the Native American experience, but they want modern readers to accept their interpretations because, retrospectively, they fit. New situations give the play's characters new meanings.

Most of these historicist critics have focused on the imposition of the English language as key to the process of colonization and the relationship between Prospero and Caliban. The Caribbean writer George Lamming was one of the first critics to suggest that language imposition functions as an essential element of colonialism; that Prospero's language constitutes Caliban's "iron cage." Through language, Prospero controls Caliban's mode of self-expression and perception, for a dialectic relationship between language and culture exists. Language influences and limits the way one perceives the world and relates to it. This (re)constituted world influences the development of language. The limitation imposed on people of the Third World by the adoption of a foreign language causes frustration, for it points to a lack of parity between possibilities for political and cultural freedom. When formal independence has come, people have been more successful in securing their physical freedom than their cultural freedom, for they are shackled to the colonizer's language. The tongue of the colonizer becomes the vehicle for self-expression, and the colonized are never free. Third World writers remain very aware of the problem of communicating with one audience in one language and thus barring a second, sometimes closer audience in one's own land of one's own people.

Some recognition, however, must be given to the liberating effects of language that Caliban himself can attest to; for though he claims only to curse, Caliban's speeches are often stirring in their beauty and power. Janheinz Jahn in Vaughan's article addresses this liberating element by suggesting that Prospero's language provides Caliban with a medium of expression for Caliban's culture. Prospero assumes that Caliban has no culture, but Caliban possesses a culture to which Prospero ultimately has no real access and that Prospero cannot control. This culture influences and interacts with the new culture that Prospero enforces. This language becomes thus "transformed, acquiring different meanings which Prospero never expected. Caliban becomes 'bilingual.' That language he shares with Prospero and the language he has minted from it are no longer identical. Caliban breaks out of the prison of Prospero's language'' (Vaughan 305).

Caliban, instead of being deprived of his culture, now has access to two cultures. He can express himself and his own heritage in a language he has made his own, even though Prospero may be deaf to the message. The emphasis thus shifts from despair over the deprivation of a native culture to pride in its tenacity and to the advantages of a double consciousness, or bilingualism.

Irony prevails, however, in the Third World's adoption of Caliban, for he ultimately remains a European artifact, a product of a brilliant *English* imagination. The use of Caliban by critics of color to criticize Western imperialism undermines these critics' attempts, for they show themselves to be still operating within a Western hegemonic structure. They are attempting to dismantle the "master's" house by using his tools.

Several additional problems surface in readings of Caliban as a symbol of the colonized. Most of these revolve around the reductive concept of the "Other." The majority of interpretations, such as Ronald Takaki's in *Iron Cages,* show Caliban as the Other who represents qualities such as powerlessness, savagery, stupidity, and uncontrolled sexuality that the colonizer wishes to project onto someone other than or different from himself. Yet binary constructions of difference, whether they be that of colonizer and colonized or the norm and the Other, embody a logic that gives "priority to the first of the dyad while subordinating the second . . . [this] logic [being] inscribed by the discourses of domination, and . . . to conform to binary difference is inevitably to corroborate the logic of domination, to underdevelop the spaces in discourse that destabilize the hegemony of dominant formations" (Lowe 24). Thus the critic basing her interpretation on the dichotomy of Prospero and Caliban, on the colonizer and the colonized, falls in the Manichean world of Western discourse and actually perpetuates the perspective that permeates this discourse.

Various indicators within the text itself militate against Caliban's being seen merely as this Other. Caliban can be seen as the first colonizer. Sycorax, his mother, through whom he claims possession of the island, comes from the old world herself. She arrives at the island and subsequently enslaves Ariel, thus herself becoming the first colonizer—one who establishes the tradition of dominance and oppression long before Prospero arrives. This also constitutes Caliban's legacy. Caliban can thus be seen as both oppressor and oppressed.

This indeterminacy forms an essential feature of Caliban's character (and of all the characters in the play). He crosses many boundaries within the text, never being wholly one thing. Adjectives that describe him range from "half-human" to "half-devil" to "half-fish" to "strange beast" to "mooncalf." Willis chooses one of these adjectives, "wild man," to demonstrate how Caliban can be viewed as both human and beast, both civilized and uncivilized. Caliban possesses the ability to learn language. He speaks in verse, unlike Trinculo and Stephano, who speak in prose; but he sometimes uses language to curse. He has the ability to reason, plot, and implement his plan to overthrow Prospero; yet his behavior is often instinctual and spontaneous. He is physically deformed and monstrous, yet able to appreciate beauty. Although Willis's reading remains Eurocentric in her definition of civilization, she points to an essential ambiguity that prevents Caliban from merely being the Other who functions as an embodiment of that which threatens the colonizer.

Interestingly, Willis uses the nonthreatening characterization of Caliban to downplay his importance. She trivializes him, describing his ambivalence as ridiculous and childlike. Her reading smacks of paternalism; for instead of seeing this ambiguity as a questioning of the concept of the Other, she replaces Caliban with Antonio as the Other.

Her characterization of Antonio as the Other rests on her adoption of Immanuel Wallerstein's categories of colonialism. To Wallerstein, the colonial enterprise operates in three domains: the core, the semiperiphery, and the periphery. The colonialism of the core involves the reinforcement and expansion of royal hegemony within England itself; colonialism of the semiperiphery involves expansion into those areas only partially controlled by England; and colonialism of the periphery is the colonialization of the Third World. Willis insists on the importance of not blurring these distinctions, and she criticizes Brown because he sees colonialism in monolithic terms. Prospero's colonial project, according to her, includes the rule of both the island and the dukedom of Milan. *The Tempest* plays the colonialism of the island against the colonialism of the core. The island becomes merely a temporary sojourn, an experiment and a means whereby Prospero might legitimately reestablish political order in Milan. Thus the essence of the play, for Willis, lies in Prospero's bringing Antonio under control and marrying Miranda to Ferdinand. Willis correctly identifies *The Tempest*'s concern with the will to power on the level of national politics; yet in her attempt to label Antonio as the Other, she falls into the same reductive trap as those critics who ignore Caliban's ambiguity to make him the Other.

Shakespeare, by creating characters who are full of contradictions, shifts the emphasis from the Other to the individual's desire to perpetuate the self, often at the expense of other people. The re-creation of self becomes more important than creating the Other, who constitutes a formulaic projection of all those attributes that Prospero or the colonizer would find threatening. Many episodes thus deal with reproduction, with a re-creation and perpetuation on biological, political, and aesthetic levels. Examples of this emphasis abound, including Sycorax's bequeathing the island to Caliban and Caliban's attempt to reproduce with Miranda: "I had peopled else / This island with Calibans" (I.ii.350–51). The masque of Ceres also dramatizes the importance of fertility and orderly succession; and Prospero by his magic tries to re-create his kingdom—an analogous act to Shakespeare's attempt to re-create a "true" theatrical fiction. This desire for re-creation, for a "brave new world," constitutes an attempt to deny death and to transcend mortality through art (V.i.87).

In addition to this emphasis on re-creation of the self, the ambiguity and the indeterminate state that characterizes not just Caliban but many other characters and scenes in the play further undercut notions of the Other. The island's location remains indeterminate, and both the natural and supernatural reside there. Miranda stands between childhood and maturity, and Prospero stands between vengeance and mercy. Even time seems to be in a state of suspension. The audience experiences stylistically a "strange repose" like that felt by Sebastian

(II.i.218) or that described in Caliban's dream scene (III.ii.138–46). This state of poetic indeterminacy complicates an ideological reading of *The Tempest,* for the play "valorizes ambiguity and irony, ironizing its own positions and insisting upon the inconclusiveness of its own conclusions. The new orthodoxy, which exalts the colonized, is as narrow as the old, which idealizes and excuses the colonizer" (McDonald 27).

This final position does not constitute a retreat into the noncontroversial, restful shadows of ambiguity and irony. Nowhere does one intend to downplay the importance of contextual literary criticism. Criticism that identifies and promotes ideological issues and that departs from traditional interpretations has been marginalized for too long. This criticism needs to be recognized. But one must remain aware of the danger of squeezing texts to fit ideology. Politics lies embedded in the aesthetic form, and neither should ever be dismissed. To do so would be to flatten the text into a mold of colonial discourse and to lose all that is rich and strange about Caliban and the text.

WORKS CITED

Baker, Houston A. Jr. "Critical Response IV: Caliban's Triple Play." *Critical Inquiry* 13 (Autumn 1986): 182–96.

Barker, Francis, and Peter Hulme. "Nymphs and Reapers Heavily Vanish: The Discursive Contexts of *The Tempest*." *Alternative Shakespeares*. Ed. John Drakakis. London: Metheun Press, 1985. 191–205.

Brown, Paul. " 'This thing of darkness I acknowledge Mine': *The Tempest* and the Discourse of Colonialism." *Political Shakespeare: New Essays in Cultural Materialism*. Ed. Jonathan Dollimore. Manchester: Manchester UP, 1985. 48–71.

Bruner, Charlotte. "The Meaning of Caliban in Black Literature Today." *Comparative Literature Studies* 13 (1976): 240–53.

Clark, John Pepper. *The Example of Shakespeare*. Evanston: Northwestern UP, 1970.

Gallagher, Susan Van Zanten. *A Story of South Africa: J. M. Coetzee's Fiction in Context*. Cambridge: Harvard UP, 1991.

Griffiths, Trevor R. " 'This Island's Mine': Caliban and Colonialism." *The Yearbook of English Studies* 13 (1983): 159–80.

Lamming, George. *The Pleasures of Exile*. London: Allison and Busby, 1984.

Lowe, Lisa. "Discourse and Heterogeneity: Situating Orientalism." *Critical Terrains: French and British Orientalisms*. From Prof. David Lloyd's English 166 Reader.

McDonald, Russ. "Reading *The Tempest*." *Shakespeare Survey* 43 (1991): 15–28.

Nixon, Rob. "Caribbean and African Appropriations of *The Tempest*." *Critical Inquiry* 13 (Spring 1987): 557–78.

Shakespeare, William. *William Shakespeare: The Complete Works*. Gen. ed. Alfred Harbage. Baltimore: Penguin, 1969.

Skura, Meredith Anne. "Discourse and the Individual: The Case of Colonialism in *The Tempest*." *Shakespeare Quarterly* 40 (Spring 1989): 42–69.

Takaki, Ronald. *Iron Cages: Race and Culture in 19th-Century America*. New York: Oxford UP, 1990.

Vaughan, Alden. "Caliban in the 'Third World': Shake-speare's Savage as Sociopolitical Symbol." *Massachusetts Review* 29 (Summer 1988): 289–313.
Willis, Deborah. "Shakespeare's *Tempest* and the Discourse of Colonialism." *Studies in English Literature, 1500–1900* 29 (Spring 1982): 277–89.

NOTE DOCUMENTATION SAMPLE

The following shows a sample page from the model research paper, indicating how one might use the note documentation system instead of the parenthetical documentation system. A page demonstrating the proper citation of notes follows the sample page of the paper.

Any reading must be made from a particular position, but it is not reducible to that position (not least because texts are not infinitely malleable or interpretable, but often certain constraints and resistances to readings [are] made of them.[1]

Historicist criticism, writes Louis Montrose, "in its antireflectionism, its shift of emphasis from the formal analysis of verbal artifacts to the ideological analysis of discursive practices, its refusal to observe strict and fixed boundaries between 'literary' and other texts (including the critic's own), this emergent social/political/historical orientation in literary studies is pervasively concerned with writing as a mode of action."[2] Using this approach, instead of studying various literary texts such as *The Tempest* as objects isolated and independent of time, one emphasizes their interaction with time. The text changes from an artifact to a social practice. Thus operating from the premise that a literary text functions as both a product of human action and also as a means whereby both readers and critics perform certain kinds of action or social practices, the recent interpretations of Caliban as a metaphor for the colonial experience by people of color gain validity.

Caliban recast stands for the countless victims of European imperialism and colonization. Like Caliban (as the argument goes), colonized peoples have been disinherited, exploited, and subjugated. Like him, they have endured and resisted European enslavement. Such readings of Caliban stem from an anticolonial sentiment tied directly to the burgeoning of both international Black consciousness and more localized national-

ist movements. *The Tempest* has been adopted as a founding
text in an oppositional lineage—in a tradition of rereading,
which in turn serves as a means of getting out from under
what George Lamming calls the "ancient mausoleum of
[Western] historic achievement."[3]

NOTES

[1]Francis Barker and Peter Hulme, "Nymphs and Reapers Heavily Vanish: The Discursive Contexts of *The Tempest*," *Alternative Shakespeares*, ed. John Drakakis (London: Methuen, 1985) 193–94.

[2]Quoted in Susan Van Zanten Gallagher, *A Story of South Africa: J. M. Coetzee's Fiction in Context* (Cambridge: Harvard UP, 1991) x.

[3]Rob Nixon, "Caribbean and African Appropriations of *The Tempest*," *Critical Inquiry* 13 (1987): 558.

Index of Authors

Abbott, E. A., 34
Adams, John Cranford, 148
Adams, Joseph Quincy, 191
Adams, Robert M., 67
Adelman, Janet, 166–67
Alexander, Peter, 40
Allman, Eileen Jorge, 85–86
Anderson, Linda, 64
Andrews, John F., 37
Archer, John Michael, 174
Atkins, G. Douglas, 168
Austin, J. L., 89

Baker, Herschel, 39
Bamber, Linda, 161
Barber, C. L., 45–46, 58
Barnet, Sylvan, 40
Barroll, J. Leeds, 153–54, 189–90
Barton, Anne, 39
Bate, Jonathan, 186–87
Bateson, F. W., 32
Battenhouse, Roy W., 116–17
Beckerman, Bernard, 40, 149
Beiner, G., 64–65
Bentley, G. E., 23, 145–46, 190
Bergeron, David M., 74–75, 168, 190
Berman, Ronald, 30
Berry, Edward, 57–58, 86–87
Berry, Ralph, 58
Bevington, David, 29, 37, 39–40, 150
Black, J. B., 183–84
Blanpied, John W., 91
Boas, F. S., 58

Bolton, W. F., 98
Booth, Stephen, 110–11, 131–32
Bowers, Fredson, 19, 24, 143
Boyce, Charles, 36
Bradbrook, M. C., 37, 133–34, 146–47
Bradbury, Malcolm, 43
Braden, Gordon, 186
Bradley, A. C., 21–22, 100–101, 112, 135, 182
Brook, G. L., 34–35
Brooke, Nicholas, 102–3
Brooks, H. F., 41
Brown, John Russell, 43, 54–55
Bruster, Douglas, 175–76
Bryant, J. A., Jr., 182
Buchman, Lorne M., 157
Bullough, Geoffrey, 23–24, 184
Burt, Richard, 174
Byrne, M. St. Clare, 145

Calderwood, James L., 88
Campbell, Lily B., 79–80, 103
Campbell, O. J., 36
Campbell, S. C., 132
Cantor, Paul A., 107
Capell, Edward, 3
Carlisle, Carol, 103
Carroll, William C., 50
Cartwright, Kent, 125–26
Cercignani, Fausto, 35, 98
Chambers, E. K., 4, 22, 136, 145, 147, 190–91
Champion, Larry S., 29, 53–54, 91–92